CRITICAL INSIGHTS

Censored & Banned Literature

CRITICAL INSIGHTS

Censored & Banned Literature

Editor
Robert C. Evans
Auburn University at Montgomery

SALEM PRESS
A Division of EBSCO Information Services, Inc.
Ipswich, Massachusetts

GREY HOUSE PUBLISHING

Publisher's Cataloging-In-Publication Data
(Prepared by The Donohue Group, Inc.)

Names: Evans, Robert C., 1955- editor.
Title: Censored & banned literature / editor, Robert C. Evans, Auburn University at Montgomery.
Other Titles: Censored and banned literature | Critical insights.
Description: [First edition]. | Ipswich, Massachusetts : Salem Press, a division of EBSCO Information Services, Inc. ; Amenia, NY : Grey House Publishing, [2019] | Includes bibliographical references and index.
Identifiers: ISBN 9781642650280 (hardcover)
Subjects: LCSH: Prohibited books--United States. | Prohibited books--United Kingdom. | Challenged books--United States. | Challenged books--United Kingdom. | Censorship--United States. | Censorship--United Kingdom.
Classification: LCC Z1019 .C46 2019 | DDC 098.1--dc23

First Printing

Contents

About This Volume, Robert C. Evans   vii

Silent Censorship and Mark Twain's *Adventures of Huckleberry Finn*,
    Alan Gribben   xiii

Critical Contexts

Censorship in Medieval England, Richard Obenauf   3

Banned, Censored, and Challenged Books: A Survey of
    Issues and Ideas, Kelly Snyder   22

Medieval Intolerance and Modern Censorship in the
    Morality Play *Mankind*, Richard Obenauf   35

Using Anything: Flannery O'Connor and Banning Books, Robert Donahoo   57

Critical Readings

The Coming Censorship of Fiction, Basil Tozer et al.   81

"Fighting Race Calumny": Efforts to Censor *The Birth of a Nation*,
    C. E. Bentley, Jane Addams, and Mary Childs Nerney   100

"Hidden Things": Self-Censorship in the Poetry and
    Career of Constantine Cavafy, Robert C. Evans   117

Banned, Bothered, and Bewildered: *Lady Chatterley's Lover*,
    Nicolas Tredell   133

Interanimations: William S. Burroughs's *Naked Lunch*, Nicolas Tredell   151

Efforts to Ban Harper Lee's *To Kill a Mockingbird*, Phill Johnson   169

To Kill a Mockingbird in Columbus, Indiana:
    A Community Divided, Robert C. Evans   187

Informal Censorship: The Literary Feud between Frank Chin and
    Maxine Hong Kingston, Liyang Dong   209

Alison Bechdel's *Fun Home*: The Gay Graphic Memoir as a
    Magnet for Censorship, Darren Harris-Fain   229

A Recent Attempt at Book "Censorship": The Conejo Valley Dispute,
    Robert C. Evans   245

Resources

Further Reading   271
Bibliography   277
About the Editor   283
Contributors   285
Index   289

About This Volume

Robert C. Evans

This volume, like all the others in the Critical Insights series, is divided into several sections. The book begins with a "flagship" essay by a major scholar. In the present case, that scholar is Alan Gribben, one of the world's leading experts on Mark Twain. Gribben also happens to be the editor of controversial editions of two of Twain's greatest works—*The Adventures of Tom Sawyer* and, especially, *Adventures of Huckleberry Finn*. It is the latter book, of course, that is widely considered one of the very greatest works in all of American literature. But it is also *Huck Finn* (as it is affectionately called) that has recently been perhaps the most often "challenged" or "banned" book of any great work of fiction, at least in the United States.

The problem, of course, is that Huck, the novel's narrator, so often uses the so-called "N" word in telling his story. That word appears over two hundred times in the course of the book, and its appearances there have frequently elicited objections from concerned readers, especially concerned African American parents whose children have been required to read the book (and encounter that word) in the public schools and in classroom discussions. Gribben, of course, knows better than almost anyone that Twain's purpose in using the "N" word was in fact to *satirize* racism (as well as to reflect, faithfully, the ways some people actually spoke in the nineteenth century).

But Gribben began to hear, repeatedly, from teachers who also loved Twain's masterpiece, that they were now reluctant to teach the book. Sometimes they feared criticism for doing so; sometimes they genuinely did not want to hurt the feelings of their African American students; sometimes both motives were involved. In any case, Gribben began to worry that Twain's great book had become the object of silent censorship: it wasn't, often, being overtly *banned* from public schools but was, increasingly, being quietly ignored or simply dropped from high school curricula. More and more, students were no longer being exposed to one of the greatest works of American fiction ever written.

Gribben decided that one way to deal with this dilemma might be to produce editions of Twain's two most famous books in which the "N" word was replaced with the less inflammatory word "slave." He knew that this alteration would arouse controversy, but he had no idea just how *much* controversy it would provoke. For weeks and even months, his decision was the subject of highly heated national and even international condemnation. Few of the people criticizing Gribben had any idea that he had devoted his entire life as a scholar to studying and celebrating Twain. Few cared that he defended himself by trying to explain that he had only wanted to make sure that *Huck Finn* was no longer silenced in American high schools. In his contribution to this book—which consists of a self-interview— Gribben explains his motives and responds to his critics.

As it happens, Gribben's interview is perhaps the perfect "flagship" essay for the present volume. Anyone who reads the entire book will see that issues of race and ethnicity have increasingly become *the* central issues (besides graphic descriptions of sexual behavior) in recent attempts to challenge, censor, or ban literature. The "N" word has become *the* most controversial word of all the terms that have led parents and others to try to limit what and how other people (especially children or young adults) can read.

Following Gribben's self-interview are four essays in the volume's Critical Contexts section. Each of these four essays is designed to offer a particular emphasis. For example, Richard Obenauf's essay on censorship in medieval England has an explicitly historical focus. This essay is designed to give students a model of how to examine any topic from a historical perspective. The next contextual essay, by Kelly Snyder, is intended to give readers a sense of the critical background to issues of censorship, not only by listing valuable secondary works on this topic but also by considering several of those works in detail. The third contextual essay—another piece by Richard Obenauf—is a kind of critical lens. In other words, it shows how the topic of censorship can be explored by focusing on one particular work (in this case the medieval morality play known as *Mankind*). Finally, the last of the four contextual essays is deliberately designed to use the method of comparison and contrast. In this case, Robert Donahoo, a leading scholar of Flannery O'Connor, compares and contrasts O'Connor's works with several others inspired by hers. It is not a coincidence that O'Connor, like Twain and others discussed in this book, is most often controversial because of her use of the "N" word. Like Twain, O'Connor intended to satirize the racists who use that word in her fiction, just as she also, like Twain, wanted to record authentically the ways people of her time actually sometimes spoke and thought. But O'Connor, again like Twain, has now become difficult to teach and discuss because she *did* use the "N" word. One value of Donahoo's piece is that he shows how fruitfully various *black* artists have responded to O'Connor's writings.

The next section of the volume—which is also the longest section—consists of ten "Critical Readings" essays. The first two of these pieces are less essays per se than compilations of historical documents. Both offer examples of the kinds of debates that flourished, in the early twentieth century, about two topics that have remained central to most debates about censorship: sex and race. The first piece reprints a 1908 article by Basil Tozer warning writers and publishers that if they did not themselves refrain from creating and issuing suggestive fiction, governments might actually impose repressive official censorship. Tozer's essay provoked various interesting responses.

The next historical piece reprints documents concerning attacks on a racially offensive film. These documents—a letter, a newspaper interview, and a detailed narrative—all grew out of efforts in 1915 to censor, suppress, or at least condemn D. W. Griffith's famous movie, *The Birth of a Nation*. This was an important early work of American cinema, but it quickly became controversial because of the ways it negatively depicted black people and, in fact, endorsed the behavior of the Ku Klux Klan. The newly-formed National Association for the Advancement of Colored People (NAACP) waged a vigorous campaign to challenge and even ban the film—a campaign the organization proudly detailed in one of its publications.

In a different kind of piece altogether, Robert Evans next looks at early poems by the great modern Greek poet C. P. Cavafy, who is also widely considered one of the great homoerotic poets of his or any other time. Evans stresses a different kind of censorship than has been emphasized previously: *self*-censorship, in which a writer cannot write what he might otherwise want to write for fear of being attacked either in print or in the flesh. In two successive essays, the English scholar Nicolas Tredell deals with two of the most famous examples of attempts at twentieth-century censorship: D. H. Lawrence's scandalous (for the time) novel *Lady Chatterley's Lover* and William S. Burroughs's perhaps even more scandalous novel titled *Naked Lunch*. Tredell explores both works less by examining actual efforts to censor them than by discussing censorship as a broader cultural and fictional theme. He shows how the ultimate failure to suppress Lawrence's book helped create a much freer attitude toward fiction from the 1960s onwards, and he shows how, in Burroughs's book, censorship—or the lack thereof—is central to the novel's own meanings.

The next two essays—by Phill Johnson and Robert Evans, respectively—deal with recent efforts to challenge Harper Lee's famous novel *To Kill a Mockingbird*. Here, again, Lee's use of the "N" word was the major point at issue. Like Twain and O'Connor, Lee used the word satirically and historically: she sought to attack racists while also reflecting, honestly, the racist language and mentality of the era in which her novel was set. Johnson's essay reports on numerous recent efforts to keep Lee's book out of public school classrooms. Evans's article focuses, in detail, on one particular case. He quotes extensively from people who either favored or rejected attempts to ban the book. Some of the evidence he cites is particularly heartfelt and revealing and suggests how difficult it can sometimes be to decide between the need to protect free speech and the desire to shield people from pain.

An essay by Liyang Dong deals with yet another kind of alleged censorship—the kind that can arise within the literary community itself, especially when two important authors are feuding with one another and bystanders feel a need to take sides. Dong shows how Frank Chin, an early and very influential Chinese American author, took offense at the fiction of Maxine Hong Kingston, a younger colleague who, according to Chin, had betrayed her people by buying into white prejudices about China, Chinese people, and Chinese Americans. Kingston, initially, felt threatened by Chin's strident criticism. Eventually, however, Kingston gained the upper hand, so that Chin later felt that he was, in effect, being censored by Kingston and her allies.

Dong's essay, like others in this book, shows how issues of race and ethnicity (and, possibly, sexism) have influenced recent examples of censorship. Meanwhile, an essay by Darren Harris-Fain (the noted scholar of science fiction and graphic fiction) explores efforts to challenge Alison Bechtdel's gay/lesbian graphic novel *Fun Home*. Like Evans's earlier essay on Cavafy, this piece by Harris-Fain explores the ways in which members of sexual minority groups have responded to efforts to censor them. The closing Critical Readings essay, by Robert Evans, offers a detailed report about a very recent controversy concerning alleged censorship. This controversy took place in 2017 and 2018 in the Conejo Valley school district in California. Sherman Alexie's novel *The Absolutely True Diary of a Part-Time Indian* was the initial title that came under suspicion, but as the controversy mushroomed it soon became clear that more than two hundred other titles might be affected by the school board's decisions.

Some members of the board wanted to flag mature books with an asterisk on syllabi and on materials available to parents. These books had already been identified, by the State of California, as intended for "mature" readers; advocates of the asterisk policy wanted to alert parents to that fact. However, opponents of the new policy saw it as an effort to censor books and deprive teachers of their right to teach what they considered appropriate. Most of the objections to books, in this case, centered around objections to mature sexual language, but supposed racial and ethnic insensitivity were also often mentioned as reasons for concern. The Conejo Valley case illustrates that debates about alleged censorship are very much alive and well in the United States today, as long before.

The final section of the present volume provides a variety of resources, including a list of suggested further reading materials, an additional bibliography, information about the editor and the contributors, and an extensive index.

Silent Censorship and Mark Twain's *Adventures of Huckleberry Finn*

Alan Gribben

What first called your attention to the issue of censorship involving Twain's most famous novel?

In 2010 the National Endowment for the Arts sponsored a Big Read initiative to encourage literacy and promote an awareness of the joys of reading. In the state where I reside, the librarians selected Mark Twain's *Adventures of Tom Sawyer*, first published in 1876, as the literary work they wished to focus on in connection with Alabama's Year of the Small Towns and Downtowns. As the scholar chosen to write an introduction to the Big Read Alabama Edition of *Tom Sawyer*, I was also tapped to travel around the state and give scheduled talks in libraries to highlight the novel's features. I visited cities as large as Birmingham and towns as small as Eufaula and Dadeville. A surprisingly large crowd of more than 100 people turned out in Valley, Alabama, thanks to a persuasive community organizer there.

What struck me more than anything else as I traveled around the state was the number of middle school and high school teachers who approached me after my talk to explain that they could no longer teach either of Twain's two most famous novels—*The Adventures of Tom Sawyer* and *Adventures of Huckleberry Finn* (1885)—in their classrooms anymore, nor even assign them in recommended reading lists. The problem was simple yet inescapable: the presence in these books of the dreaded N-word, two syllables so potent in their lingering vitriol and racist connotations that they cannot be fully spelled out in newspapers or even pronounced on television or radio shows without major repercussions.

After listening to these disturbing reports from perplexed teachers—all of whom lamented that these fine books were now off-limits in their public school classrooms—I went home, reached for a first edition of *Tom Sawyer*, and carefully counted the N-words appearing in the table of contents, the captions to illustrations, and the text: nine N-words occurred in that novel. There were far, far more of these in a first edition of *Huckleberry Finn*, I could assume. No wonder the school boards, principals, curriculum directors, and (in many cases) the teachers themselves had become squeamish about assigning these books in Deep South schools where only a century and a half had passed since millions of enslaved African Americans were finally liberated from unpaid toil and violent oppression.

I had not grown up in the South but rather in a small railroad town in Kansas. The grip of discrimination reached there, too, however; during my childhood the balconies in the three movie theaters were reserved for "colored" patrons. Our nearby county seat had an official-looking sign at the city limits notifying such people to be sure to leave the vicinity by sunset. The civil rights era of the mid-1960s coincided with my college years at the University of Kansas at Lawrence, and I energetically joined in picketing and demonstrating against this type of bigotry. I even endeavored to integrate my fraternity house and the campus Greek system (and only a single vote prevented my fraternity house from revoking my membership by the mandated two-thirds majority).

When did you decide to prepare an alternative edition of Twain's two novels?

One night, driving home from yet another library talk after which teachers gathered around me to vent their frustration about being denied the opportunity to analyze Twain's influential fiction with their students, I realized with a start that it lay within my capacity to attempt a remedy for this vexing type of classroom censorship. During my graduate student years at the University of California at Berkeley I had been employed as an editorial assistant for the Mark Twain Project, a publishing venture in the Bancroft Library that was issuing new texts of Twain's writings. I had written the introductions and explanatory notes for five of Twain's notebooks and had helped edit and proofread other portions of his writings.

What if I were to edit two virtually identical versions of Twain's best-known novels, *Tom Sawyer* and *Huckleberry Finn*?

The only difference between them would be the translation of the racial epithets in one version; that alternate text would render the N-word as *slave* and Injun Joe (Huckleberry Finn's term for the villain in the first of the paired novels) as *Indian Joe*. The other edition of the novels would retain Twain's original language. They would have identical pagination, making it possible for teachers and students to have a choice about how they wish to encounter this reading experience.

I wrote up my idea for these two kinds of texts and contacted the same press, NewSouth Books, that had published the Big Read Alabama edition of *The Adventures of Tom Sawyer*, seeking an appointment with the publisher, Suzanne La Rosa, or the editor-in-chief, Randall Williams. To my surprise both of them attended the presentation I gave in their office about how this innovation might solve, at least temporarily, the prohibition against teaching these novels in public schools. They conferred briefly and then came back with a positive answer: their press would undertake this challenge. I added then, mainly to placate my conscience, that textual purists were not likely to be happy with this manipulation of Twain's words, even though there would be an accompanying volume with his original language. (I was thinking of the fact that I myself would formerly have opposed this compromise, inasmuch as it went against all of my graduate school instruction as well as my training at the Mark Twain Project.) "There are liable to be some hostile reviews," I predicted. Randall Williams, a veteran of the civil rights struggles whose office was once firebombed by the Ku Klux Klan, almost seemed to welcome the prospect of opposition. "Bring it on!" I remember him saying.

Were there any particular difficulties you faced while preparing the edition?

My wife, Irene Wong, assisted me in preparing the two alternate versions. We scanned copies of the first editions of Twain's novels, proofreading carefully for the inevitable typographical errors and altering the derogatory racial labels in what we named the NewSouth Edition (in tribute to the intrepid press that was bringing out this experiment in resolving a problem that had stymied classroom instruction about Twain's works). The publisher decided that the NewSouth Edition would precede the Original Language Edition by a few months, since the latter version had considerable competition in the marketplace whereas the NewSouth Edition had none.

The main difficulty we faced, one that greatly concerned Suzanne La Rosa, was the task of making teachers and professors aware that they would soon have an alternative edition available if they wished to try it. She repeatedly told me about the terrible odds against bringing attention to any new book among the hundreds of thousands published each year. "I just hope we can somehow get the word out to classroom instructors about this new development," said La Rosa. Neither of us knew then that notifying the world about our book would soon be the least of our problems.

As soon as NewSouth Books sent out an advance press release to advertise the impending N-word-free *Tom Sawyer* and *Huckleberry Finn*, Mark Schultz of *Publishers Weekly* wrote a major article on January 3, 2011 announcing this news. Suddenly the media world exploded over the concept of tampering with Mark Twain's phrasing. Reporters from television, newspapers, magazines, and radio besieged the publishers (and me), seeking interviews and details. Among the news organizations covering this were NBC, CBS, BBC, NPR, the New York *Times*, the Washington *Post*, the *Wall Street Journal*, the *International Herald Tribune*, the *Guardian*, the London *Times*, the *Irish Times*, and the *India Times*. This premature frenzy caught us off guard, as it were; Irene and I had not quite finished editing the texts and I was still putting the finishing touches on my (differing) introductions and explanatory notes for the two novels. In a flurry of activity we stayed up all night, working at the kitchen table, and early in the morning of January 9 we completed and submitted the entire manuscript to the publisher and editor-in-chief. Incidentally, in that hectic process we misread one of our handwritten figures in counting up the number of N-words that appeared in the table of contents, captions to the illustrations, and text of the first edition of *Huckleberry Finn*; we accidentally launched the combined NewSouth Edition of *Mark*

Twain's Adventures of Tom Sawyer and Huckleberry Finn with an introduction that cited a mistaken figure of 219 rather than 215 total usages of the N-word in Twain's first edition of *Huckleberry Finn*. That slip eventually became rather comical as we watched this erroneous figure repeated endlessly in dozens of articles, editorials, and op-ed columns. We had inadvertently created a minor hoax that affected information sites everywhere on the Internet. At first chagrined by our slipup, we gradually concluded that Twain, an inveterate prankster, would no doubt have relished our unintentional feat of instigating a fake number that will be carried to the far corners of the world for decades to come.

There then followed an excruciating monthlong wait until the book finally became available for purchase on February 5, 2011; in that long interval the members of the media and the writers of letters to the editor basically pummeled NewSouth Books and me, even though none of them had yet seen a copy of my introduction and notes, which explained and justified the rationale for offering an optional version of Twain's books. Nearly all of the brouhaha centered on Twain's masterpiece, *Adventures of Huckleberry Finn*; hardly any of the commentators mentioned its prequel, *The Adventures of Tom Sawyer*. The commentators' urge to sensationalize the event, to cast the situation as an uppity professor in the Deep South believing that he could "improve" on Mark Twain's prose, seemed to overwhelm them. Twain's admonitions that "phrasing is everything, almost," that "the difference between the *almost* right word & the *right* word is really a large matter," and that "it's the difference between the lightning bug & the lightning" were tirelessly quoted to me, as though I—the author of the two-volume *Mark Twain's Library: A Reconstruction* (1980) and several dozen published articles about Twain's intellectual background—needed basic instruction about Twain's tenets for good writing.

What kinds of reactions did you expect?
I had naively (as it turned out) assumed that the authors and scholars who had previously consulted my substantial work on the topic of Twain's library and reading would give me the benefit of the doubt,

despite the media's sensationalizing of these optional editions for classroom reading, but such was not the case. On January 7, only four days after the *Publishers Weekly* online announcement, the eminent Mark Twain biographer Ron Powers, who had written *Dangerous Water: A Biography of the Boy Who Became Mark Twain* (1999) and *Tom and Huck Don't Live Here Anymore: Childhood and Murder in the Heart of America* (2001), impulsively blogged about "the vapid, smiley-faced effrontery" of my endeavor. This was the same Ron Powers who, at a conference on The State of Mark Twain Studies in August 2005 at Elmira College, where he was the keynote speaker to celebrate the publication of his *Mark Twain: A Life* (2005), arose from his book-signing table when I approached him with my copy of his book and embraced me, telling me what a great asset my study of Twain's reading had been to him in writing his biography. Now, in 2011, without ever having seen my book or its explanatory introduction, he castigated my "desecrated edition" of *Huckleberry Finn* as "an evisceration of America's great novel" and referred me to the instructive work of another Mark Twain scholar, Shelley Fisher Fishkin, who supposedly could set me straight about "the legitimacy of racial slurs" in Twain's novel. "Is Twain's inspired irony really so hard to grasp?" asked an exasperated Powers. He had special contempt for my "distinctly vanilla-flavored publisher," cherry-picking through hundreds of the NewSouth Books titles to extract two titles that he suggested—falsely—were indicative of longstanding Deep South prejudices. He proceeded to remind this "Alabama-based publisher of books with ingratiating titles" about the arrest of Rosa Parks and the sacrifices made at Selma as though Randall Williams and Suzanne La Rosa had never been made aware of the civil rights movement. Throughout Powers's denunciation he blithely assumed that all teachers have complete choice about what they can teach, and that only "enfeebled and . . . intimidated" instructors would be unable to discuss a book with 215 N-words in today's integrated public school classrooms. Randall Williams, a veteran and historian of the civil rights movement who had been the founding director of the Southern Poverty Law Center's Klanwatch Project and whose credentials regarding racial justice are unimpeachable, was flabbergasted by Powers's ill-informed and slanted blog. I, on the other hand, simply felt that I had irretrievably lost an author-friend I had long admired.

Did anything about those reactions surprise you?
The penalty for my breaking ranks with my fellow American literature scholars has been silent but effectual. The candidates for whom I have written letters of recommendation since then have almost unanimously been rejected for fellowships and other awards, which seems to me a way of striking back at my action by vetoing anyone I support. My attendance at academic conferences is usually received huffily. My perception is that I have been given a massive professional cold shoulder.

Perhaps most significant of all, the scholars who wrote to NewSouth Books and requested review copies of the two NewSouth Books editions never followed through with any reviews. Despite some groundbreaking points in my introductions that explored the necessity of Tom Sawyer's role, discussed the pairing of these companion works, cast new light on Ernest Hemingway's often misunderstood praise for *Huckleberry Finn*, and probed the deeper messages of that novel, together with an extensive inventory of Twain's satirical targets and a bibliography of scholarly studies, these editions went virtually unreviewed in any premier journals, an unheard-of thing. Rather than analyze the merits of my volumes the reviewers went mute. If this is not silent censorship of the most virulent type, then what is?

Were you surprised by the national and international attention the edition received?
The amount of radio and newspaper coverage that the NewSouth Edition of *Huckleberry Finn* elicited would astonish the publisher and me. Katie Couric had a few brief words with me on the NBC televised evening news. NPR stations independently transmitted several interviews. Drive time talk show radio jockeys and I argued vociferously as their listeners wended their way to work or commuted back home. A Canadian radio network pitted me in an

on-air debate against a Canadian professor who asked, "But what if your edition takes hold and becomes the version taught in most classrooms?" As I recall it, the moderator of that little set-to evinced a Canadian superiority regarding the racial harmony that Canada had peaceably and perfectly long ago attained. Ireland struck me, in several radio interviews, as being perhaps the nation most at ease in using the N-word; the Irish with whom I held on-air arguments were passionate defenders of that racial slur as just another word, it appeared to me. Over and over my opponents in these interviews and in printed newspaper editorials and magazine columns accused me of censorship and likened me to bowdlerizers, book banners, and book burners. Prominent political cartoonists hammered at this alleged instance of rampant censorship. Dave Granlund's cartoon depicted a gigantic alligator labeled *Censors* about to devour a tiny figure of Mark Twain afloat on a copy of *Huckleberry Finn.* Oliphant portrayed Twain, smoking a cigar in heaven, receiving the news that "the political correction Nazis have re-written Huck Finn and Tom Sawyer to expunge the offending n-word! Do you have a comment?" as nearby angels cover their ears in fearful anticipation of his furious objection. Margulies drew an incensed Mark Twain demanding of the editor (me), "Don't touch my junk!" Ramirez's cartoon in the Houston *Chronicle* showed an indignant Twain asking, "you CENSORED parts of *Huck Finn?*" followed by an obscenity issuing from his mouth that the newspaper (in the cartoon) had to censor. Stahler in the Columbus *Dispatch* sketched a vending machine displaying a newspaper headline: "Twain's '*Huck Finn*' censored." Only a single cartoonist—Jim Day in the Las Vegas *Review Journal*—took a different view; he pictured a television viewer watching a newscaster reporting the "controversy" swirling around "the new, sanitized version of Mark Twain's classic book" while a cobwebbed copy of *Huckleberry Finn* is used as a doorstop, with Twain's famous maxim printed in the forefront of the cartoon: "Classic: A book which people praise and don't read."

It seemed to me that the cartoonists along with the op-ed writers and columnists (all of whom, by the way, chastely avoided printing the very word they were attacking me for translating) lacked any basic notion of what those terms *censorship* and *ban* actually mean. After all, I was trying to *restore* these novels to the classroom where they are currently verboten; it was not I but the teachers, curriculum directors, principals, and school boards who were quietly banning them from the students' eyes. What is more, my publisher would also bring out in 2011 my Original Language Edition of the same books—so how could this possibly amount to either censorship or banning?

I had spent my entire scholarly career promoting and praising Twain's works (see www.alangribben.com), not denigrating him. A little online reading on my detractors' part would have revealed to them that *censorship* normally and more accurately refers to governmental or religious prohibitions against the publication, sale, or distribution of a certain book or type of books. I was in no way interfering with the printing, sale, or distribution of the dozens of other editions of these novels by Mark Twain. My publisher and I were simply adding two more editions to the ample supply from which customers could choose. Nor did I possess any authority—or, for that matter, any wish—to "ban" Twain's writings. In fact, the bibliographies in my editions recommended various other editions of these novels for further reading.

Do you feel that your critics had any legitimate points?

Leaving aside Ron Powers's unfair slams, I found myself having considerable patience with those who objected to any alterations in Mark Twain's texts. Graduate programs in English emphasize the sacredness of an author's final textual decisions and the Mark Twain Project at the University of California at Berkeley, where I had been employed for eight years, strives to present to readers the most accurate possible rendition of his writings, working directly from his holograph manuscripts where possible.

However, the majority of the objectors to the NewSouth Edition of Twain's two novels had never undergone the experience of trying to teach them in racially mixed classes. I had introduced these books into my assigned readings at three institutions where I taught: Elmira College (a summer course), the University of Texas at Austin (seventeen years), and Auburn University at Montgomery (twenty-eight years). During all of these forty-five years of classroom teaching I have never once pronounced the N-word in front of students; I have always translated it as *slave*. In the household where I was reared my parents would never have tolerated that word, in the integrated public schools I attended it was (quite literally) a fighting word, and in my college days I had protested against such demeaning concepts and attitudes.

What do you think were some of the weaknesses in your critics' arguments?

Virtually all of the denouncers of the NewSouth Edition of *Tom Sawyer* and *Huckleberry Finn* made two fallacious assumptions. First, that teachers in public schools have complete control over what they are permitted to teach. This is not true in any classrooms except those designated as special honors classes, where teachers are given more leeway in selecting their materials. Curriculum directors generally issue a list of approved readings for public school teachers. Moreover, school boards and principals have learned from bitter experience that announcements about curriculum matters can quickly degenerate into nasty newspaper and Internet headlines. Thus their reading lists are now constructed and released in utter silence, the best possible example of true censorship and yet difficult to prove because of the wide range of other books listed for teachers to adopt.

Second, those who loftily sermonize that Twain's novels can offer "a teachable moment" and advise teachers and college instructors merely to teach the N-word-laden passages "sensitively" do not realize that they are demanding an impossible task. The N-word is so culturally charged with implications of permanent and inescapable inferiority that it can do incalculable harm to young African American readers, and it still registers bias that is uncomfortable to older students as well. Several African American men wrote to me to say that the day their teacher discussed one or the other of these two novels in class remained one of the worst and most embarrassing days of their lives.

Who came to your defense, and why?

Quite a few of my former students wrote in support of my character and my tendencies as a classroom teacher. Some of them were now prominent in their field. Rick Riordan, a well-known writer of mythic science fiction novels, defended my classroom style and what he took to be my good intentions here. A large number of teachers verified my points about the utter impossibility of introducing a book with 215 N-words into classrooms amid today's racially heated atmosphere. I even heard from a few English professors, one of them at Hofstra University, who admitted to eliminating Twain's *Huckleberry Finn* from their reading lists as requiring too much precious classroom time to soften the blows of the N-word by exploring its etymology and explicating Twain's commitment as a realist author to capturing the actual speech of uneducated characters along the Mississippi River during the 1830s and 1840s (the period in which Twain set his novels). I had rather expected that at least a few African American professors of English might speak out in my favor, but several of them explained to me privately that they could not afford to get mixed up in this particular controversy. "That word sticks to you," remarked one of them. "If you are a black educator you become enmeshed with a terrible word that clings to your identity."

How has the edition fared?

NewSouth Books reports that my editions of *Tom Sawyer* and *Huckleberry Finn* have climbed into the ranks of the firm's top sellers, and their annual sales are steadily increasing. The Original Language Editions do surprisingly well, too. Moreover, the initial controversy over these books may have helped them find the educators who could best put the editions to use, and the massive publicity in 2011 brought NewSouth queries and submissions from distinguished authors and agents who had not previously heard of the press.

Have reactions changed over the years?

As far as I know, only one writer, a columnist for the St. Louis *Post-Dispatch*, retracted in 2013 her 2011 remarks, recalling that "I was part of the crowd crying about the sacrosanct nature of Twain's original text" and acknowledging that she had altered her opinion after her fourth-grade daughter was exposed to an oral rendition of a Twain short story that included the N-word. A few high school instructors, including Hugh H. Davis in North Carolina, have let me know that they have tried the alternate NewSouth Edition in classrooms with predominantly African American enrollments and have experienced encouragingly positive results (despite the students' occasional confusion about when Twain explicitly meant to refer to a slave instead of the N-word).

If you had to do it all over again, would you?

The experiment I undertook still seems well worth the abuse. And in today's world of Internet trolls and bloggers, there assuredly *was* abuse. Within a few weeks of the *Publishers Weekly* article my office computer registered 443 strongly objecting emails, most of them unsigned and a great many of them seeming to take pleasure in an opportunity to throw the N-word around in denouncing me and my edition. A significant percentage of these profane missives alluded to their worship of the late comedian George Carlin; that is to say, they classified the N-word as simply another one of the curse words that Carlin asserted should always and everywhere be accessible to speakers and writers, just like the S-word and the F-word. But to my mind, a word attaching itself only to a designated racial minority is hardly the same as the vulgar profanities Carlin cherished. Anyway, by contrast only 170 messages arrived that congratulated and thanked me. (Another 469 emails sought more information, seemed to be cautiously on the fence, or else requested interviews or correspondence with me.) A few people contacted my department chair, demanding that he fire or punish me. An anonymous online objector who claimed he was an Auburn University student vowed that he would seek me out and give me a thrashing, but he never showed up. NewSouth Books also received their share of hate mail and a warning that an organized and determined group of objectors would be picketing their premises on a certain day, but that never materialized, either; Montgomery, like much of the South, can get some very chilly, windy weather in January.

This furor would not abate until the Arab Spring uprisings and the Fukushima nuclear disaster in Japan altered the news cycle. Another televised event also had an impact. On June 12, 2011, Byron Pitts on CBS television's *60 Minutes* interviewed Randall Williams of NewSouth Books within the context of two Minnesota high school teachers' contrasting approaches to *Huckleberry Finn*. One of the Minnesota teachers pronounced the N-word in her classroom; the other teacher declined to do so. Then the high school students responded with candid remarks about their reactions to the two tactics. The hurt expressed by an African American student in the N-word-spoken classroom vividly brought home the pain and the power of the racial insult. More than anything else that transpired during 2011, this revealing *60 Minutes* segment cooled the ardor of the pro-N-word crowd.

I was certainly glad that I had chosen to take my concept to an independent press that had a deep commitment to free speech and racial justice; few if any university presses or large commercial publishers would have withstood the wave of denunciations that NewSouth Books endured. There truly seemed to be an orchestrated campaign to halt the publication of the NewSouth Edition. Suzanne La Rosa and Randall Williams never had second thoughts about their determination to see this edition published, promoted, and distributed. In standing resolutely against the tide of indignant and angry critics who demanded that they stop the presses before the book could be released, were they not in effect combating outright censorship of a book?

The ironies in this entire episode are both deep and rich. Those intellectuals who deemed themselves most progressive in their racial attitudes suddenly marshaled their utmost efforts against the publication of a book that would in effect cause less injury to the feelings of young African Americans. Normally these were people who would denounce any examples of censorship or book banning, yet here they were, demanding that NewSouth Books stop the presses and retract a book before it had even reached print.

Absolutely hilarious is the fact that by bringing out this translated edition I managed a political miracle in today's divided national loyalties. The Far Left and the Far Right astoundingly found themselves in mutual agreement about something: that these NewSouth Editions should be banned. The Far Left saw the use of *slave* rather than the N-word as a nefarious attempt to hide America's racist past (as though a substituted word denoting an enslaved and abused people is not in itself sufficiently horrendous), whereas the Far Right interpreted the edition as yet another kowtowing capitulation to political correctness, a knuckling under to the demands of sensitivity agitators. In all fairness I should have received a bit of credit for the fact that on this one particular issue— whether or not my editions should be banned—I healed for several months the immense breach between our current political attitudes.

If the current silent censorship of Twain's novels proceeds unabated in the public schools, *Tom Sawyer* and *Huckleberry Finn* will soon be less and less familiar to teachers and students except in private academies. Very few colleges require courses in nineteenth-century American literature, and thus the vast majority of young Americans will complete their education without ever having any classroom contact with these works. How much longer will they seem famous or relevant under these conditions in the future? We will extinguish two classics merely for the sake of a single detested noun.

Whenever I teach Twain's novels I offer my students their choice of texts—the original or the translated version. Most African American students opt for the NewSouth Edition, but a number of the white students choose it, too. (Some of the African American students who go with the Original Language Edition have told me that they want to show their classmates, and themselves, that they can take the insults and not be affected.) In any event, by skipping over the superficial subject of the N-word—which I am convinced Mark Twain never foresaw as the main point of his books—we are quickly able to get into the far deeper challenge that *Huckleberry Finn*, especially, throws at us. Huck Finn's narrative implicitly asks us to examine our relationship to our culture and make certain that we ourselves are not conforming to outdated, inhumane behavior that demeans and injures our fellow humans in ways to which we have become inured. As I taught Twain's *Huckleberry Finn* over the years, its narrator's faulty assumptions gradually made me aware that by assigning Twain's paired novels—without offering any other options to my students—I myself was participating in the dissemination of hurtful language that even the novels' artistic accomplishments could not excuse at this point in our civilization.

My more permanent scholarly legacy will be my studies of Mark Twain's library and reading, but I take some satisfaction in having offered students and teachers a choice in how a great American work and its prequel can be reintroduced into their classrooms.

CRITICAL
CONTEXTS

Censorship in Medieval England

Richard Obenauf

Censorship is a form of intolerance. Exerted by institutions rather than by individuals, censorship today generally refers to the prepublication approval of a text or to the condemnation of a work after it has been published. Before the invention of print, however, censorship also involved other methods of enforcing ideological conformity in works, such as altering manuscripts or destroying them. Additional forces that shape literary decisions through intimidation are more accurately understood not as censorship but as other forms of intolerance.

Censorship is often difficult to prove. Scholars of medieval literature and history must contend with handwritten manuscripts on animal skin that have been damaged by fires, floods, insects, and other forces. The most effective form of censorship—condemnation that leads to the elimination of every copy of a text—leaves no trace. Through the centuries, some documents have been inadvertently altered, and others intentionally mutilated. Many medieval works survive in a single manuscript, while countless others have simply been lost to the passing of time. Here I offer a brief account of premodern censorship in England while focusing on the problems in defining and proving censorship in the Middle Ages. We will see that the roots of formal print censorship may be found in earlier forms of intolerance and that during the Middle Ages intolerance was arguably a more effective form of control than censorship.

Medieval English society was highly hierarchical and demanded rigid conformity. This strict hierarchy, sometimes referred to as the Great Chain of Being, was predicated on the idea that everything in existence had a specific rank in the universe, with God at the top, followed by angels, humans, animals, plants, and minerals, each category with its own hierarchy. This system promoted the divine right of kings, but because everything had its place in this order, kings and peasants alike were understood to have defined roles and duties to fulfill. Censorship and intolerance sought to promote political and religious conformity by eliminating people and ideas that were perceived to pose a threat to this social structure.

A Medieval Model of Censorship

For premodern periods, G. H. Putnam's two-volume *Censorship of the Church of Rome and its Influence upon the Production and Distribution of Literature* (1906) remains the authority on church censorship, throughout Europe as well as in England. Putnam demonstrates that the medieval church provided a framework for censorship in general that would remain long after Henry VIII broke ties with Rome, a point that seems not to be clearly spelled out elsewhere. The most important book on censorship specifically in England is Frederick Seaton Siebert's 1952 *Freedom of the Press in England 1476-1776: The Rise and Decline of Government Control*, which briefly acknowledges earlier statutes but draws primarily on contemporary documents, including licenses, proclamations, royal patents, and laws. Johannes Gutenberg had developed a printing press with movable type in Germany circa 1440, but his invention did not reach England until William Caxton set up the country's first printing press in Westminster Abbey in 1476. Starting with the year of Caxton's first printed publication, 1476, Siebert traces a nearly linear path from oppression to freedom as practical and civil matters. Thus medieval precedents do not inform his work, nor any of the scholarship based on his work, such as Annabel Patterson's 1984 *Censorship and Interpretation:The Conditions of Writing and Reading in Early Modern Europe.*

Patterson describes early modern (post-1476) techniques for evading censorship in the pulpit, on the stage, and in the press, through an interpretive strategy she calls the "hermeneutics of censorship." For Patterson, all three arenas were carefully controlled because all three routinely attempted to influence politics. "There is no question but that early modern censorship was inefficient and incoherent," writes Patterson (13). The limitations on toleration in the Middle Ages may help to explain why from a twentieth-century perspective early modern censorship might have appeared inefficient and incoherent. Patterson's argument does not take into account earlier signs of intolerance that, in my view, made censorship and other forms of intolerance the logical tools for preserving the social order in the medieval and early modern periods.

Setting out to discover ways canonical early modern writers evaded the censor, Patterson searches for moments of interpretive ambiguity that become evidence of the "hermeneutics of censorship." Although her model has been influential in the field of censorship, because it hinges on ambiguity, it seems to me that Patterson's criticism is impossible either to prove or to disprove. Some recent scholarship on censorship has begun to reevaluate Patterson's hypothesis, but not by examining earlier forms of intolerance. For example, Cyndia Susan Clegg has written a series of books on censorship: *Press Censorship in Elizabethan England* (1997), *Press Censorship in Jacobean England* (2001), and *Press Censorship in Caroline England* (2008). Like Patterson and Siebert, Clegg follows the official record carefully, and like the others she focuses on the direct connections between texts, laws, and events.

Debora Shuger, also writing from a literary perspective, tackled the subject in her book *Censorship and CulturalSensibility: The Regulation of Language in Tudor-Stuart England* (2006). Shuger finds two models of censorship in early modern England, one stemming from classical Rome and designed to prevent defamation, the other stemming from the Church of Rome and designed to safeguard against heresy. More recently, Randy Robertson's book *Censorship and Conflict in Seventeenth-Century England: The Subtle Art of Division* (2009) is narrowly focused on a single period. He notes that "Clerical and lay controls of the printed word—mechanisms of both prepublication and post-publication censorship—existed as early as 1479" (2). And indeed, as we shall see, the roots of such censorship are to be found in the religious, social, and political intolerance of the medieval period.

Although not explored by these scholars, the medieval roots of censorship can be clearly traced into the early modern period. The history of church censorship, from the second century through the Reformation, was aimed at preventing heresy. Putnam begins his study on *The Censorship of the Church of Rome* by pointing out that "Church censorship may be said to have begun as early as 150" (1.1). In subsequent centuries, he writes, numerous edicts cautioned the faithful "against the pernicious influence of various works classed as heretical, and the heretics who had been concerned in the production and circulation of such writings were threatened with penalties ranging from confiscation of property to imprisonment, excommunication, and death" (1.1-2). Although the famous *Index* of books banned by the Catholic Church did not emerge until 1559, Putnam points to several medieval predecessors for this list, all created at the direction of the Church. "After the middle of the 13th century," he notes, "the papal condemnations of specific books frequently included the specification of names of the examiner or examiners, usually one or more of the cardinals" (1.24). He explains that in a Bull issued by Alexander IV in 1256 against a tractate of William Saint-Amour, of Paris, "the Pope says that his action is based upon the report of four cardinals, to whom had been confided the task of examining the work. All copies are ordered to be burnt within eight days, under penalty of excommunication" (1.24).

The emphasis in Putnam's example is on religious conformity, with severe religious consequences for failure to comply. Uniformity is created literally by eliminating the criticism of Church doctrines while simultaneously sending a message that authors of heretical works would meet a similar fate at the hands of these same censors. The spiritual well-being of English communities called for excommunication, and with it, eternal damnation, as the consequence for refusing to conform. Compliance appears to have been so much the norm that cases of public condemnation were notable in their day and continue to stand out in the historical records.

Revision for Ideological Conformity

Censorship is understood differently in the age of manuscripts than in the age of print. In the age of print, censorship applies to the prepublication inspection or approval of a work, or to the destruction or condemnation of a work once it has been published. For the age of manuscripts, Raymond Clemens and Timothy Graham offer a more useful definition. "Censorship," they write, "is the correcting of a text to bring it into ideological, rather than factual, correctness" (110). Among the various reasons for the systematic destruction of books, Clemens and Graham single out religious zealotry and ideological and social change in particular (67). They note that such acts were justified in a New Testament passage in which "the newly converted Christians of Ephesus gathered together their old books on the magical arts and burned them," which began "a long history of Christian purification by fire of pagan or heretical works" (67). After this evidence of the voluntary destruction of heretical books by early Christians, Clemens and Graham have little to say at that juncture about censorship until the sixteenth century (67) and the Index of Banned Books (68). The paucity of evidence of texts modified during the Middle Ages suggests that destruction through force, rather than revision by the author, was the norm. Christopher de Hamel, a key authority on illuminated manuscripts, has privately confirmed to me that he could not recall having noticed a single instance of a surviving medieval manuscript that had been censored in such a way as to bring it into ideological conformity ("Re: Censorship of medieval manuscripts"). This leads him to agree that censorship by forced revision may well postdate Gutenberg's development of the printing press.

A survey of the textual notes for Geoffrey Chaucer's *Canterbury Tales* (ca. 1387-1400), which exists in a staggering 83 surviving manuscripts, suggests that most variants in that work arise from aesthetic and linguistic correction inherent in scribal transmission rather than from forced amendment or censorship for ideological reasons. In the satire "The Summoner's Tale," for example, the same friar who accepts "persecucioun for rightwisnesse" (1909), later threatens to get his revenge through "disclaundre" or slander:

'Madame,' quod he, 'by God, I shal nat lye,
But I on oother wyse may be wreke,
I shal disclaundre hym over al ther I speke,
This false blasphemour that charged me
To parte that wol nat departed be
To every man yliche, with meschaunce!' (2210-15)

The textual variant here, which replaces "disclaundre" with "sclaundre" or even "diffame" (*Riverside Chaucer* 1131), merely substitutes closely related synonyms for slander and does not appear to change the meaning at all. The satire itself does not seem to be censored in the various manuscripts, which is not surprising, for, as Penn Szittya has emphasized, antifraternal satire against corrupt friars was not only tolerated but even popular and socially acceptable in the late fourteenth century.

On the other hand, one of the most famous lines from the *Tales* occurs when the host insults Chaucer's literary ability and cuts short his tale of Sir Thopas: "'By God,' quod he, 'for pleynly, at a word, / Thy drasty rymyng is nat worth a toord![']" (928-29). According to Corpus Christi College MS 198, however, "'By God,' quod he, 'pleynly I the say / thou schalt no lenger rymen heere today[']" (*Riverside Chaucer* 1131). But again, this change points to aesthetic rather than ideological sensibilities, I think, and while it is a memorable difference it is not a strong instance of Clemens and Graham's definition of censorship as "correcting ... a text to bring it into ideological, rather than factual, correctness" (110). And because the alteration appears in only one manuscript, the well-known lines do not appear to have been taken as sufficiently offensive to merit true revision.

Anita Obermeier has recently argued that Chaucer created "three distinct literary censorship scenarios, corresponding to, but not necessarily overlapping with, his three roles of translator, compiler, and author" (81). Searching for evidence that authorial "self-criticism might function as a mechanism to circumvent censorship" (81), Obermeier has suggested that the *Manciple's Tale* from the *Canterbury Tales* "can be read as a veiled and encompassing metaphor about the quandary offensive authors face unless they employ apology strategies," adding that "the tale paints a metaphoric picture of a medieval poet's precarious relationship to a potentially irascible monarch, which we might see in Chaucer's and Gower's relationships to Richard II" (81). She notes that "Richard was extremely touchy about personal criticism, threatening imprisonment for offenders, and in the 1397 royal declaration pronounced disparagement of his person as treason and thus a capital offence" (90). Elsewhere I have argued that Chaucer's *Parlement of Foules* may well have been a daring attempt to see how far he could go in testing the king's tolerance. Like Obermeier, I rely on formal, thematic, and historical data for evidence of self-censorship, since Chaucer appears to have written his poetry in such a way that it would not be considered ideologically offensive and thus not in need of revision. This sort of self-censorship, therefore, should be understood as the effect of intolerance, but not as censorship in a strict definition of the term.

A stronger case for censorship can be made in the revisions of William Langland's *Piers Plowman*, which exists in three versions and survives in more than fifty manuscripts. The earliest version, the A-text, was likely composed ca. 1367-70, when many of the ideas that John Wycliff would later garner attention for were not considered particularly dangerous even if they were technically heretical. A later revision, the B-text, dates from ca. 1377-79 and is significantly longer. During the 1380s, in what is referred to as the C-text, Langland would overhaul his poem once more to distance himself from views that were now deemed heretical. Kathryn Kerby-Fulton has observed that the Blackfriars' Council of 1382 banned several ecclesiastical and theological opinions as heretical, including three "of which the B-text falls foul" ("Langland and the Bibliographic Ego" 75). She explains that when these passages from the earlier B-text are compared against the later C-text, "we find that in each case Langland made significant alterations in his final version so as to suppress the ideas most likely to offend" (75). By the Clemens-Graham standard, Langland may be said to have censored himself in a way that Chaucer did not. However, since Langland himself apparently carried out these revisions, rather than someone other than the author acting after the fact to bring the text into ideological compliance, I suggest that strictly speaking these alterations should be seen as evidence of intolerance rather than as censorship.

Kerby-Fulton has found evidence of a form of censorship in the mid-fourteenth century that fits more faithfully with Clemens and Graham's model. In one striking example that involved three poems in London, British Library, Cotton Cleopatra B.II, she writes that "Two of the three poems ('Preste' and 'Heu') are heavily cancelled (as none of the other contents of the manuscripts are) with large Xs—large enough to give the suitable *appearance* of cancellation or censorship, but still allow the poetry to be read" (*Books Under Suspicion* 164-65). She takes this to be "the perfect form of functional ambiguity or self-protection" (165), giving a nod to Patterson's theory. But such perfunctory cancellation could hardly be said to "[correct] a text to bring it into ideological, rather than factual, correctness" (Clemens and Graham 110), for no correction has taken place. In a more convincing example, Kerby-Fulton points to a Joachite manuscript, Bodleian Library, MS Laud Misc. 85, by Henry of Costesy, that has been heavily mutilated. She believes this is because, given a "contemporary papacy that was burning Franciscan Spirituals, it would be difficult to finesse *any* interpretation of these verses in a Franciscan commentary that could appear uncontroversial" (86). But she also notes that Henry's treatment of all these verses had been removed from the Laud copy: "What is missing runs from Apocalypse 13:9 . . . to the discussion of the number of the beast. . . . The torn portion runs, then, from John's own covert appeal to the reader to 'decode' into another such appeal" (86). "Whoever tore this section out was knowledgeable enough about Franciscan Joachite exegesis to know it could be trouble," she writes, adding that "What survives is Henry's overt focus on Islam as the main external threat to the church and some of his numerical theories to calculate how long Islam would endure" (86). In her view, "Henry's focus on Islam, for instance, sounds *prima facie* like a safe externalizing of the Apocalypse's threats as coming from outside the church, but this is in part a code for anyone 'with an ear'" (86). The removal of some passages, while leaving another that seemingly also ought to have been excised (because it deals with the taboo topic of predicting the Apocalypse), suggests that even banned topics could be tolerated in the right context. In this way, while the *text* does not appear to have been modified, the *manuscript* has physically been altered to "bring it into ideological, rather than factual, correctness," as Clemens and Graham put it (110).

While Clemens and Graham's definition of censorship is based on medieval manuscript culture, some of the best evidence for it comes in manuscripts from the first century of print rather than from the Middle Ages. Clemens and Graham observe that the "most drastic method of censorship, the burning of books, leaves little room for survival" but that in some cases "censorship involved lesser forms of intervention such as the erasure of offending passages" in manuscripts (110). They are able to give a more concrete glimpse into the relationship between censorship and manuscripts, albeit *after* the dawn of print, in the aftermath of Henry VIII's break from Rome:

> Because the universal authority of the pope was no longer recognized in England, some owners of medieval manuscripts obliterated the word *papa* (pope) when they came upon it; if the word appeared in the genitive case, *pape*, they sometimes erased just the first letter, leaving *ape*! (110)

They add that even "greater care was taken to expunge references to Thomas Becket, the pro-papal archbishop of Canterbury who defied King Henry II and in 1170 was murdered in his cathedral by Henry's liegemen," for at the height of his dispute with Rome in 1538, "Henry VIII destroyed Becket's shrine at Canterbury and issued a proclamation condemning his memory, eliminating his feast day from the calendar, and ordering all images of him to be removed from churches and all references to him in service books to be erased" (110-11). They proceed to demonstrate the effectiveness of Henry's proclamation with the example of Chicago, Newberry Library, MS 35, "a fifteenth-century Book of Hours made in Bruges for use in England" (111). This manuscript was owned by the Gonstone-Mildmay family, which was closely linked to the crown. Clemens and Graham's illustration is worth repeating here because it demonstrates the social pressure to conform on a very small scale in private libraries. They note that the family zealously complied with the 1538 proclamation:

Becket's name has been scraped out both for his feast day (29 December) and for the commemoration of the translation of his relics (7 July). A further erasure of his name occurs within the litany, and the memorial to him within the suffrages of the saints has been vigorously crossed out—although the facing-page illustration of his martyrdom has not been tampered with. Nor is this the full extent of the book's censorship. Within the text known as the Seven Joys of the Virgin, a reference to an indulgence of one hundred days granted by Pope Clement to anyone who should recite the text aloud has been expunged [...] and at other points in the manuscript, objectionable passages of text have been masked from view with sheets of paper pasted over them. (111)

Here we have a clear example of censorship implemented by subjects who are eager to demonstrate their obedience to the new head of the Church. This phenomenon is a clear continuation of a culture of intolerance in the service of obedient conformity.

In addition to the examples mentioned by Clemens and Graham, Allen Frantzen has pointed to the sixteenth-century figure Matthew Parker, Anne Boleyn's chaplain, who published early printed editions of Anglo-Saxon texts. According to Frantzen, many "Anglo-Saxon manuscripts are physically defective, and the texts they contain are aesthetically (as well as sometimes physically) defective" (45). He writes that

These defects—whether physical (burns, tears) or aesthetic (faulty meter or grammar)—are invitations to editors to reconstruct or "write," and thereby interpret, that which they claim only to restore. The hermeneutic moves of Parker and his assistants go well beyond anything scholars today would imagine. They wrote in many manuscripts in red chalk, leaving marks that usually, but not always, took the form of notes and comments. (45)

But what Frantzen finds most significant about their endeavor, aside from the rigor they applied to their print editions (45-46), is the ideological adjustments they made to texts which they assumed "had been tampered with late in the Anglo-Saxon era, or during the Conquest, when Lanfranc reformed monasticism and so altered scribal (and textual) culture, and that, as a result, evidence of both the pure early Church and its degradation had been destroyed" (45). Frantzen thus observes that the "charge that earlier scholars had rewritten texts for political ends is richly ironic, for those activities describe precisely the scholarly endeavors of [John] Bale and Parker and his assistants" (46) working in the age of print.

Frantzen provides a further example of such ideological revision of an Anglo-Saxon text in the mid-sixteenth century, Worcester manuscript, Cambridge, Corpus Christi College 265, which was donated to the college by Parker. According to John Foxe, "words denying the Real Presence" ('Non est tamen hoc sacrificium corpus eius,' p. 177) were erased; they were restored to the manuscript by [Parker's secretary John] Joscelyn from an Exeter manuscript, Cambridge, Corpus Christi College 190" (46). Frantzen states that after complaining

> about the rewriting of early sources by corrupt Roman clergy, Foxe demonstrated a canny sense of textual emendation. His re-editing of the "Easter" homily deliberately distorted the text to sharpen its polemical edge. His rewriting shows that he too understood the need to "rase out" information contrary to his own views. (46)

Again, that the best-known examples of formal censorship of medieval documents—that is, edits and revisions, rather than mutilation or destruction—occur after the Reformation suggests two things. First, it suggests that censorship and related forms of intolerance in the Middle Ages were widespread and effective. Second, it suggests that conditions changed in the early sixteenth century such that censorship became more formalized.

The Chilling Effect of Medieval Intolerance

Other forms of intolerance could, for purposes of discussion, be seen to act as censorship during the Middle Ages. According to Ian Forrest, "Treason and heresy had been intimately linked since Innocent III's decree *Vergentis* of 1199, which proposed that punishments for treason should also be applied to heresy, since attacking the majesty of Christ was in fact worse than attacking the majesty of a secular ruler" (150). Despite "the spiritual nature of the crime," says Forrest, "heresy was an offence that secular authority, in this case the English crown, had a duty to resist, as protector of the church and guarantor of peace between men" (28). All forms of publication, written and oral, were therefore tightly controlled throughout the Middle Ages. Medieval intolerance and censorship, however strict or draconian they may appear by later standards, were part of a coherent worldview that provided the foundation for policies of intolerance and censorship well into the age of print.

Forrest points to the oral component of even written publication in the Middle Ages. "As a marker of heresy," he writes, "literacy has perhaps been overestimated by historians and literary scholars, because ours are literate disciplines relying upon literate sources, and we naturally privilege them in our interpretations" (183). However, he also explains that

> Because the written word is by its very nature recorded for posterity while the spoken word is not, legislation such as the constitutions issued by [Archbishop Thomas] Arundel in 1409 have elicited greater excitement for the censorship of writing than for the restrictions on preaching and speaking. (183)

Hence, for Forrest, the "key to understanding the place of writing in the detection of heresy ... is to examine how the authorities saw the *use* of books, bills, and libels within the context of oral communication" (183). H. Leith Spencer adds that when, "as [Thomas] More said of the Constitutions, 'this is a lawe that so many so longe haue spoken of, and so fewe haue in all this whyle rought ['cared'] to seke whyther they say trouth or no,' we too must enquire further." He clarifies that the "constitution of special interest for a study of preaching is the first, in which Arundel defined the circumstances that permitted a man to preach and prescribed certain limits to the contents of sermons" (165). Spencer outlines the specifics of this forerunner of print censorship that originated with Arundel's Constitutions and persisted as a way to enforce intolerance:

First, "no secular or regular which is not authorised by the law, or otherwise specially privileged, to preach the word of God shall take upon him the office or use of preaching the said Word of God, or in any wise preach to the people or clergy in the Latin tongue, or in any vulgar tongue, within churches or without, except he first present himself to the Diocesan of that place where he intendeth to preach and of him be examined." (165)

Arundel was attempting to leave no loopholes: unlicensed preaching was prohibited in any language and in any place without explicit prior permission. After proper examination, the candidate was issued a license, "the terms of which may vary at the diocesan's discretion, and which he must show to the incumbent of the parish where he intends to preach" (165). The responsibility of enforcement fell on both parties:

Indeed, the incumbent, for his part, must demand to see the license before allowing the visitor to preach in his church. Because, as Arundel put it, "this wholesome statute might seem to bring hurt by means of exactions of money, or any other difficulty," the examination of the candidate and the provision of the license should be performed without delay and free of charge. (165)

It is significant that, as Spencer notes, "this statute regulated visiting preachers" (166). Arundel's intolerance of unlicensed preaching was designed, in effect, to censor unapproved ideas and prevent them from entering a community. This intolerance of nonconformity of ideas, manifested here through a form of intolerance closely resembling censorship, was understood as a necessary method for maintaining stability throughout society during the English Middle Ages.

The rigid control imposed by early modern censorship of needing to secure official approval and a prepublication license would hardly have been necessary in the Middle Ages, since it was then understood that disseminating dangerous ideas or criticizing authority would not be tolerated. Kerby-Fulton has proposed that in the Middle Ages, "effective 'censorship,' as we understand it, was ultimately impossible, indeed, in any absolute sense an impractical task in the age before print" (17). In her view, this is because manuscript culture "was not much amenable even to *authorial* control, let alone authoritarian control. Imposing modern notions of publication on medieval authors has resulted in all kinds of misunderstanding about what book censorship, or even self-censorship, is or could be in late medieval England" (17). She writes that

> In the period before print, and therefore before the attempts to control book production through licensing that prevailed during the Renaissance and Reformation, we cannot assume the kind of state- or church-centered power structures that made New Historicism so enticing for the study of later periods. Contrary to what those models have taught us, manuscript culture was, in fact, an enormously empowering mode of publication for the adventurous author. (17)

She has thus hypothesized that because "reproduction time was slower, texts could be more easily kept, at least early on, within reading circles, where oral delivery to a select group allowed yet more freedom," noting that some of the texts she examines "make overt pleas—whether we take these at face value or not— to the reader to keep the circulation 'secrette.' The vast majority of medieval manuscripts contain little or no or inaccurate authorial attribution, and little concrete evidence of ownership" (17).

Given the precaution taken on even small scales of publication, it is evident that authors and readers alike feared the intolerance and persecution they might suffer should they be associated with the authorship or possession of dangerous texts. An author's need to control the circulation of his or her ideas points to a kind of self-censorship that was apparently well understood by a culture that lived under the constant pressure to conform or else to hide nonconformity. The need to keep a text "secrette" exposes the daily pressure to conceal nonconformity and reveals the pervasiveness and effectiveness of the intolerance that served to restrict the circulation of ideas during the Middle Ages.

Although both preaching and teaching required a license, Forrest aligns preaching more with publication in medieval England, because teaching was private (67). Harold Love, meanwhile, stipulates that various modes of publication (at least in the seventeenth century but with implications for the Middle Ages) are linked in the sense of

> movement from a private realm of creativity to a public realm of consumption. The problem is to determine whether any given text— in our case a text transmitted through handwritten copies—has made this transition. We will need to recognize both a "strong" sense in which the text must be shown to have become publicly available and a more inclusive "weak" sense in which it is enough to show that the text has ceased to be a private possession. (36)

Following Love's definition of publication, then, a text that asks readers to keep "secrette" would fall under the "weak" sense of the term, and if circulation is indeed controlled, such a text should belong to a category closer to private conversation or instruction than to publication. In another sense, however, by the time an idea was uttered it was as good as published in the Middle Ages. And as Kerby-Fulton has found, some documents were dangerous enough that their circulation needed to be controlled, even if the texts themselves were not destroyed: she shows that books could be hidden, both literally, such as under lock and key (74), and figuratively, such as by "changing the author's name but leaving the text intact, or by cutting out the rubric or colophon," or by miscataloging the work, or by other ruses (74). Once again, that these strategies were apparently necessary points to intolerance and underscores the danger implicitly associated with some texts. A text that could exist only within such narrow limits (such as being kept completely secret or nearly secret) cannot be considered to be published in a meaningful sense and such a text would be aligned more closely with other private forms of communication.

Conclusion

One consequence of the emphasis on conformity (that is, a desire not to stand out) in the Middle Ages is that many works, whether innocuous or provocative, have no identifiable author. Indeed, the culture of anonymity worked to the advantage of those who wished to circumvent censorship and related forms of intolerance. Nicholas Watson has pointed out that fifteenth-century religious works tend to be "carefully anonymous" (833). He adds that for "writers of English theological works whose names we know—apart from Pecock, hagiographic poets such as Capgrave, Kokenham, and Lydgate . . . and, of course, Margery Kempe—we have to wait until the early sixteenth century" (833). On the one hand, it is tempting to see anonymity—whether in ownership, authorship, or some other stage of publication—as one way of evading the rules of censorship and therefore making some small "win" for toleration. On the other hand, the very fact of anonymity points to a recognition that, at least in the wrong hands, some ideas were dangerous enough that they should be tightly controlled, if not destroyed altogether.

There are some further paradoxes in understanding intolerance that served to restrict the circulation of ideas within manuscript culture, both before and after movable type. One of Love's central theses in *The Culture and Commerce of Texts* is that scribal publication in the age of print "was one of several means of acquiring and transmitting . . . privileged information, not meant to be available to all enquirers" (177). He demonstrates that manuscript culture was useful for preserving and circulating documents only within specific circles, with the purpose of holding an advantage over others who could not access that information. It is distinct from church or state censorship, in which dangerous works are destroyed for the sake of the greater good. Thus it is not an exact parallel to compare medieval (or even Renaissance) practices to keep documents in the right hands with the practices Love describes, such as when Thomas More was granted special permission in March of 1527 to read "heretical books in order that, following the example of the King (Henry VIII), More might be enabled to make good defence of the Catholic Faith against the new heresies" (Putnam 2.258). Likewise, Kerby-Fulton turns to a "collection of Joachite materials owned by Richard de Kilvington, dean of St. Paul's (1353-61)." She writes that "Kilvington's *Liber excerptionum abbatis Joachim* (British Library, MS Royal 8.F.XVI) contains an anthology of genuine and spurious works" and the "physical manuscript itself ... is full of puzzles." She explains that "even though the book deals with issues a hundred years old, Kilvington himself seems to have been nervous that the *Liber* might get loose" (89). She describes his scheme: "His full name appears in a neat early *anglicana formata* hand on the top of every second page (that is, every odd-numbered page)—a highly unusual, and unusually thorough, way of marking medieval book ownership" (89-92). On this evidence she concludes that

> his could only be an act of unprecedented caution, because, given the quire structure, if the book were unbound (and the staining of the outer leaves strongly suggests it was), no single loose bifolium would go into circulation without the dean's name on it somewhere. It looks then, as if even a highly placed fourteenth-century church official could not own a copy of a Joachite text without making provision in case it, or even part of it, went astray. (92)

Both Thomas More's need for permission to read censored materials and the earlier example of Kilvington's branding each leaf to prevent circulation highlight a mindset in which conformity was established and maintained by suppressing publication effectively. In these examples, access to unsound ideas was restricted for the sake of the community, not just spiritually but also literally. Falsehood, not truth, was censored—and rightly so according to this worldview in which conformity was valued above all else.

Works Cited

Chaucer, Geoffrey. *The Riverside Chaucer*. 3rd ed. Edited by Larry D. Benson, Houghton Mifflin, 1987.

Clegg, Cyndia Susan. *Press Censorship in Caroline England*. Cambridge UP, 2008.

_____. *Press Censorship in Elizabethan England*. Cambridge UP, 1997.

_____. *Press Censorship in Jacobean England*. Cambridge UP, 2001.

Clemens, Raymond, and Timothy Graham. *Introduction to Manuscript Studies*. Cornell UP, 2007.

de Hamel, Christopher. "Re: Censorship of medieval manuscripts." Received by Richard Obenauf, 20 June 2015.

Forrest, Ian. *The Detection of Heresy in Late Medieval England*. Clarendon, Oxford UP, 2005.

Frantzen, Allen. *Desire for Origins: New Language, Old English, and Teaching the Tradition*. Rutgers UP, 1990.

Kerby-Fulton, Kathryn. *Books under Suspicion: Censorship and Tolerance of Revelatory Writing in Late Medieval England*. U of Notre Dame P, 2006.

_____. "Langland and the Bibliographic Ego." *Written Work: Langland, Labor, and Authorship*. Edited by Steven Justice and Kathryn Kerby-Fulton, U of Pennsylvania P, 1997, pp. 67-143.

Love, Harold. *The Culture and Commerce of Texts: Scribal Publication in Seventeenth-Century England*. U of Massachusetts P, 1993.

Obermeier, Anita. "The Censorship Trope in Geoffrey Chaucer's *Manciple's Tale* as Ovidian Metaphor in a Gowerian and Ricardian Context." *Author, Reader, Book: Medieval Authorship in Theory and Practice*. Edited by Stephen Partridge and Erik Kwakkel, U of Toronto P, 2012, pp. 80-105.

Patterson, Annabel. *Censorship and Interpretation: The Conditions of Writing and Reading in Early Modern England*. U of Wisconsin P, 1984.

Putnam, George Haven. *The Censorship of the Church of Rome and Its Influence Upon the Production and Distribution of Literature: A Study of the History of the Prohibitory and Expurgatory Indexes, Together With Some Consideration of the Effects of Protestant Censorship and of Censorship by the State*. 1906. 2 vols. Benjamin Blom, 1967.

Robertson, Randy. *Censorship and Conflict in Seventeenth-Century England: The Subtle Art of Division*. Pennsylvania State UP, 2009.

Shuger, Debora. *Censorship and Cultural Sensibility: The Regulation of Language in Tudor-Stuart England*. U of Pennsylvania P, 2006.

Siebert, Frederick Seaton. *Freedom of the Press in England 1476-1776: The Rise and Decline of Government Control*. U of Illinois P, 1952.

Szittya, Penn. *The Antifraternal Tradition in Medieval Literature*. 1986. Princeton UP, 2014.

Spencer, H. Leith. *English Preaching in the Late Middle Ages*. 1993. Clarendon, Oxford UP, 2002.

Watson, Nicholas. "Censorship and Cultural Change in Late-Medieval England: Vernacular Theology, the Oxford Translation Debate, and Arundel's Constitutions of 1409." *Speculum*, vol. 70, no. 4, 1995, pp. 822-64.

Banned, Censored, and Challenged Books: A Survey of Issues and Ideas_____

Kelly Snyder

Some of the most helpful general overviews (as opposed to narrow or specialized studies) of the topic of banned, censored, or challenged works of literature are organized in very similar ways. They tend to focus on individual works, first by offering plot summaries of those texts and then by providing histories of efforts to ban, censor, or challenge them. One example of this very helpful kind of reference volume is *120 Banned Books: Censorship Histories of World Literature*, by Nicholas J. Karolides, Margaret Bald, and Dawn B. Sova. The sections on censorship history included in this work are often quite long, covering many decades and numerous examples of efforts to suppress either parts of works or entire works. The same sort of approach to organization appears in various later, separate volumes involving the same authors. These include Dawn B. Sova's *Banned Books: Literature Suppressed on Social Grounds*; her similar volume *Banned Books: Literature Suppressed on Sexual Grounds*; Margaret Bald's *Banned Books: Literature Suppressed on Religious Grounds*; and Nicholas J. Karolides's *Banned Books: Literature Suppressed on Political Grounds*. Finally, two more titles in this very valuable series are also worth consulting. Both were written by Sova: *Banned Plays: Censorship Histories of 125 Stage Dramas* and *Forbidden Films: Censorship Histories of 125 Motion Pictures*. Taken together, these seven volumes are probably the most helpful general studies in existence on the controversial topic of banned, censored, or challenged works of literature (and cinema).

Also useful are two other helpful overviews: *Book Banning*, edited by Ronnie D. Lankford (2007), and its sequel, also titled *Book Banning* (2012), edited by Thomas Riggs. These works, rather than offering histories of attempts to suppress individual texts, instead offer diverse general arguments from various points of view, in opposition to—and also in favor of—efforts to control what others read, listen to, or view. Thus, if one wants to know, specifically, the censorship history of any particular work, the books by Karolides and colleagues are especially helpful resources. But if one wants to know, more generally, why and how people have either opposed or sometimes endorsed censorship, the books edited by Lankford and Riggs are very much worth consulting. These two books reprint essays by a wide variety of authors, and have the valuable result of offering numerous arguments both for and against (although mainly against) what is often very broadly called *censorship*. In this essay, I survey a range of representative arguments about this broader issue.

Persis M. Karim

In a 1997 article titled "The New Assault on Libraries," Persis M. Karim opened by emphasizing an apparent paradox: "How does a society that vigorously and sacredly regards its right to freedom to speech, so willingly and unquestionably engage in censorship on a regular basis?" (n.p.). He then answered his own question:

> The answer, of course, is that book banning, the most widespread form of censorship in the U.S. today, is aimed specifically at children, and is successfully practiced using the rationale that we are protecting the youth of this country from the potentially dangerous effects of the ideas and representations contained within these so-called undesirable books. (n.p.)

Karim noted, however, the irony of the fact that "while hundreds of books are removed from course lists and libraries every year, children can watch television (unmediated by adults) that is chockful of sex and violence" (n.p.). Karim observed that while the constitution does protect the right to free speech, there "is no amendment that protects our right to have access to information." This, he thought, was "one of the reasons why the practice of banning or challenging books so readily takes place." People who ban, censor, or challenge reading materials generally think they are protecting young people from "potentially 'dangerous' and 'offensive' materials." But Karim argued that the danger is not in the actual act of reading itself, but rather, the possibility that the texts children read will incite questions, introduce novel ideas, and provoke critical inquiry. This wasn't always the case, however. Most challenges to and bans of books prior to the 1970s were primarily focused on a concern over obscenity and explicit sexuality. A smaller percentage of books like Harper Lee's *To Kill A Mockingbird* were challenged or banned because of how they might depict a particular group or community. (n.p.)

Karim claimed, however, that the "concerted ideological attacks on materials in the schools began in the late 1970s with the founding and rise of a number of right-wing political action groups." After mentioning several organizations, Karim asserted that these "groups and individuals began challenging books based not on dirty words and depictions of sex, but because of the representation of 'a criticism, explicit or otherwise, of free-enterprise, patriotic, or fundamentalist Christian dogma'" (n.p.).

In an especially interesting passage, Karim suggested that the

attack on books because of their content and ideas, in fact, has everything to do with the way that changes in the public schools have reflected a greater emphasis on access to information. A greater emphasis on a twentieth-century American-focused curriculum, in lieu of a nineteenth-century British one, has meant that literature and ideas that were previously considered too controversial or that simply reflected a range of U.S. cultures, interests, and historical movements (other than those of white and middle-class culture), have been introduced to students in school curricula and in libraries. Books written from the point of view of Blacks, Chicanos, Asians, and, of course, those books that reflect the perspective have forced us to consider other truths. (n.p.)

Karim maintained that a list of banned and challenged books from 1995 to 1996 showed a

disproportionate number of books written by black, Chicano, and homosexual authors represented on its pages; these books are frequently the target of campaigns by parents and right-wing groups which claim these books are unfit to be read and taught to children in schools. Challenges to and bans on books in the U.S. are motivated by the fear that these books will threaten someone's authority—that of a parent, a teacher, a state, an ideology, a lifestyle—or that these and those who read and teach them won't be learning or teaching the "right" kind of values to maintain that authority. (n.p.)

According to Karim, groups interested in censoring materials often focus on materials taught in specific classes. He asserted, however, that a library "is different than a classroom. It represents an unmediated, unsupervised space, where a child or adolescent is more or less free to wander among the shelves and check out those books that might not be available in school libraries or at home." Karim suggested that a library "in some ways is a more democratic and free space—those who use it do so voluntarily and can obtain books which represent a diverse spectrum of ideas and cultures" (n.p.). Karim, of course, objected to any censorship. In fact, he claimed that when

> parents began policing libraries and their children's reading and borrowing patterns, they have effectively made the banning and removal of books unnecessary. If you make children afraid of the consequences of reading and asking questions, you make them so leery of a place like a library that they no longer want to go there. This, in my opinion, constitutes the more heinous aspect of censorship: making children and young people afraid to read, question, criticize—all necessary and fundamental aspects of maintaining anything that can be called a democracy. (n.p.)

Sharon Cromwell

In a 2005 article entitled "Banning Books from the Classroom: How to Handle Cries for Censorship," Sharon Cromwell offered an overview of recent attempts at censorship and also of legal rulings regarding the issue. But Cromwell additionally provided much practical advice to teachers about how to deal with complaints about particular books.

Cromwell opened the article by suggesting that "the best method of handling controversial material is to have a clearly stated policy [and] parental participation." Even when controversies do arise, Cromwell said, "a school should attempt to explain the issue, provide a copy of the school's policies, and inform the complainant of the review process" (n.p.).

She then noted that "advocates of banning certain books maintain that children in grades K-12 will be harmed if we don't protect them from inappropriate materials and opponents are equally heated in insisting that censorship of books and other curriculum materials violates the academic freedom and diversity of thought protected by the U.S. Constitution." She named several classic works of literature that have been banned from schools over the years, such as "Shakespeare's *Hamlet*, Nathaniel Hawthorne's *Scarlet Letter*, and Mark Twain's . . . *Adventures of Huckleberry Finn*." Some of the most challenged books in 1997 included "R. L. Stine's *Goosebumps* series, *I Know Why the Caged Bird Sings* by Maya Angelou, and *Catcher in the Rye* by J. D. Salinger" (n.p.). According to Cromwell, a report by the National School Boards Association (NSBA) found that "challenges of school materials are common throughout the United States; nearly one-third result in materials being withdrawn from schools or their use curtailed" (n.p.). Cromwell raised the following questions: "do opponents of banning books believe that any book is appropriate for teaching in school? And where should the line be drawn between books that are appropriate and inappropriate?" (n.p.).

Regarding legal trends and issues in censorship, Cromwell mentioned that "Supreme Court cases that deal with censorship issues show a broad trend toward supporting the schools, but they also caution educators to remain aware of values, including minority values, in the communities they serve." She then said, "experts have cited the First Amendment of the Constitution as protecting both students' rights to know and teachers' rights to academic freedom. At the same time, parents have the right to protest books or materials that they consider damaging to their children" (n.p.).

Developing a consensus within communities and preventing cries for censorship were, in Cromwell's opinion, key ways to deal with such cries. She quoted suggestions from Larry Mikulecky designed to aid in these efforts:

- Ask parents to contribute to developing school reading programs.
- Give recommended, rather than required, reading lists.
- Have files of professional reviews that support materials.
- In collective bargaining agreements, negotiate clauses that protect academic freedom and call for agreed-on selection processes.
- Discourage the concept that only one text can be used to teach a specific theme. (n.p.)

The best way to avoid unnecessary controversy, according to Mikulecky, is to do the following:

- Meet with the complainant and attempt to resolve the issue.
- If that fails, request a written complaint detailing the questionable material, the bad effect it is thought to have on students, and what replacement materials are suggested.
- Give the complainant a copy of published district policies for controversial materials and explain the procedure to be followed.
- Have a review committee provide the school board with a final report.
- Inform the complainant of the review process and when committee meetings are slated.
- Provide an appeals process.
- While the complaint is being explored, keep the controversial material available. (n.p.)

Ultimately, Cromwell asserted, the "challenge is not to avoid censorship, but to meet it head on with adequate policies and procedures that provide an open forum for deciding what should—or should not—take place in public schools."

Rebecca Hagelin

Not all commentators on book banning have sympathized completely with the views of many teachers and librarians. In fact, in an essay entitled "Are Your Kids Reading Rot?" Rebecca Hagelin warned parents that some teachers and librarians were attempting to force their own narrow values on society at large. Hagelin believed that while "we as a society have been taught to believe that any reading is good for adolescents, it is important to consider the kinds of books that children are reading" (n.p.). She examined some books that the American Library Association (ALA) had recommended for young readers and found that they contained "curse words and graphic sexual information" (n.p.). Hagelin suggested that "a parent should review a child's reading material beforehand" and said "it is a parent's responsibility—not the ALA's and not an educational institution's— to decide what a child should read." She later explained that the American Library Association "exerts great influence over what reading materials teachers assign their students" and claimed that this material "may be highly inappropriate for your child" (n.p.).

Hagelin reported that while she was "reading a book that was located in the Young Adult section of the library," she began "to read passages so cheap and trashy that [she] could scarcely believe [her] eyes" (n.p.). She did not have to get very far in this book before "the first of many uses of the term 'mother—' showed up and several scenes described sexual acts between teenagers in graphic detail." The next recommended book for teens Hagelin looked through "was equally as nauseating" because of offensive details, such as "a sexual act between fourth-graders and graphic details of sex between teenagers that included a homosexual encounter" (n.p.).

Hagelin alleged that the ALA "is quick to call anyone who questions its decisions a 'censor'" and asserted that "part of our responsibility and privilege as parents is to be the ones who determine what is and is not appropriate for our own children" (n.p.).

Stephanie Beckett

Similarly skeptical about the motives and conduct of the ALA was Stephanie Beckett, who explained her reasoning in an article published in 2006 in the *Daily Texan*. Beckett began by asserting that "Banned Books Week has a major flaw: some books *should* be removed from libraries." She argued that "while no parent is able to control a child's behavior at all times, schools cause parental concern when they allow children access to inappropriate materials." Beckett alleged that "Banned Books Week is less about celebrating intellectual freedom than demonizing concerned parents" (n.p.).

Beckett described Banned Books Week as "not a protest of governmental book banning, because such book banning does not actually exist in our nation" but a "movement sponsored by the American Library Association (ALA) to stop private citizens from asking certain library collections to remove certain books from the shelves." She saw Banned Books Week as "silly" and suggested that the "requests by private citizens actually added to the public debate about books and did not amount to censorship" (n.p.).

Regarding parental involvement in the books children should be reading, Beckett asserted that "parents need to look out for kids, and this extends to the ability of parents to help guide their kids' reading material." After citing the most challenged book in the United States in 2005 (including *It's Perfectly Normal: Changing Bodies, Growing Up, Sex, and Sexual Health*), she posed the following question: "Can you blame parents for wanting their elementary school aged kids to learn about sex in a supervised manner rather than by independently reading a (rather graphically illustrated) sex education primer?" (n.p.). Beckett argued that "children do not have all the same rights as adults—they cannot smoke, drink, or give consent to have sex with an adult. These restrictions on children take into account the fact that kids are immature and too inexperienced to understand the complexity of certain issues" (n.p.).

Beckett conceded that even though Banned Books Week presents several challenges for communities, "it would obviously be wrong for every challenge to end in the banning of a book from a library, even a school library" (n.p.). She held that, if this were true, "books that just have unpopular opinions would end up becoming unavailable for public consumption" (n.p.). The goal of Banned Books Week, according to Beckett, was "really just to label people as uncultured, narrow-minded and generally un-American if they are concerned that a book is inappropriate for a particular library collection." She maintained that official complaints, such as challenges, are key to monitoring which books are in a library's collection. She said, "Surely the ALA does not believe that all possible reading materials, such as clearly pornographic books, should be included in school library collections" (n.p.). She added that "without any kind of community involvement like the challenging process, school libraries could include just about anything in their collection that any particular librarian deemed appropriate." In her final paragraph Beckett called Banned Books Week a "disheartening thing that, by trying to demonize the legitimate concerns of private citizens," minimizes "the true viciousness of nations that actually do ban books" (n.p.).

Chelsea Condren

In contrast to Beckett, Chelsea Condren claimed in 2013 that "Banned Books Week celebrates readers everywhere and encourages us to pick up a book whose content has, at some point, been questioned." She noted that "chances are you love a book that has ended up on a banned books list, although you might not realize it yet. Everything from the *Harry Potter* series, to Toni Morrison's *Beloved*, to Harper Lee's *To Kill a Mockingbird,* has been challenged in a public or school setting" (n.p.). Condren later stated that "religious leanings might have something to do with inclinations to ban a book. But I would say that's because religious viewpoints also shape ethical and moral viewpoints—not because society's religious [persons] are leading the attack on freedom to read." Condren pointed out that "the most common imitators of book challenges are parents, and the most common settings for book challenges are schools, school libraries, and public libraries [...] books are most frequently challenged by concerned parents who believe materials are unsuitable for children or teens" (n.p.). Condren maintained that "we can't shield our children from racism and sexism, but we can teach them how to understand these issues more comprehensively." Condren closed her essay by suggesting that "book banning isn't about quality control;

it's about thought control" and then declared that "in banning books we are not protecting anyone from anything, we are only oppressing them" (n.p.).

Regan McMahon

Like Condren, Regan McMahon recently argued that in fact kids *should* read banned books and outlined several reasons to support this claim. McMahon asserted that "reading banned books offers families a chance to celebrate reading and promote open access to ideas, both of which are keys to raising a lifelong reader" (n.p.). She noted that ideas and literature that are considered offensive change over time and reported that the ALA argues that challenges to such ideas and literature "pose a threat to freedom of speech and choice—freedoms that Americans hold dear and are worth standing up for" (n.p.). McMahon listed five reasons that kids *should* read banned books. She claimed that "today's edgy is tomorrow's classic," that "there's more to a book than the swear words in it," that "kids crave relatable books," that "controversial books are a type of virtual reality," and that kids who read banned or challenged books "will kick off a conversation" about why a book has been deemed controversial (n.p.).

McMahon later stated that "original work pushes boundaries in topic, theme, plot, and structure. What is shocking today may be assigned in English class five or ten years from now if it has true literary merit" (n.p.). She also claimed that "many books have been banned for language that your kid has encountered before or will soon." She thought, in fact, that "a character's language may add realism to the story, or it may seem gratuitous or distracting—your kid can evaluate" (n.p.).

McMahon insisted that

> banned books often deal with subjects that are realistic, timely, and topical. Young people may find a character going through exactly what they are, which makes a powerful reading experience and helps the reader sort out thorny issues like grief, divorce, sexual assault, bullying, prejudice, and sexual identity. (n.p.)

McMahon argued that because controversial books explore complex topics like "sexuality, violence, substance abuse, suicide, and racism through well-drawn characters," kids exposed to such books could "contemplate morality and vast aspects of the human condition, build empathy for people unlike themselves, and possibly discover a mirror of their own experience" (n.p.). She then posed several questions: "what did people find so disturbing in a book that they wanted to ban it, and to what extent was it a product of its time or did it defy social norms of its era?" (n.p.). Ultimately, McMahon declared that "reading a challenged book is a learning experience and can help your kids define their own values and opinions of its content" (n.p.).

Ron Charles

Obviously, it would be possible to continue offering pro and con positions for many more pages. Perhaps, then, it is worth closing the present essay by summarizing an article by Ron Charles, of the *Washington Post*, who managed to present *both* sides of the issue in an intriguing piece published in that paper.

Charles had "been irritated for a long time by Banned Books Week," which he saw as often "shrill and inaccurate" (n.p.). He felt that Banned Books Week sometimes "appeared to exaggerate a problem that's largely confined to our repressive past." He said that "Banned Books Week is pitched at such a fervent level that crucial distinctions are burned away by the fire of our moral certainty, which is an ill that wide reading should cure not exacerbate." He asked "what books are actually effectively 'banned' in the United States today?" and answered that "the titles on the Top 10 Most Challenged list, in fact, sell hundreds of thousands of copies every year" (n.p.).

But then Charles interviewed one of the country's top librarians, James LaRue. LaRue raised the following possible scenario:

> Let's say you're a young gay kid, and you go to your library, and David Levithan's *Two Boys Kissing* has been removed, and so you don't know that it's there. You don't have a credit card to get it from Amazon. You can't hop in a car if you're 14 years old and drive to a bookstore. (n.p.)

For such reasons, LaRue stated, a "ban is not a trivial thing. It's a deliberate suppression of a viewpoint that has real consequences for people." According to LaRue, "trying to remove [a book] from the library says that other people's children don't have the rights to read it, which is the hallmark of an intolerant society." Ultimately, in response to such arguments, Charles supposed he was "glad we have Banned Books Week" because, as LaRue argued "it encourages us to reflect on what we're not discussing" (n.p.).

Common ground between individuals, LaRue further declared, can be found in "the library because everyone is welcome. Even the books on our shelves may disagree with each other, but there's a tacit understanding that this is a place where you have the right to investigate choices and make up your own mind" (n.p.). Charles, reacting to such logic, went from doubting the value of Banned Books Week to thinking that it still served a useful purpose.

Works Cited or Consulted

Bald, Margaret. *Banned Books: Literature Suppressed on Religious Grounds*. Rev. ed., Facts on File, 2006.

Beckett, Stephanie. "Banned Books Week Is Hypocritical." Greenhaven Press, 2008. EBSCOhost, libproxy.aum.edu/login?url=http://search. ebscohost.com/login.aspx?direct=true&db=edsgov&AN=edsgcl. EJ3010489204&site=eds-live.

Charles, Ron. "Do We Really Still Need Banned Books Week?" *Washington Post*, 26 Sep. 2018. https://www.washingtonpost. com/entertainment/books/do-we-really-still-need-banned-books-week/2018/09/26/80e924be-c0fd-11e8-90c93f963eea204_story. html?utm_term=.ec3c0b45d91e.

Condren, Chelsea. "Why Do We Ban Books, Anyway?" *The Hub*, 27 Sep. 2013. www.yalsa.ala.org/thehub/2013/09/27/what-makes-a-book-ban-worthy.

Cromwell, Sharon. "Teachers Should Prepare for Book Challenges." Greenhaven Press, 2008. EBSCOhost, libproxy.aum.edu/ login?url=http://search.ebscohost.com/login.aspx?direct=true&db=e dsgov&AN=edsgcl.EJ3010489215&site=eds-live.

Hagelin, Rebecca. "Are Your Kids Reading Rot?" *The Heritage Foundation*, 16 Aug. 2005. www.heritage.org/marriage-and-family/commentary/are-your-kids-reading-rot.

Karim, Persis, M. "Books Are Often Banned." Greenhaven Press, 2001. EBSCOhost, libproxy.aum.edu/login?url=http://search.ebscohost.com/login.aspx?direct=true&db=edsgov&AN=edsgcl.EJ3010037213&site=eds-live. 4 Feb. 2018.

Karolides, Nicholas J. *Banned Books: Literature Suppressed on Political Grounds*. Rev. ed., Facts on File, 2006.

_____., Margaret Bald, and Dawn B. Sova. *120 Banned Books: Censorship Histories of World Literature*. 2nd ed., Facts on File, 2011.

Lankford, Ronnie D., editor. *Book Banning*. Greenhaven, 2007.

McMahon, Regan. "5 Reasons Why Your Kids Should Read Banned Books." *Workingmother.com*, 19 Sep. 2018. www.workingmother.com/why-your-kid-should-read-banned-books.

Riggs, Thomas. *Book Banning*. Greenhaven, 2012.

Sova, Dawn B. *Banned Books: Literature Suppressed on Sexual Grounds*. Rev. ed., Facts on File, 2006.

_____. *Banned Books: Literature Suppressed on Social Grounds*. Revised edition. Facts on File, 2006.

_____. *Banned Plays: Censorship Histories of 125 Stage Dramas*. Facts on File, 2004.

_____. *Forbidden Films: Censorship Histories of 125 Motion Pictures*. Facts on File, 2001.

Medieval Intolerance and Modern Censorship in the Morality Play *Mankind*

Richard Obenauf

When medieval authorities dealt with material they considered offensive or unacceptable for some reason, their default ethical position was what we would describe as intolerance, not what we would consider to be censorship. What we now think of as censorship did not appear in England until the arrival of the printing press in 1476 and the Reformation in the next century. Intolerance as I characterize it in this essay did not merely seek to preserve the status quo. Reaching beyond that objective, intolerance also sought to uphold a rigidly hierarchical social structure that was believed to save souls as well as to provide order and safety. As I explain earlier (see my essay "Censorship in Medieval England" in this volume), it is more useful to focus broadly on manifestations of intolerance in the Middle Ages than to search for evidence of the specific form of intolerance we now call censorship.

Medieval authors published their works in a climate of intense intolerance. As a result, many medieval works were so guarded in their commentary on contemporary politics that it is now very difficult to detect the criticism these authors wished to register. In this essay I focus on *Mankind*, an allegorical play that obscenely satirizes church corruption and therefore risked incurring official disapproval. In most other ways, however, this work roundly condemns heresy and disobedience more broadly. I will argue that this representative late medieval entertainment can show us how intolerance shaped culture as well as popular drama on the eve of the Renaissance. *Mankind* also offers surprising support for tolerance in the form of appeals for mercy. Mercy is personified as the play's dominant figure and, in keeping with the play's Christian focus, must both condemn sin but implore sinners to seek forgiveness, thus showing how close to tolerance intolerance could come.

Mankind and Its Political and Religious Context

Mankind is a kind of medieval allegorical drama known as a *morality play*, whose main character is a personification of all of humankind as it was then understood. *Mankind* was written during the upheavals of the late fifteenth century, including the Wars of the Roses (1455-1485). Its author was most likely an anonymous monk in East Anglia, possibly at the abbey of Bury St. Edmunds, writing around 1470 or 1471, and hence immediately before the arrival of the printing press in England in 1476.

Mankind concerns a cosmic battle between good and evil, with humans caught in the middle of this allegorical warfare. Concepts like vice are comically portrayed through the device of personification. *Mankind* was almost certainly written by an agent of the church for dogmatic purposes; in other words, it was written by the faithful for the faithful. The play opens with the first of ten or so sermons, as these speeches are often called, by Mercy (1-44), who serves as spiritual advisor to Mankind and to the audience. Mischief interrupts this sermon and is joined by the other vices (New-Guise, Nowadays, and Nought) in making fun of Mercy's seriousness (45-185). Mankind then introduces himself and describes his condition of being made of a body and a soul, cursing his flesh as a "stinking dunghill" that corrupts his soul (186-216). Mercy informs him that the life of man on earth is a battle between good and evil, instructing him to resist the temptations of the flesh and other worldly temptations (217-44). Mankind works in his field and staves off the temptations of the vice characters (245-330).

However, the vice figures are successful at tricking the audience, first into joining in an obscene Christmas carol and second into paying to see the spectacular devil Titivillus (331-528). Titivillus is visible to the audience but invisible to Mankind and thus easily tricks Mankind into giving up his work and joining the vice figures in sin (529-661). Mischief and his band of vices hold a mock court where Mankind swears his allegiance to their wicked ways of crime (662-733). Further antics ensue until Mankind is about to hang himself out of despair, believing he is no longer worthy of mercy, at which time Mercy pleads with him to seek forgiveness, which he finally does (734-900). The play ends with yet another sermon in which Mercy beseeches the audience to renounce sensual pleasures and beg for mercy so that they, too, may achieve everlasting life (901-14).

One of the playwright's possible concerns is the danger of theological error, although this appealing line of research has perhaps been overstated. According to Lynn Forest-Hill, "In the fifteenth century those who erred most problematically were the Lollards, whose activities appear to have been particularly problematic in East Anglia" (19). The followers of John Wycliff (ca. 1330-1384), pejoratively known as Lollards, had been perceived by religious and secular authorities alike to threaten the religious and political unity of England, and new measures of intolerance against them were imposed beginning with the Blackfriars Council of 1382, affirmed by an act passed by Parliament in 1401 known as the *De heretico comburendo*, and perhaps most famously by the Constitutions of Oxford under Archbishop Thomas Arundel in 1409. Because Wycliffite heretics were involved in open rebellion, including an uprising led by John Oldcastle in 1414, they made a convenient political target and were persecuted well into the sixteenth century. Some critics have suggested that the play's language and themes may be dramatizing "issues of ecclesiastical discourse that had been politicized in the Lollard and anti-Lollard rhetoric of the fifteenth century" (Ashley). Even Forest-Hill, who has advanced some of these arguments, concedes that the "play's message is not aimed at an audience of those who have erred, but takes the form of a dramatization of specific, or perhaps allegorical, contexts in which error may occur" (19). And indeed, it is difficult to imagine why an attack on heresy would need to be as veiled as some modern critics have suggested, given the record of persecution of heretics by both the Church and the state. As we will see, rather than concealing heretical ideas, the play clearly ridicules and condemns a variety of types of error, including blasphemy.

Other attempts to find veiled criticism that might point to signs of self-censorship in *Mankind* have also come up short, in my view. In addition to reading *Mankind* as a morality play that operates on two levels (literal and spiritual), some recent critics have hinted at another level of allegory (political), which suggests that we might take aspects of *Mankind* as evidence of political intolerance and self-censorship during the Lancastrian Readeption, when Henry VI briefly reclaimed the throne during the Wars of the Roses. Jessica Brantley and Thomas Fulton, for example, have claimed that "The unstable world of late-fifteenth-century England shaped the text in several distinct ways, for Mankynde's relationship with the world around him is often cast in political terms that indict secular as well as ecclesiastical authority as suspect and unstable. The play projects the problems of the monarchy onto the untrustworthy world of local politics embodied by the Vices" (344). For instance, when the actors take up a collection from the audience during the performance (in what is usually regarded as the first known instance of commercial acting in England), Brantley and Fulton suppose that the demand for money "might have suggested to its audience the church's collection of tithes. But the appeal for money can also be seen in relation to taxation or other ways in which secular power enriched itself. Edward IV was renowned for his avarice" (341). However, given the play's overt criticisms of corruption in the Catholic Church, it is unlikely that the political satire would be so guarded. Besides, it seems to me that the fund-raising effort for those staging the play (whether they were traveling actors or young monks remains debated) is more plausibly understood as moral satire in which members of the audience are tricked into betraying their own morals and their own souls.

Both possibilities depend on the device of allegory in order to criticize through satire. The playwright uses a similar device in a number of other instances to show the audience how easy it is to fall into disobedience; by manufacturing peer pressure to coerce the audience into paying to see a spectacular devil, the playwright traps the audience with the same skill the devil Titivillus uses against Mankind. Furthermore, once Titivillus comes out, he mentions specific members of the community by name. Master Huntington of Sawston, William Thurlay of Hauxton, Picharde of Trumpington, William Baker of Walton, Richard Bollman of Gayton, and William

Patrick of Massingham (505-15), in addition to the unnamed members of the audience, are gently reminded that they are personally responsible for the misfortune that befalls Mankind at the hands of Titivillus. Because they are singled out for having helped bring out this devil, these named men have incurred an additional sin for which they must repent. Far more than targeting the king's avarice, the playwright seems to be targeting the audience's sinful desire for worldly delights, an appropriate theme for a morality play. Ultimately, the playwright does not appear to condemn any political figures or secretly to offer political advice. The political impulses I see in this play merely generate topical humor for a small and sympathetic coterie without necessarily testing the audience's tolerance in that way.

The Limited Tolerance of Patient Amendment in *Mankind*
Even if it is not possible to make a convincing argument for hidden political commentary that might point to intolerant forces resembling self-censorship in *Mankind*, the play's central theme of avoiding sin and repenting error is emblematic of medieval intolerance. In fact, it may well be that the playwright avoided making even veiled commentary on topical political and religious controversies in order to push the envelope in other ways. As John A. Geck has pointed out, the play was most likely written in 1470-1471 and performed as part of the Shrovetide festivities in 1471, quite possibly on Saturday, 23 February 1471 (33). During the pre-Lenten activities of Carnival, medieval English society was more tolerant of boisterous mockery and scatological humor (Ashley). By teaching sound doctrine and by staging the play at Shrovetide, the *Mankind* playwright was able to deploy shockingly vulgar language in the service of entertaining and instructing his audience, as well as offering some targeted attacks on corruption within the Church.

Mankind asserts traditional authority even as the players disrupt the peace in order to lure the audience into sinning. Despite its rowdy humor, the play ultimately aims for peace and does not undermine the authority of traditional power. *Mankind* often shows what *not* to do, teaching its audience not to make the wrong choice, even when it comically portrays sin. The playwright does not appear to make a meaningful distinction between heresy and other kinds of sin. Nevertheless, there are many ways to go wrong, the play suggests, but very few ways to go right. It is therefore important to make the right choices, the play teaches. Hence, as didactic literature, this play is intolerant of error, even if the play does not represent evidence for the censorship of erroneous or heretical ideas. In fact, both its thematic elements and its structure point to a limited degree of tolerance which permitted people to correct their error to avoid the need for harsher and more disruptive punishment.

We will now examine the evidence for tolerance in *Mankind*, especially forms of tolerance that might serve to amend error and thereby enforce conformity. The political philosopher Michael Walzer has proposed five kinds of toleration: resignation to difference for the sake of peace; a benignly relaxed, passive indifference to difference; a principled recognition that others have rights even if they exercise them in unattractive ways; openness or even curiosity; and finally, an enthusiastic endorsement of difference (10-11). In *Mankind* I see four main tests of tolerance, which Walzer might refer to as "tests of adhesion" or "rituals of membership" (31). The first such test of adhesion centers on the introduction of the main characters (Mercy, Mankind, and the vice figures), in which Mercy and Mankind do not tolerate the vice characters and in which the vice figures also participate in their own rituals of membership in their slapstick comedy. The second ritual of membership involves the audience, rather than Mankind, when the vice figures seduce the audience into singing a lewd song and paying to see a devil. The third test of adhesion centers on Mankind as he falls into sin and is persuaded first by Titivillus and then by the other vice characters to abandon Mercy's teachings. The final ritual of membership in this morality play is the ending, in which Mankind enthusiastically endorses Mercy's teachings and thus achieves salvation. Taken together, these events suggest that medieval intolerance was sometimes tempered by a limited form of tolerance that also served to enforce conformity.

The First Test of Tolerance: Intolerance of Vice

The first test of tolerance in *Mankind* suggests that avoiding sin and begging for mercy were two important imperatives for medieval Christians. In the opening lines of the play, Mercy explains that God sent his own son to be crucified because of humans' inherently disobedient nature (1-4). Mercy addresses the "sovereigns" in the audience with a lesson that he will repeat many times throughout the play in his instructions to the character of Mankind:

> O soverence, I beseche yow yowr condicions to rectifye,
> Ande with humilité and reverence to have a remocion
> To this blissyde prince that owr nature doth glorifye,
> That ye may be particable of His retribucion. (13-16)

In "beseeching" the audience, Mercy implies a possibility of rectifying one's condition by changing one's inclination ("remocion"), signaling a limited degree of tolerance and even a genuine desire for the audience to change their ways. However, this stance of toleration is no higher on Walzer's scale, I think, than a resigned acceptance for the sake of peace. Mercy is not benignly indifferent to sin: he insists that his teachings are of universal importance. For example, Mercy indicates that his teachings apply to an audience of varied social status: "O ye soverens that sitt, and ye brothern that stonde right uppe, / Prike not yowr felicites in thingys transitorye!" (29-30). Religious doctrines and philosophical advice that apply to all humans are paired here with a strict hierarchy, which likewise none may escape, often described as the Great Chain of Being, in which each person has a specific role to fulfill. The need to follow Mercy's teachings is pitched as a ritual of membership in which all of humankind is expected to participate. Failure at this important test of adhesion results in damnation, while endorsing it leads to salvation.

Mercy's speech is interrupted by the vice figures, Mischief, New-Guise, Nowadays, and Nought, who illustrate the pervasiveness of worldly temptations (45-161). For example, New-Guise urges the minstrels to play a common dance with such force that they burst their bellows. The vice characters even get into a slapstick fight over dancing to this music that turns so violent that Nought worries he might break his neck (72-81). They try to include Mercy, but of course Mercy refuses their invitation, a signal that he does not tolerate their actions: "Nay, brother, I will not daunce" (90). The vice characters' banter and slapstick humor in harassing Mercy and each other provide a satiric contrast to Mercy's explanation of Christian rituals of membership by acting out an alternative test of adhesion, one which would be better for humankind not to participate in. When they exit, Mercy offers another sermon, this time specifically on the subject of avoiding these and other worldly temptations: "This condicion of leving, it is prejudiciall— / Beware thereof! It is wers than only felony or treson" (166-67). Mercy suggests that humankind should not tolerate their sinful "condition of living," since it is worse than felony or treason. By equating sinful behavior, represented allegorically by song and dance, with felony or treason, Mercy's intolerance of sinful behavior would seem to fall below Walzer's scale. In critiquing Walzer's scale, the political historian John Christian Laursen has proposed a simpler scale, with "organized, systematic, violent persecution" at one end and "respect, endorsement, and celebration" at the other (3); Mercy's intolerance here would fall at the far low end of Laursen's simplified scale.

In his first speech, Mankind expresses his intention not to tolerate worldly temptations (190-93), stating that one can find salvation only by submitting to God's wishes and overcoming one's own desires. The didactic nature of his speech suggests that enthusiastic endorsement—found at the high end of Walzer's scale—of Mercy's teachings ought to be the default choice. Note, however, that Walzer's fifth kind of toleration is the enthusiastic endorsement *of difference*, and both Mankind and Mercy have only endorsed sameness, while condemning the error of succumbing to temptation. Mankind explains that he is composed of "a body and of a soul, of condicion contrarye— / Betwix them tweyn is a grett division. / He that shulde be subjecte, now he hath the victory" (195-97). He laments that his "soull, so sotyll in thy substance, / Alasse, what was thy fortune and thy chaunce / To be associat with my flesch, that stinking dungehill?" (202-04). As medieval literature often suggests, and perhaps as our own experience confirms, it is not always easy to do as we are told.

According to the author of *Mankind*, humans have little choice but to strive to overcome their condition as human and prone to error, but sin is tolerated so long as it ceases and the sinner repents. Still it is better not to tolerate sin in ourselves, but to avoid it in the first place, a sort of self-censorship in living. Mercy repeatedly instructs Mankind that he will be rewarded in the next life for resisting temptation in this life:

> The temptacion of the flesch ye must resist like a man,
> For ther is ever a battel betwix the soull and the body:
> *Vita hominis est militia super terram.*
> Oppresse yowr gostly enmy and be Cristys own knight!
> Be never a cowarde ageyn yowr adversary:
> If ye will be crownyde, ye must nedys fight.
> Intende well, and Gode will be yow adjutory. (226-32)

Mercy states that his doctrine is "convenient" (i.e., sound) (844), and in his sermons he either warns Mankind that he is about to be tested or helps to usher him back to spiritual safety after he has fallen prey to various temptations. Mercy repeatedly advises Mankind to do as he is instructed in order to reach eternal bliss (278-84, e.g.). The play stresses that avoiding temptation and following God's orders are moral and religious imperatives, and yet the playwright allows for redemption even as he condemns sin. Thus, the *Mankind* playwright suggests that humans have free will and are prone to making wrong choices. Unlike many medieval writers, who saw free will as a threat to the peace because choice can enable people to go astray and therefore cause harm to others, the author of *Mankind* takes a more patient approach. Humans may need much guidance, if not also coercion, in order to keep themselves in check and contribute to social stability through their conformity, but the possibility of redemption leads this author to favor limited tolerance over intolerance or outright persecution.

Despite the intolerance necessary in didactic literature, *Mankind* points to a stance of limited toleration. On the one hand, Mercy consistently instructs Mankind to steer clear of temptation: "My name is 'Mercy.' Ye be to me full hende; / To eschew vice I will yow avise" (219-20). But on the other hand, the play sometimes also points to a stance of moderation that might be seen as a form of tolerance in this play. Mercy says, "Take that is to be takyn, and leve that is to be refusyde" (185). David Bevington glosses this as "Use moderately those things God intended you to enjoy, and refuse what should be refused." Part of staying on the path to salvation, the play suggests, is abstinence from things which should be refused; at the same time, not everything is to be refused. In this way, the playwright signals that moderation could function as a form of tolerance.

Indeed, Mercy openly advocates moderation rather than strict abstinence from activities he openly deems harmful:

> Distempure not yowr brain with goode ale nor with win[e].
> 'Mesure is tresure'; I forbid[d]e yow not the use.
> Mesure yowrsylf ever. Beware of excesse.
> The superfluouse g[u]ise I will that ye refuse;
> When nature is suffisyde, anon that ye ses[s]e. (236-40)

Since humans require sustenance in order to survive, it is overindulgence that Mercy warns against. Moderation may thus be seen as one of Walzer's middle kinds of toleration, such as a relaxed indifference or perhaps even a kind of moral stoicism. Given the danger associated with excess, however, I do not think Mercy's moderation would qualify as openness or endorsement. Mercy further illustrates this point using the example of a horse that will obey his master when hungry but that will disobey when overfed:

> If a man have an hors, and kepe him not to[o] hye,
> He may then reull him at his own dysiere;
> If he be fede over-well he will disobey
> Ande, in happe, cast his master in the mire. (241-44)

On an allegorical level, Mercy's proviso suggests that a man who has overindulged in worldly pleasures may rebel against God. When one fails to control one's own bodily urges, Mercy teaches, each person has the potential to land his own soul in the mud, soiling everyone else in the process. The danger of luxury and overindulgence are a constant in medieval literature as well as in moral satire, also a didactic genre. It is through this limited tolerance of moderation that order is maintained in society.

In addition to advocating moderation, Mercy also preaches patience, and the *Oxford English Dictionary* suggests that patience is in fact synonymous with tolerance: "Forbearance or long-suffering under provocation; *esp.* tolerance of the faults or limitations of other people" ("Patience"). Mercy counsels Mankind to follow the biblical example of Job (285-88), again signaling that Mercy will tolerate sin in the context of the play's depiction of falling into sin and the subsequent need for repentance. By framing the irreverence of the center part of the play with an overt reminder of Mercy's patience, the playwright suggests, in effect, that Mercy tolerates the blasphemy that follows. It can be argued that this framing device, in addition to the pre-Lenten liberty of a Shrovetide performance, serves as a way of licensing depictions of sin which might not otherwise have been permissible.

Tests of Misplaced Tolerance

Soon after Mercy counsels patience, the action is again interrupted by the vice figures and the introduction of Titivillus in the second major test of tolerance in the play. In this center portion of the play (323-725), both the audience and Mankind are trapped in the very vices that Mercy has been advising the audience and Mankind alike to avoid. In this mayhem, Nowadays says to "Make rom, sers, for we have be longe! / We will cum gif yow a Cristemes song" (331-32). The singing of a Christmas carol would seem to be a virtuous activity, and Nought encourages audience participation in this putatively worthy activity: "Now I prey all the yemandry that is here / To singe with us, with a mery chere!" (333-34). However, it is not until after the audience has begun singing, and it would be awkward not to continue the call and response, that the song is revealed to have been a trap: "It is wretyn with a coll, / He that schitith with his hoyll / But he wippe his ars clen, / On his breche it shall be sen" (335-41, repetitions omitted). The focus then shifts back to Mankind's struggle to ward off temptation, and he makes an earnest effort to work in his field while the vice figures engage in some slapstick comedy (344-453).

The "worschipfull soverence" of the audience are then tricked, a second time, into betraying their virtue in favor of worldly pleasures. This time, the actors take up a collection, refusing to bring out the spectacular devil Titivillus until after the audience has paid. Nowadays explains that Titivillus "is a worschipp[f]ul man, sers, saving yowr reverens. / He lovith no grotys, nor pense of t[w]o-pens: / Gif us rede reyallys, if ye will se his abhominabull presens" (463-65). Eventually, the actors are satisfied and Titivillus emerges, only to show himself to be the embodiment of craftiness. "Ever I go invisibull—it is my jett," he says (529) as he tells the audience how he is going to trick Mankind into abandoning his work in the field. The play's coarse humor and blasphemy, always spoken by vice characters, appears to license a limited form of toleration that, I argue, served to amend the sinner. For the play's original audience, these irreverent moments seem to be licensed not only by Mercy's patience, by its performance during Shrovetide festivities, or by the device of associating such sin with allegorical representations of sin, but also by the play's didactic purpose of teaching redemption on the condition that one ceases one's sinful ways. Moreover, in succumbing to this peer pressure, the audience may be said to tolerate sin even as the play instructs them not to tolerate it.

The third major test of adhesion is when Mankind must decide whether he will endorse Mercy's teachings or instead tolerate or even endorse worldly temptations. For example, Titivillus places a board in Mankind's field to discourage him from working as he should and then mixes weeds in with his seeds (532-38). Many of the temptations staged in this center portion of the play involve earthly temptations with consequences that are both temporal and spiritual. By inhibiting Mankind's ability to produce a good harvest of crops, Titivillus aims to starve him in this life and corrupt him for the next. The plan works, and Mankind soon abandons his work and his prayer. He is useless to himself and to society. After succumbing to the ploys of the invisible Titivillus, Mankind is much more susceptible to more apparent temptations; it is easier for him to tolerate (or even endorse) the sinful and criminal ways advocated by Mischief, Nowadays, New-Guise, and Nought. Mankind, like the audience before him, bows to peer pressure. Nowadays brags that he has stolen from a church: "I have laburryde all this night. W[h]en shall we go din[e]? / A chirche her[e]-beside shall pay for ale, brede, and win[e]: / Lo, here is stoff will serve" (632-34). In his turn, Mischief boasts that he escaped imprisonment, killed the jailer, and hints that he may have raped the jailer's wife: "The chenys I brast asundyr, and killyde the jailere, / Ye[a], ande his fayer wiff halsyde in a cornere— / A, how swetly I kissyde the swete mowth of hers!" (643-45). In his descent into sin, Mankind then dreams that Mercy was hanged, which leads him to vow his allegiance to the vices (655-58). On its surface, the play moves from intolerance of sin at the opening to a stance of patience that served to amend; now the play would seem to endorse sin. Instead of being held accountable for their crimes in a court of law (much less in God's final judgment), the vices hold their own court which parodies the legal system and results in a perverse verdict in which Mankind swears his loyalty to New-Guise, Nowadays, Nought, and Mischief. Mankind is instructed to rape all the women of the country while their husbands are out (703-04), to rob, steal, and kill as fast as he can (710), to skip Sunday mass and instead join the vices for a meal at the alehouse (710-12), and to become a highwayman, mugging his victims and then slitting their throats (714-16). To each of these instructions, Mankind affirms, "I will, ser." Mankind thus enthusiastically endorses sin, and in so doing no longer accepts Mercy's teachings. The play could hardly be said to endorse these sinful and criminal acts, since the playwright clearly indicts them through this mock trial by showing what not to do. Both Mankind and the audience are now in a position to beg for Mercy's patience.

Mankind's Ultimate Test: Repentance and Conformity

Mankind may participate in misplaced rituals of membership, but it is still not too late for him to repent. As is common in morality plays, the tension created by the uncertainty of whether or not Mankind will repent represents both the final test of adhesion in this play and the ultimate ritual of membership for Christians. When Mercy returns, he is in a strong position to offer a sermon on the fickleness of human nature, comparing man's inconsistency to a weather vane: "As the fane that turnith with the winde, so thou art convertible" (749). He prays on behalf of Mankind, whose sins he is tolerating in the hopes of amendment (756-59). Mankind's fickleness is then illustrated as he continues his trajectory into a life of crime, sin, and worldly pleasures (772-810). Just as Mankind is about to hang himself in despair that it is too late for him to repent, Mercy intervenes and begins a dialogue in which he counsels repentance:

> Yowr criminose compleynt wo[u]ndith my hert as a lance!
> Dispose yowrsylff mekly to aske mercy, and I will assent.
> Yelde me nethyr golde nor tresure, but yowr humbyll obeisiance—
> The voluntary subjeccion of yowr hert—and I am content. (816-19)

In his despair, Mankind says that "It is so abhominabyll to rehers my iterat transgrescion, / I am not worthy to have mercy by no possibilité" (821-22). Mankind's repeated transgressions, however, are countered by Mercy's unwavering patience. Mercy maintains that Mankind must always repent because "The justice of God will as I will, as himsylfe doth preche: / *Nolo mortem peccatoris, inquit,* iff he will be redusible" (833-34). Here, Mercy is quoting Ezekiel 33:11 to the effect that he does not wish the death of a sinner before he has had the will to repent, another sign of his patience (and therefore of his limited toleration).

Despite his patience, however, Mercy also says, "Sinne not in hope of mercy! That is a crime notary. / To truste overmoche in a prince, it is not expedient. / In hope, when ye sin, ye thinke to have mercy: beware of that aventure!" (845-47). In acknowledging that the possibility of redemption is not a license to sin with the intention of repenting later, Mercy signals that he extends his patience in the service of helping sinners to amend their ways. He repeats:

Offend not a prince on trust of his favour, as I seyd before.
If ye fele yoursylfe trappyd in the snare of your gostly enmy,
Aske mercy anon; beware of the continuance!
Whill a wo[u]nd is fresch, it is provyd curabyll by survery,
That, if it procede ovyrlong, it is cawse of gret grevans. (854-58)

In preaching that Mankind should always seek mercy through repentance, Mercy is patient. But his patience is limited by the spiritual need to repent quickly and to cease sinful behavior as soon as possible. He is able to forbear sinful activities inasmuch as he wants to prevent them and help amend the sinner. Mercy's patience, moreover, may now be seen to resemble his stance of moderation, which I believe should be seen as a form of limited toleration that served to promote conformity. Elsewhere I have forwarded a model of intolerance wherein conformity was achieved by relentless intolerance during the English Middle Ages; in this model, limited forms of toleration may be preferred over outright coercion but often mask coercive force and nevertheless act in the service of intolerance (Obenauf 44-96). I believe Mercy's patience is suggestive both of Walzer's first kind of tolerance and of my model of medieval intolerance because it appears to exert pressure on those who have fallen into error to reform their ways.

Both the trajectory of the play's action and Mercy's sermons suggest that patience is understood in this play as a form of tolerance. Mercy may dislike sin but he is willing to tolerate it so long as the sinner repents. In this way, Mercy seems to be at Walzer's lowest level of toleration: for the sake of peace, he allows the sinner time to repent. However, this toleration is predicated on the condition that the sinner agrees to go and sin no more, or, in other words, to amend the fault. Indeed, Mercy tolerates, perhaps even endorses, those sinners who amend their ways and agree to sin no more. This endorsement is not endorsement of difference; it is an example of a kind of toleration that might exemplify the goal of tolerance in the Middle Ages. This form of tolerance I detect in the Middle Ages, and that Walzer's scale fails to consider, is the acceptance of someone as a peer for having met the expectations of sameness. It demands a lack of disobedience and therefore differs from Walzer's scale in that difference is not celebrated. Because sin is renounced and then forgiven, acceptance comes not from the acceptance of difference, but from the unacceptable being made acceptable. This is the goal of censorship, enforced here through both tolerance and intolerance.

Modern Censorship and the Literary Canon

The clearest cases of censorship of medieval texts postdate the medieval period (Obenauf 18-39), and this is the case for *Mankind*. The play's central teaching of avoiding sin and repenting error is doctrinally sound and may have bought good will with the authorities, who then tolerated elements in this play that pushed the limits of vulgarity in its targeted criticisms of Church corruption. However, by the time the play was rediscovered in the late nineteenth century and began to circulate in the early twentieth century, publishers and teachers, rather than ecclesiastical authorities, appear to have taken issue with some of its scatological and sexual content. I will conclude this essay by considering some of the ways this play has been suppressed, whether in whole or in part, in the age of print.

In Bevington's estimation, "*Mankind* is a culmination of the most popular elements in the late medieval English stage. As such, it appears to be more representative than the restrained *Everyman*, with its less typical plot of the coming of Death, its absence of burlesque comedy, and its textual affinity to continental drama" (*From Mankind to Marlowe* 17). It is likely that many plays like *Mankind* were staged in the late Middle Ages but that the manuscripts containing the texts of similarly earthy plays were lost long ago for any number of reasons. It is clear that the morality play was a popular genre of the late Middle Ages, and a number of examples survive, though none as raucous as *Mankind*. The best known of these, by far, is *Everyman*, which exists in both manuscript and early printed versions. Now as when it was first written, *Everyman* contains little

---

offensive material and so it is easy to understand how it has come to represent the entire genre in college courses.

In *Everyman*, a character representing humanity (Everyman) is warned that God is keeping a ledger of his activities and repentance and that he will be judged when he dies. Its simple plot concerns Everyman's attempt to get spiritual help from others, only to learn that he must find his own salvation. He dies at the end of the play. *Everyman* offers little social criticism and little questionable material. At about 925 lines, it is short enough that it can represent the genre without overwhelming a syllabus. Consequently, *Everyman* has dominated college reading lists as a representative example of the morality play. However, *Everyman* is devoid of the vice figures and the comedy they generate in other morality plays. The warnings against worldly temptation that make *Mankind* so effective are utterly missing in *Everyman*. Meanwhile, teachers who assign *Everyman* inevitably struggle to show their students the evolution of the genre when they subsequently read Christopher Marlowe's *Doctor Faustus* and any number of Shakespeare's plays. Both as a stand-alone play and as a representation of the form, *Everyman* pales in comparison to *Mankind*, which is sometimes regarded as "the first English comedy" (Duffin 14).

I propose that the dominance of *Everyman* in the literary canon may be seen as a form of suppression of other, perhaps more relevant exemplars, such as *Mankind*, and may be understood as a kind of censorship. For instance, *Ottemiller's Index to Plays in Collections* (2011) records some 136 editions of *Everyman* printed since 1900, but just eight editions of *Mankind*. In part, this may be due to the superior textual condition of *Everyman*, given that *Mankind* survives in just one damaged manuscript. The Norton anthology of English literature contains only *Everyman*; recent exceptions include the less frequently taught Broadview anthology, which prints both *Everyman* and *Mankind*, and the Longman anthology, which omits *Everyman* and instead presents students with a modern acting translation of *Mankind*. What might account for this imbalance?

The reason for omitting *Mankind* in favor of *Everyman* surely lies in the vulgar, blasphemous, and scatological content in

Mankind, initially made permissible by the play's performance as part of the Shrovetide festivities and its doctrinally sound lesson. Since both plays are religious allegories about the need to prepare for judgment day, thematically there is no obvious reason to favor *Everyman* so heavily. At approximately 910 lines, *Mankind* poses no more imposition on a course's reading load than *Everyman*, and, it seems to me, *Mankind* much more captures the lived experience of medieval people as well as the spirit of the genre with its earthy folk humor, especially as it manifests in other canonical works like *Doctor Faustus* and Marlowe's satirical portrayal of the Seven Deadly Sins.

In addition to the scatological Christmas carol (335-43), *Mankind* contains a number of other obscene references, some much more vulgar than the purported "merry cheer" with which the vice characters trick the audience into sinning. For example, Nowadays pokes fun at Mercy's learnedness by asking him to translate the following lines from English into Latin: "I have etun a disch-full of curdys, / Ande I have schetun yowr mowth full of turdys" (131-32). Nowadays ups the ante by boasting that he has received a pardon for his sins from a Pope Pocket ("wallet") who sells indulgences to those who perform oral sex on this corrupt pope's wife: "If ye will put yowr nose in his wiffys sokett, / Ye shall have forty days of pardon" (144-46). Mercy responds to both by exclaiming, "This idyll language ye shall repent! / Out of this place I wolde ye went" (148-49). The play is filled with many other references to excrement, most of them highly vulgar and comical, but others used to lofty ends. For instance, Mankind's woe that his body is a "stinking dunghill" (204) is a valuable insight into the human condition in the late Middle Ages. And, to repeat, the playwright never uses such imagery merely to entertain; these moments always serve to warn against pursuing worldly amusement.

In addition to the overwhelming preference for the subdued *Everyman* over the raunchy *Mankind* in anthologies and on syllabuses, *Mankind* has also suffered from outright censorship. Only a handful of early scholarly editions printed the play in its entirety, including *The Macro Plays* (edited by F.J. Furnivall and

Alfred W. Pollard for the Early English Text Society in 1904) and *Recently Recovered "Lost" Tudor Plays* (edited by John S. Farmer for the Early English Drama Society in 1907 and printed in a light translation). However, these aimed to present medieval curiosities to specialists in the field rather than to students or those unfamiliar with the period.

I trace the explicit censorship of passages of *Mankind* back to its first printed edition, John M. Manly's *Specimens of the Pre-Shak[e]sperean Drama*, Vol. 1, from 1897. According to Bevington, Manly's edition was based on an inaccurate transcription by Eleanor Marx, the daughter of Karl Marx (*The Macro Plays* xxi). Bevington adds that Alois Brandl's 1898 edition, published in Strassburg and with German commentary, is also based on Marx's transcription. By including the obscene Christmas carol, Brandl signals that Marx had transcribed the song in full rather than redacting it in her copy of the manuscript. This is clear evidence that Manly or his publisher, rather than his source, had censored the song. In Manly's edition, Nought invites the audience to join in the "merry cheer," but he reproduces only the first line ("It is written with a coal"), and states in a footnote that New-Guise and Nowadays "reply with the same line; each of the four lines of the vulgar song is similarly treated" (328). Manly's edition fails to censor the other vulgar, blasphemous, and scatological material in the play, such as the reference to the corrupt Pope Pocket. This suggests that even a scholarly readership of obscure medieval texts in the late nineteenth century would be more offended by a song sung by vice characters who personify various forms of temptation than they would by references to other forms of blasphemy.

Joseph Quincy Adams's *Chief Pre-Shakespearean Drama*, published by Houghton Mifflin, was the standard textbook for half a century, from its publication in 1924 and subsequent reprinting in 1952 until it was supplanted by Bevington's *Medieval Drama* in 1975. Bevington states that Adams reproduces "nearly all of *Mankind*" (*The Macro Plays* xxv). That is to say that Adams does not print all of *Mankind*, or, to put it more bluntly, that he censors it. Adams is at most half correct when he writes that "the humor becomes at times exceedingly vulgar; and the literary skill of the writer is unusually poor" (304). To the contrary, the *Mankind* playwright deftly vacillates through parodies of a number of genres and demonstrates a deep knowledge of Scripture. The play is much more complex and more rich than Adams gives it credit. I would argue that the lines he redacts are the most illuminating evidence of the author's expert ability to use coarse and even blasphemous language in the service of moral instruction. Adams excises at least four key passages, stating that they were "omitted because of obscenity" or "unprintable." These include the references to taunting Mercy about filling his mouth with turds and the subsequent joke about Pope Pocket (307) and the Christmas carol and related banter (311). Nevertheless, Adams prints a number of references to shit without glossing them or calling attention to them; in other cases he offers a plausible gloss while allowing the possibility of an obscene pun, such as Nought's complaint that he has "shot" himself in the foot and that his foot is foully "over-schett" (i.e., "overshot" / covered in shit) (321). A century ago, Adams signals, students who were mature enough to comprehend the theological satire of *Mankind* nevertheless needed to be shielded from a little scatological humor.

It is truly remarkable that obscene Christmas carols and jokes about sex with a corrupt pope's wife could be performed in the fifteenth century as part of Shrovetide festivities, yet could become "unprintable" in the twentieth even in academic contexts. The recent inclusion of *Mankind* in the Broadview and Longman anthologies is a welcome step toward giving students a more honest picture of the late Middle Ages. By censoring this play, well-meaning editors and teachers have deprived students of a compelling example of the medieval Christian worldview that vice is everywhere, and that it is easy to fall into sin even with the best of intentions.

Thus, *Mankind* is a representative example of medieval intolerance and modern censorship. To be sure, writers in the Middle Ages often deployed devices like allegory in order to disguise ideas that might be considered blasphemous or treasonous, and a great deal of recent scholarship has endeavored to tease out daring topical commentaries in texts written in intolerant regimes. Nevertheless, in this essay I have disagreed with recent critics who have attempted to uncover such hidden messages in *Mankind*, in part because the play is so brazen in its attacks and in its obscenity, even by medieval standards. Instead, I have emphasized that the play is still a product of a highly intolerant society that valued conformity and obedience and that stressed the need to repent after even the most minor of transgressions. In looking for moments of toleration in the play, we have seen that tolerance in late medieval England served the same goal as intolerance. Both exerted pressure on the faithful to go and sin no more.

Works Cited

Adams, Joseph Quincy, editor. *Chief Pre-Shakespearean Dramas: A Selection of Plays Illustrating the History of the English Drama from its Origin Down to Shakespeare*. 1924. Houghton Mifflin, 1952.

Ashley, Kathleen M. "*Mankind*: Introduction." TEAMS Middle English Texts, University of Rochester, 2010. d.lib.rochester.edu/teams/text/ashley-mankind-introduction.

Bevington, David M. *From Mankind to Marlowe: Growth of Structure in the Popular Drama of Tudor England*. Harvard UP, 1962.

_____, editor. *The Macro Plays: The Castle of Perseverance, Wisdom, and Mankind: A Facsimile Edition with Facing Transcriptions*. Folger Shakespeare Library, Johnson Reprint Corporation, 1972.

Brandl, Alois, editor. *Quellen des weltlichen Dramas in England vor Shakespeare. Quellen und Forschungen*, vol. 80. Karl J. Turner, 1898.

Brantley, Jessica, and Thomas Fulton. "*Mankind* in a Year without Kings." *Journal of Medieval and Early Modern Studies*, vol. 36, no. 2, 2006, pp. 321-54.

Duffin, Ross W. *Some Other Note: The Lost Songs of the English Renaissance Comedy*. Oxford UP, 2018.

Farmer, John S., editor. *Recently Recovered "Lost" Tudor Plays*. Early English Drama Society, 1907.

Forest-Hill, Lynn. "*Mankind* and the Fifteenth-Century Preaching Controversy." *Medieval and Renaissance Drama in England*, vol. 15, 2003, pp. 17-42.

Furnivall, F. J., and Alfred W. Pollard, editors. *The Macro Plays: Mankind, Wisdom, and The Castle of Perseverance.* Early English Text Society, 1904.

Geck, John A. "'On yestern day, in Feverere, the yere passeth fully': On the Dating and Prospography of *Mankind.*" *Early Theatre*, vol. 12, no. 2, 2009, pp. 33-56.

Laursen, John Christian. "Orientation: Clarifying the Conceptual Issues." *Religious Toleration: "The Variety of Rites" From Cyrus to Defoe.* Edited by John Christian Laursen, St. Martin's, 1999, pp. 1-12.

Mankind. ca. 1470-1471. *Medieval Drama.* Edited by David Bevington, Houghton Mifflin, 1975, pp. 903-38.

Manly, John Matthews, editor. *Specimens of the Pre-Shak[e]sperean Drama*, vol. 1. Athenæum Press Series. Ginn, 1897.

Obenauf, Richard Thomas. *Censorship and Intolerance in Medieval England.* Loyola University Chicago, 2015. ecommons.luc.edu/luc_ diss/1651.

Ottemiller, John H. *Ottemiller's Index to Plays in Collections.* 8th ed. Edited by Denise L. Montgomery, Scarecrow, 2011.

"Patience, def. 1b." *The Compact Oxford English Dictionary*, New Edition. Clarendon Press, Oxford UP, 1991.

Walzer, Michael. *On Toleration.* Yale UP, 1997.

Using Anything: Flannery O'Connor and Banning Books_____

Robert Donahoo

Almost from its inception, the fiction of Flannery O'Connor has raised flags about its suitability for the public. If O'Connor's letters are to be believed, John Selby, her editor at Rinehart while she was working on *Wise Blood*, found her drafts too unconventional, lacking in objectivity, damaged by "aloneness," angular (*Collected Works* [hereafter *CW*] 881), and "unpleasant" (*CW* 882). But John Crowe Ransom may hold the distinction of first putting on record an objection to O'Connor's work because of its most frequently criticized aspect: its treatment of race. Writing to O'Connor about her submission to the *Kenyon Review* of "The Artificial Nigger," Ransom stated: "There's one other matter that Rice and I are a little bothered over: whether we ought to have 'nigger' in the title. I hate to insult the black folk's sensibilities. [Peter] Taylor thinks it doesn't matter, especially when 'nigger' is the only word a colloquial Southern story could use, in the text. Rice and I wonder what you would think of: THEY GOT TO HAVE AN ARTIFICAL ONE. It's in your text. Please say what you think as to this" (Ransom 180). What she thought "as to this" became fodder for the larger debate about O'Connor's work and race:

> About the title: I don't think the story should be called anything but "The Artificial Nigger." But if this title would embarrass the magazine, you can of course change it. I think the story as a whole is much more damaging to white folk's sensibilities than to black; and that if I must eliminate the word from the title, I must eliminate it everywhere it occurs in the story. Following Mrs. Tate's advice, I never allow the omniscient narrator to use it. . . . I don't know if this is a problem that comes only to the burdened Southern conscience or not. I have been worried by it before and I don't treat it lightly and I have not made up my mind what one must do, but in this case I think the title is impersonal-sounding enough to stand as it is. In any case,

I do not like "They Got to Have an Artificial One." That is entirely too colloquial for a title. If you change it, please call it "The Good Guide." ("To John Crowe Ransom" 181-82)

The story went on to appear in the *Kenyon Review* in the spring of 1955 and, in the same year, in O'Connor's first collection of short stories, *A Good Man Is Hard to Find*. She confessed to Ben Griffith "I have read The Artificial Nigger several times since it was printed, enjoying it each time as if I had had nothing to do with it" (*CW* 932). She makes a similar comment to her friend Betty Hester: "I suppose The Artificial Nigger is my favorite" (953), and, in a letter to Maryat Lee she calls the story "probably the best thing I will ever write" (1027).

Scholarship has been less sure, and in the decades since O'Connor's death, the most consistent challenge to a triumphalist view of O'Connor's art has been based on the issue of race. As early as 1968, two scholars published essays critical of the story's ending (Byrd 243; Hays 267). In 1976, Melvin Williams went beyond "The Artificial Nigger" to declare all O'Connor's "Black characters are for the most part only 'issues' instead of people" (130). Two years later, Claire Kahane began an article by declaring "The Artificial Nigger" "one of Flannery O'Connor's finest short stories" (183) while also asserting that her "Negro characters . . . are usually *negative* racial stereotypes, ignorant, lazy Sambos, conventional comic accessories to the main concerns of plot" (184). When, following the availability to scholars of O'Connor's unedited correspondence to Maryat Lee, Ralph Wood published an essay seeking to come to terms with her "unsavory remarks about blacks" and her lack of "sympathy with the civil rights crusade of the 1960s" (Wood 90), the author's private communiqués added fuel to the debate about the handling of race in her fiction.[1]

In the summer of 2000, the issue of O'Connor and race got down to the practical business of actually limiting access to her work in the seemingly unlikely setting of Opelousas Catholic High School in Louisiana's Lafayette Parish. According to news reports in the Baton Rouge *Advocate*, Bishop Edward O'Donnell of the Diocese of Lafayette pulled *A Good Man Is Hard to Find and Other Stories* from the school's eleventh-grade literature reading list after "a group of African Americans was upset" by the title, "The Artificial Nigger," and by the use of the word "pickaninny" in "A Good Man Is Hard to Find." The Bishop qualified his decision by declaring that his action was "not a banning of the book," and he commented, "I think [O'Connor]'d be hurt, and she would feel misunderstood. But we have to understand that some people also feel hurt and misunderstood. I am not in a position to tell them when they should feel insulted and when they should not" (Schultz 3). One of leaders who pressed for the book's removal from the school's required reading list was a local businessman, Patrick Fontenot, who noted the complaints by white parents about another book on the list: the King James Bible which, until 1962, was not approved for Catholics to read. "The white parents were raising hell about it," the paper quotes Fontenot saying, "[b]ut I should read nigger, nigger, nigger and open my mind. Well, I've been flooded with it" (Schultz 3).

The incident sparked several printed cries of dismay and outrage, with O'Connor defenders tending to soak their reactions in irony. Writing in the Baton Rouge *Advocate*, Danny Heitman states that the "ruckus" sent him back to reading O'Connor's work again. "It's been edifying. . . . I don't know whether to chide O'Connor's critics, or thank them" (1C). The conservative, nationally distributed *Weekly Standard* couched the issue more broadly:

> Thanks to Bishop Edward J. O'Donnell's abject surrender to the forces of political correctness, a southern Catholic school . . . has the dubious distinction of being the first recorded school in America to ban the southern Catholic writer Flannery O'Connor.
>
> In fact, the bishop's edict goes further. . . . [I]n ordering the elimination of O'Connor's volume, [it] directed that "no similar books" replace it: All books containing those racial epithets are forbidden, regardless of context.
>
> Mark Twain? Gone. William Faulkner? A dead letter. Black authors Ralph Ellison, Toni Morrison, James Baldwin, even local writer Ernest J. Gaines? Banished without reprieve. (Dreher 33)

The Catholic journal *Crisis* added this:

> The only Catholic admitted by mainstream secular literary critics
> to the canon of 20th-century American authors now excised
> by Catholics. A major southern writer involved in the project of
> explaining southerners to themselves, now prohibited in a set of
> southern schools. A woman known in her own day for her *anti-
> racism* now placed on the forbidden list on the grounds of racism.
> (Bottum 48)

O'Connor on Banning

While such sentiments are balms to many a literary if not literal
heart, they ignore O'Connor's own stance on banning—something
she did not unequivocally oppose. Her correspondence makes clear
that she accepted the Catholic Church's Index of Prohibited Books.
In a letter to Caroline Gordon dated 20 May 1953, she writes jokingly
but tellingly, "There was a man at Yaddo who used to say [André]
Gide was the 'great Protestant spirit.' I was glad they put him on the
Index as it meant I wouldn't have to read him. Otherwise I would
have thought I had to. If I had charge of the Index, I'd really load
it up and ease my burden" (O'Connor and Gordon 63). When, in
1957, a reading group organized by "the local Episcopal minister"
and meeting at Andalusia to discuss "theology in modern literature,"
added Gide to the group's list of readings, O'Connor wrote to her
friend Father James McCown, "You said once you would see if you
had the faculties to give me permission to read such as this. Do
you and will you? All these Protestants will be shocked if I say I
can't get permission to read Gide" (*CW* 1057-58). After McCown
responded positively, she wrote to him again:

> I am very much obliged for your taking the time to find out about
> the permissions etc. I will use the *epikia* [a dispensation] and also
> invoke that word, which is very fancy. I have for the time being led
> them away from Gide, with the good reason that he is to be had in no
> 35cent [sic] edition and we are all in the 35¢ class. I am afraid though
> that they are headed for Sartre—also on the Index. So if you can
> include him in with Gide, I'd be obliged. (*CW* 1060-61)

Beyond her personal reading, she was also willing, for political reasons, to prevent her own work from being published—even though, as her willingness to accept Ransom's editorial change to the title of "The Artificial Nigger" to get it published suggests, she was anxious to spread her reputation. In 1956, she wrote to her editor Denver Lindley instructing him to "drop the matter of publication [of *Wise Blood*] in any Russian-occupied country. They would probably use the Misfit to represent the Typical American Business Man..." (*Habit of Being* 151). In short, far from being adamantly opposed to book bans under any conditions, O'Connor both sees their necessity and submits her personal decisions to the Church.

Even more detailed is her discussion of a situation that has some facets in common with the one at Opelousas Catholic High School. "Fiction Is a Subject with a History—It Should Be Taught That Way," an essay first published in the *Georgia Bulletin* in 1963,[2] directly addresses "two recent instances in Georgia" where "parents have objected to their eighth and ninth grade children's reading assignments in modern fiction" (*CW* 849). Though O'Connor gives few specifics about these incidents, she does name the two books involved—John Steinbeck's *East of Eden* and John Hersey's *A Bell for Adano*—and describes parents stumbling upon "passages of erotic detail or profanity and tak[ing] off at once to complain to the school board" (*CW* 849). Yet far from belittling the parents, O'Connor takes aim at teachers who allow their choice of subject matter to be selected by students: "the teacher assigns what he thinks," she writes, "will hold the attention and interest of the students. Modern fiction will certainly hold it" (850). She adds, "No one asks the student if algebra pleases him or if he finds it satisfactory that some French verbs are irregular, but if he prefers Hersey to Hawthorne, his taste must prevail" (850). O'Connor argues that the reading of modern fiction needs to be prepared for by knowing the history of the novel form, how it has changed over time. Essentially, she argues for reading to occur in historically constructed educational contexts. Essential to her case is her theoretical view of the experience of reading modern fiction:

The [modern] author has for the most part absented himself from direct participation in the work and has left the reader to make his own way amid experience dramatically rendered and symbolically ordered. The modern novelist merges the reader in the experience; he tends to raise the passions he touches upon. If he is a good novelist, he raises them to effect by their order and clarity a new experience—the total effect—which is not in itself sensuous or simply of the moment. Unless the child has had some literary experience before, he is not going to be able to resolve the immediate passions the book arouses into any true total picture. (*CW* 851)

O'Connor is, obviously, *not* endorsing the burning of books in the streets or denying authors free speech; rather she is suggesting something akin to the movie rating system most of us know well enough today, though her criteria of admission are more stringent than age: "Whether in the senior year students should be assigned modern novelists should depend both on their parent's consent and on what they have already read and understood" (*CW* 851-52).

Putting aside the feasibility of such a system of reader control, O'Connor had to be aware of its potential to affect her own fiction— especially since her novels alone are marked by the use of prostitutes, profanity, and murder (*Wise Blood*) as well as arson, child murder, and homosexual rape (*The Violent Bear It Away*). Moreover, in stressing, as she does, the need to be able to process "dramatically rendered and symbolically ordered" material, she raises questions related to the racial material in her fiction. Are readers well enough trained in how fiction works to separate the racist language of, say, "The Artificial Nigger" from the potentially antiracist "new experience" being formed by the "total effect"? Or, more brusquely, should O'Connor's work at some level be banned?

If anyone is expecting an answer to that question, they are about to be disappointed. Individuals in a democratic society need, as O'Connor does, to weigh the matter for themselves, book by book, story by story. Nevertheless, several important factors merit consideration—at least for an informed rather than an emotional decision.

O'Connor and African American Writers

High in priority among these factors is the significance of O'Connor for African American artists who make use of or turn to her work. Such ties have not been insignificant. In 1975, little more than a decade after O'Connor's death, Alice Walker published "Beyond the Peacock: The Reconstruction of Flannery O'Connor" in *Ms* Magazine, where she recreates a conversation with her mother as they drive to visit the O'Connor farm, Andalusia. "I like her," Walker tells her mother, "because she could *write*" (Walker, *In Search* 46). She further praises *Mystery and Manners*, the first collection of O'Connor's nonfiction, as "the best of its kind I have ever read" (48). But perhaps best known is her evaluation of O'Connor's depiction of African American characters:

> That she retained a certain distance . . . from the inner workings of her black characters seems to me all to her credit, since, by deliberately limiting her treatment of them to cover their observable demeanor and actions, she leaves them free, in the reader's imagination, to inhabit another landscape, another life, than the one she creates for them. This is a kind of grace many writers do not have when dealing with representatives of an oppressed people within a story, and their insistence on knowing everything, on being God, in fact, has burdened us with more stereotypes than we can ever hope to shed. (52)

The O'Connor-Walker connection, however, goes beyond Walker's praise or opinion of O'Connor's work. According to Walker scholar Nagueyalti Warren, in 1966, after reading O'Connor's fiction as a student at Sarah Lawrence College in New York, Walker wrote "a story that can be seen as the missing part of O'Connor's story, 'Everything That Rises Must Converge'" (1). Not published until 2014, the story titled "Convergence: The Duped Shall Enter Last: But They Shall Enter" "covers the same period as O'Connor's story—post-1957 and the integration of public buses, but pre-full civil and human rights in the South" (1). Far from a simple imitation, "Convergence" offers several key and clearly intended reversals of the details of O'Connor's story. Instead of the would-be intellectual and pretentious Julian, Walker substitutes an angry young African

American women home from college who drives to an exercise class—not Julian's white overweight mother, but her small traditional mother who believes she is "satisfied wid where I is" ("Convergence" 7) and complains that "you all young'uns . . . don't know your place" (6). And while, like Julian's mother, the mother in Walker's tale is assaulted after reaching out to help a young man of a different race, she does not suffer a stroke and die. Instead, she joins a sit-in at a drugstore's whites-only soda counter and closes Walker's story by "slurping her coke complacently, as if this wasn't the first time she'd been able to sit down with it" (12). As a result, while O'Connor's story is often viewed as using the topical issue of race to broach theological issues (see, for example, Coles 42-3; Giannone 175-78; Desmond 68-70; Lake 181-83), Walker's tale reverses the stress: "Convergence'"s mother stops singing "Je-sus ke-ee-p me ny-aer the cross" (6) to take up social justice actions.

At the same time, O'Connor's presence is not in the story merely to be lectured, corrected, or punched in the gut. Along with the obvious reference to O'Connor's "The Lame Shall Enter First" in Walker's subtitle—"The Duped Shall Enter Last: But They Shall Enter"—the story is laced with images and phrases from across O'Connor's canon. Early in "Convergence" Adrianne and her mother mirror Mary Grace and the "well-dressed" (*CW* 635) mother in "Revelation" with Adrianne's mother telling her, "I don't know what's the matter with you. Your daddy and me scrapped and saved to send you to school ... and whut do we git for it? Nothing but disrespect and abuse from you who ain't even dry behind the ears yet" (3; compare *CW* 644). Where O'Connor's Mrs. Turpin carries on nightly unvoiced conversations with Jesus about race (*CW* 636, 642), Adrianne "conduct[s]" a "mental angry monologue" with Jesus: "And I tell you right now Jesus . . . I don't want nothing to do with you if you desert little fools like Mama who never did nobody no harm and send them flying through a goddamn white mob trying to make some goddamn stupid white boy go to school and make good marks so his 'poor ma and pa' won't end up in the 'horspital'" (10). More subtly, the language of Ruby Turpin's description of black protesters who "[l]ay down in the middle of the road and stop traffic" (*CW* 653) as well as "Revelation"'s vision at that story's end (*CW* 654) can be heard in a description of protesters uttered by "Convergence"'s mother: "I seen a whole lot of peoples who ain't got no respect for themselves and nobodies else out marching and gallivantin' around like they think they know more'en anybody's else whut's been going on in the world. . . . I know whut's been going on, and a whole lot of marching and sanging ain't going to change nothing" (7).

Links in "Convergence" to other O'Connor stories range from the humorous description of the mother's car that "chocked and gurgled, and snorted and farted and finally quit altogether" before finally lurching down the road (4), looking like a close relation to the Carters' 1920s Ford that Mr. Shiftlet resurrects in "The Life You Save May Be Your Own" (*CW* 173, 178) to more serious mentions of people being "mix-placed and mis-placed persons" ("Convergence" 6), recalling "The Displaced Person"—a link encouraged by a woman with a "jutting hillock of stomach" (5) recalling Mrs. Shortley (*CW* 285) and the mother's adage that "the secret of success is that you makes do wid whut you got" ("Convergence" 7) echoing the Judge's advice: "The devil you know is better than the devil you don't" (*CW* 299). Add these slight references to "Good Country People" ("Convergence" 4; *CW* 267) and "Greenleaf" ("Convergence" 5; *CW* 518) and O'Connor's presence is unmistakable. What that presence means in this one story and the distance that presence stretches into Walker's mature work is something scholarship needs to explore, but without reading O'Connor, an understanding of Walker's development and her sense of her literary past are lost or at least incomplete.

While Toni Morrison has been less effusive in her praise of O'Connor and not, to my knowledge, had O'Connor directly impact her fiction, she has pointedly discussed O'Connor's racial work as valuable in understanding African American culture. Her 1990 book of literary criticism, *Playing in the Dark: Whiteness and the Literary Imagination*, makes two brief comments on O'Connor. The first notes the failure of readers to see the "connection between God's grace and Africanist 'othering' in Flannery O'Connor" (14)—

clearly a call not to ban O'Connor but to study further her use of race. Slightly more developed is her discussion of "The Artificial Nigger" in the context of "common linguistic strategies employed in fiction to engage the serious consequences of blacks" (67). Morrison reads Mr. Head's "triumphantly racist views in that brilliant story" as the result of "dehistoricizing allegory"—a process in which "difference is made so vast that the civilizing process becomes indefinite—taking place across an unspecified infinite amount of time" (68). In this way, Morrison offers a path to understanding Mr. Head's lack of historical progress—his failure to reject racism—despite his realizations about his soul. In doing so, she uses O'Connor's story to identify and illustrate the nation's ongoing struggle with and toleration for racism that might well suggest insights stretching beyond O'Connor's time to at least recent United States election cycles.

Along with mentions in at least one public address after *Playing in the Dark* (O'Neil), Morrison has a more extended analysis of "The Artificial Nigger" in her most recent book of criticism, *The Origin of Others*. Here, Morrison reads the story as "a carefully rendered description of how and why blacks are so vital to a white definition of humanity" (20). Her sense of the story as illustrating an education by which Nelson "has been successfully and artfully taught racism" that leads him to believe "he has acquired respectability, status" (24) may have little in common with traditional theological readings of the tale, but Morrison shows "successfully and artfully" how the work of a white writer—O'Connor—is important for understanding African American experience whatever the author's intentions.

O'Connor and Nonliterary African American Art
Moreover, African American artists outside the field of literature also have benefited from encounters with O'Connor's fiction. In 2005 Benny Andrews, an artist whom the *St. James Guide to Black Artists* describes as "a social realist" who "believes that art elevates people, glorifies people's pasts, and builds self-pride" (Tenabe 17), published six prints illustrating O'Connor's story "Everything That Rises Must Converge" for the Limited Editions Club of New York.[3]

Andrews might be thought to be an odd artist for such work, as he was known as much for his social activism as for his art. Indeed, civil rights leader and congressman John Lewis eulogized Andrews in the foreword to a 2013 exhibition catalogue this way:

> For Benny there was no line where his activism ended, and his art began. To him, using his brush and his pen to capture the essence and spirit of his time was as much an act of protest as sitting-in or sitting-down was for me. I can see him now: thinking, speaking, articulating what needs to be done and in the next few moments trying to make real what he had been contemplating. He was honest to a fault, and I think it was his determination to speak the plain truth that shaped his demand for justice and social integrity. He never aligned with any political group, but would offer the full weight of his support to anyone he thought was standing for truth. ("Overview")

In his afterword to the illustrated volume of O'Connor's story, Andrews delineates at some length the distance between himself and O'Connor:

> … we existed, during her lifetime, in two very different worlds; in fact in many ways two opposing worlds. This woman was to us, the African-Americans of her time, a "white lady." We spoke of them "white ladies" like one would speak of unworldly creatures, like moss growing high up on tall trees out of reach of mere earthlings, us. (41)
> … Flannery O'Connor would not have given me an audience during her lifetime. I would have never been invited to her home or probably been given much time to say anything of significance at her lectures. (41-42)
> … As I moved out into the bigger world I resisted "the society that she fed on." I became the kind of Negro that she didn't like, the James Baldwin kind, a militant. (42)
> … the news that we read in the Atlanta papers meant different things to us. The "troubles between the races" as it was often discreetly put in the papers, didn't say the same thing to her that it said to me. The stories about Negroes being beaten for not observing the segregation laws meant different things to us. The "mixing of the

races up North" meant different things to us. What we hoped for and dreamt of were different. (42-3)

Given their differences, Andrews's assertion that "Flannery O'Connor in my mind is a great writer" jumps out like one of O'Connor's "large and startling figures" (*CW* 806), and that is one of his claims about what he finds in her fiction: "She confronts the leaping flames and churning waters" (43). He clearly knows O'Connor beyond the one story he illustrates, commenting on her published letters, "she reveals as much about the culture she lives in as she does about herself" (43). As for her connection to his own art—his justification for illustrating her work—Andrews writes, "Now I am challenged to bring those two parallel lines together. I see her writings to be so much bigger and more everlasting than her society's traditions. Like any person attempting to be creative, to seize anything that can be of use in forging a work that is bigger and more significant than the ordinary, I see her work as being of use in making a more powerful force than our two parallel lines make" (43-44). Defining what this use is, he borrows from O'Connor's vocabulary: "The portions of the story that I chose to illustrate originate in O'Connor's deteriorating old world, one that would end in a death that would haunt her descendants. Those choices make this volume a convergence, and it is my hope that they rise and in their rising converge two different worlds" (44).

The six etchings that illustrate the volume show Andrews putting these ideas into practice. The earliest one in the volume is also the only one in which only white figures appear: a blonde, thin Julian leans against a door, his face downcast and sullen. His mother's back is to the viewer as she sets her green and purple hat on her head and stares into a full-length mirror where her image, in contrast to the precision of the rest of the etching, is a faded red blur (4). Here is the deteriorating old world of O'Connor's time. Four of the etchings are set on the bus: the entrance of the black man in a suit (11); the entrance of the black woman in her purple and green hat and her young son (25); the four principals sitting on opposite sides of the bus, facing each other, with the chasm of the aisle growing wider as it nears the viewer's perspective (29); and the moment when Julian's mother holds out a penny to the young black child as his mother and Julian look on in outrage and anger (33). Here are Andrews's parallel lines—the two racial worlds and their uncertain divides made visible. Yet it is the sixth and final etching that stands out. It looks more like a draft than a finished work; the vibrant colors of the other etchings are absent; faint lines suggest a Julian-figure standing over his mother stretched on the sidewalk as a dark stain of a cloud begins to cover them. Only the mother's black purse and her green and purple hat hint at the style of the other five pieces (39). In his afterword, Andrews comments only on this final image:

> The final illustration, like the ending of O'Connor's story, remains open-ended. Neither offers definitive solutions. The Negro and the white lady have met down at the crossroads, but that's just where they are, at the crossroads. It is up to the reader of the story and the viewer of my art work to look at two Southerners and wonder, wonder, and hopefully wonder more. (44)

This wonder and wondering about race that Andrews finds in O'Connor's story has become the basis for his own attempt at similarly suggestive work in his own medium. In interacting with O'Connor's racial work, he finds a generating force for his own African American art, which he sees as redemptive of the old racial divide—in his words, a convergence that is made possible only because O'Connor's fiction remains to be read.

In 2004, in a different medium, Bill T. Jones—a modern dancer and choreographer whom Michelle Dent in *The Drama Review* has labeled "one of the consummate choreographers of our time" (27)— staged *Reading, Mercy and the Artificial Nigger*. Using a condensed but unsanitized version of O'Connor's words, in Allen Robertson's description, "as if they were a soundscore" (Robertson), two narrators on opposite sides of the stage read the story while dancers perform "movement sequences" that mirror the text "in highly formalized and abstract ways" (Dent 29). In contrast to the seemingly straightforward O'Connor narrative, the two main characters, Mr. Head and Nelson, are "personified not by one pair but by five pairs of dancers" (Kisselgoff E3) without regard to the race or gender given in the story. Donald Shorter, an African American dancer who performed "a Mr. Head," recalls the parts were assigned based on height: "The shorter dancers were going to be Nelson and the taller dancers were going to be Mr. Head," with the characters distinguished on stage by having the Nelson dancers wear olive-colored suits and the Mr. Head dancers dressed in black (Shorter).

A gay African American man, whom reviewer Anna Kisselgoff sees as "refusing to be contained in a system" and "making people uncomfortable" (E3), Jones at the time of the production was asked by a New York *Times* interviewer, "Why base a dance on Flannery O'Connor's short story?" He replied:

> I have for so long been trying to get away from messages or obvious meaning in my work. And not to be condescending to writers, but I always think writers work with something more tangible than dancers do in terms of words and what they mean. For me, dance is free of the literal. But then I ran into a story that stopped me in my tracks because I again realized there was real power in words. I see "Artificial Nigger" as a journey by two characters who are dubious in every sense of the word. Who are they? What do they really believe? They claim to be Christians, but there is a great deal of anger and resentment and fear in them. Mr. Head actually has a moment where he realizes he is a great sinner in having betrayed Nelson. But then there appears the artificial nigger. A-ha! The artificial nigger, if you accept Mr. Head's religious rationale—the Lord forgives in proportion to our sins—represents a kind of grace. This moment of grace enables Mr. Head and Nelson to heal the rift between them.... And while O'Connor seems to make a connection between religion and race, this story ultimately isn't about race. It's about the dynamic between two people, the grandfather and the grandson. And if it takes a shocking title like "The Artificial Nigger" or my accepting a very casual use of a very hurtful word to get at something about human nature, then I have no qualms about embracing it. (Jones AR 6)

For Jones, O'Connor's story, then, becomes a tool to see beyond race, to bring together, using Benny Andrews's image, the parallel lines converging into a common humanity.

Like Andrews's illustrations, too, Jones's work is open-ended—a quality emphasized in the dance by replacing the lawn statue with a simple "chair from the stage [that] levitates so that it is floating at the center of a moon projected on the backdrop" (Dent 30). This shift pushes to an extreme the artificialness of the object Mr. Head and Nelson wonder at and are steered by toward reconciliation, thus stressing the constructedness of their racial views. Donald Shorter describes his own progress to such an understanding as one of Jones's dancers: "My attachment to the piece had been from inside it, and it involved fear because 'Oh my God, I have to do this right!' But now I'm looking at it from a different lens, being able to be outside it again. I like the fact that it's not a Disney transformation where it's like 'Oh my gosh, I love black people!' It's more of a realistic level of awareness that the characters and audience get about their relationship to race" (Shorter). Critic Michelle Dent goes further:

[Jones] lets O'Connor's text speak for itself, as both a reflection and an incrimination of the author and the society from which she drew her material. The meeting with the "artificial nigger" is, after all, every white American's history. The audience is left straining to make sense of the dance and, by inference, of today's social systems. (30-31)

Such straining can be avoided by refusing to interact with O'Connor's writing, but for Jones this ability to involve the audience is important for black art. Establishing a correlation between O'Connor's words and his own medium of dance, "a disjunction" is made visible "between what is seen and heard. . . . These disjunctions throw everything into question: what is really happening here, both on stage and in the viewer's head?" (Jones AR 6). For Jones, then, O'Connor's work is worth keeping alive and being presented to multiracial audiences far different from the world depicted in her work because it provides a significant musical-like theme for his art to riff on.

Returning to O'Connor: *The Violent Bear It Away* and "The Artificial Nigger"

As powerful as such views are, they take us back to O'Connor's writing itself to seek a reason for why her work has such an impact, suggesting that the work itself is ironically the best argument against banning it—despite its obvious racial offenses. Consider a passage, seldom, if ever, addressed when considering the need to limit access to her work. The passage, marked by racially offensive language, occurs in the first chapter of O'Connor's second novel, *The Violent Bear It Away*. Young Tarwater is at his great-uncle's still taking deep swigs from the old man's stock of moonshine:

> Take it easy, his friend said. Do you remember them nigger gospel singers you saw one time, all drunk, all singing, all dancing around that black Ford automobile? Jesus, they wouldn't have been near so glad they were Redeemed if they hadn't had that liquor in them. I wouldn't pay too much attention to my Redemption if I was you. Some people take everything too hard. (*CW* 358)

This passage goes out of its way to emphasize the racial slur, placing it not only in the detailed image of black singers dancing around a Ford but underscoring it with the sneeringly humorous line about the debt their religious fervor owes to alcohol. Yet read in the context of the entire novel, it is also a defining moment for the "friend" who just a few pages earlier had been only a "voice of the stranger" (345) spoken by Tarwater before gradually solidifying into a distinct form as simply "the stranger" (345) and now in this passage has become "his friend." Consequently, this passage, because of the racial slur, defines this "friend" as racist and links that racism to a discouraging of Tarwater's interest in "Redemption." With this launch into the friend's character, the reader can follow him through the course of the novel until he merges with another figure known only as "the stranger": "a pale, lean, old-looking young man" wearing "a lavender shirt and a thin black suit and a panama hat" (469) who drugs Tarwater, carries him into the woods, and most likely rapes him (471-72). That O'Connor starts this line of character development by linking the stranger/friend with racism is a strong indictment of that racism—an indictment that is made possible by the racist slur that serves as a foundation defining his character. Even if we accept O'Connor's tendency to insist on reading the theological themes in her work, this passage suggests that she is using racism as a way to identify and mark evil—a move that hardly encourages it.[4]

In "The Artificial Nigger" something similar is going on, though the final twist of the story makes the outcome more interesting. As scholars have noticed,[5] two traits mark Mr. Head. First, his delusion is emphasized in the story's opening passage in which he sees his shack through moonstruck eyes: his floor boards are "silver," his pillow ticking "brocade," and the moon "wait[s] for his permission to enter" as the chair on which his trousers lie becomes a servant, "stiff and attentive as if it were awaiting an order." Even his pants "had an almost noble air" (210). In such a light, his eyes have "a look of composure and of ancient wisdom as if they belonged to one of the great guides of men. He might have been Vergil summoned in the middle of the night to go to Dante, or better, Raphael, awakened by a blast of God's light to fly to the side of Tobias" (210). It is in light of such delusion that his second quality appears: his unrelenting use of the N-word—especially in the scene on the train with the coffee-colored man—that shows his racism. The story has prepared a context for his language, and in doing so his character is revealed to the reader as flawed long before his own realization of himself as "a great sinner" for whom "no sin was too monstrous for him to claim as his own" (231). It's this revelation that marks the story's attack on racism—a revelation that uses the racist language as one of the foundational levels of Mr. Head's character.

Does this mean that O'Connor shouldn't or can't be banned or set aside because of her reliance on racist language? The answer is probably no, but it underscores the cost of doing so. It also points to an interesting aspect of her writing that is often overlooked. In an interview with Gerard Sherry in 1963, O'Connor was asked her thoughts on "[w]here the pulpit is failing as a medium of instruction" (100). After asserting, "I am in no position to say what the general level of preaching is today in the Church," she launches into a story about a "connection" of hers "who married a Baptist." After twelve years of going to the Catholic church with his wife, the Baptist converted to Catholicism, and O'Connor asked him "Whatever got you interested?" The man replied, "Well, the sermons were so terrible, I knew there must be something else to it to get all those people there Sunday after Sunday"—to which O'Connor comments, "The Lord can use anything, but you just think He shouldn't have to" (100). O'Connor's fiction has a similar take on racism. It uses anything—even the language of racism itself—to critique the failings of her culture. But that doesn't stop us, every time we read or teach her, from wishing it didn't have to.

Notes

1. The focus on race and anxiety about it has not abated in the current century. Two essays with very different tones that address it are the ones by Pugh and Caron cited below. An MLA publication, *Approaches to Teaching Flannery O'Connor*, set for release in 2019, will have two essays about teaching race in O'Connor: Doreen Fowler's "Race and Grace in Flannery O'Connor" and John Duvall's "O'Connor and Whiteness Studies."

2. This essay is included in *Mystery and Manners*, the 1969 collection of O'Connor's nonfiction prose edited by Robert and Sally Fitzgerald, where it has the title "Total Effect and the Eighth Grade." The notes for *Mystery and Manners* state that the title in that volume is the one on the essay manuscript (*MM* 236), but neither those notes nor the ones in *Collected Works* explain how the title in the *Georgia Bulletin* came to exist.

3. Images of Andrews's illustrations can be found on line by searching "Benny Andrews Everything that Rises Must Converge." One of the best sites is www.limitededitionsclub.com/everything-that-rises-must-converge, which has five of the six illustrations and Andrews's afterword.

4. Such a move is hardly unique to O'Connor. Mark Twain's presentation of Pap in chapter six of *Adventures of Huckleberry Finn* has Pap overusing racist language and ideas as he rails against the "govment" that prevents a free black man from being sold "till he'd been in the State six months" (66, 67). This saps him of any potential for a sympathetic response and gets him "agoing on so" that he falls over

"the tub of salt pork" (67). Such a depiction paves the way for the unemotional announcement of his death near the novel's end.

5. Representative discussions of Mr. Head's limitations include Cheatham 476-77, Monroe 71, Oates 157, and Asals 81-2, but in some form this topic appears in most scholarly discussions of the story.

Works Cited

Andrews, Benny. "Afterword" and Illustrations. *Everything That Rises Must Converge*, by Flannery O'Connor. Limited Editions Club, 2005, pp. 4, 11, 25, 29, 33, 39, 41-44.

Asals, Frederick. *Flannery O'Connor: The Imagination of Extremity*, U of Georgia P, 1982.

Bottum, Joseph. "Flannery O'Connor Banned." *Crisis*, vol. 18, no. 9, Oct. 2000, pp. 48-49.

Byrd, Turner F. "Ironic Dimension in Flannery O'Connor's 'The Artificial Nigger.'" *Mississippi Quarterly*, vol. 21, no. 4, 1968, pp. 243-51.

Caron, Timothy P. "'The Bottom Rail Is on the Top': Race and 'Theological Whiteness' in Flannery O'Connor's Short Fiction." *Inside the Church of Flannery O'Connor: Sacrament, Sacramental, and the Sacred in Her Fiction*. Edited by Joanne Halleran McMullen and Jon Parrish Peede, Mercer UP, 2007, pp. 128-64.

Cheatham, George. "Jesus, O'Connor's Artificial Nigger." *Studies in Short Fiction*, vol. 22, no. 4, 1985, pp. 475-79.

Coles, Robert. *Flannery O'Connor's South*. U of Georgia P, 1993.

Dent, Michelle. "Checking the Time: Bill T. Jones's American Utopia." *The Drama Review*, vol. 49, no. 2, 2006, pp. 24-47.

Desmond, John F. *Risen Sons: Flannery O'Connor's Vision of History*. U of Georgia P, 1987.

Dreher, Rod. "Banning Flannery." *Weekly Standard*, 11 Sept. 2000, pp. 33-34.

Duvall, John. "O'Connor and Whiteness Studies." *Approaches to Teaching Flannery O'Connor*. Edited by Robert Donahoo and Marshall Bruce Gentry, MLA, forthcoming.

Fowler, Doreen. "Race and Grace in Flannery O'Connor." *Approaches to Teaching Flannery O'Connor*. Edited by Robert Donahoo and Marshall Bruce Gentry, MLA, forthcoming.

Giannone, Richard. *Flannery O'Connor: Hermit Novelist*. U of Illinois P, 2000.

Hays, Peter L. "Dante, Tobit, and "The Artificial Nigger." *Studies in Short Fiction*, vol. 5, no. 3, 1968, pp. 263-68.

Heitman, Danny. "Some Kind Words for Flannery O'Connor." *The Advocate* [Baton Rouge, LA], 15 Sept. 2000, p. 1C. *Newsbank*.

Jones, Bill T. "Dance; The Sincerest Form of Flannery." Interviewed by Fletcher Roberts. *New York Times*, 1 Feb. 2004, AR 6. www.nytimes. com/2004/02/01/arts/dance-the-sincerest-form-of-flannery.html.

Kahane, Claire. "The Artificial Niggers." *Massachusetts Review*, vol. 19, no. 1, 1978, pp. 183-98.

Kisselgoff, Anna. "Dance Review: Race and Redemption, from the Page to the Stage." Review of *Reading, Mercy and the Artificial Nigger*, choreographed by Bill T. Jones, *New York Times*, 5 Feb. 2004, p. E3. www.nytimes.com/2004/02/05/arts/dance-review-race-and-redemption-from-the-page-to-the-stage.html.

Lake, Christina Bieber. *The Incarnational Art of Flannery O'Connor*. Mercer UP, 2005.

Monroe, W. F. "Flannery O'Connor's Sacramental Icon: 'The Artificial Nigger.'" *South Central Review*, vol. 1, no. 4, 1984, pp. 64-81.

Morrison, Toni. *The Origin of Others*. Harvard UP, 2017.

_____. *Playing in the Dark: Whiteness and the Literary Imagination*. Vintage, 1993.

Oates, Joyce Carol. "The Action of Mercy." *Kenyon Review*, vol. 20, no. 1, 1998, pp.157-60.

O'Connor, Flannery. *Collected Works*. Edited by Sally Fitzgerald, Library of America, 1988.

_____. *Habit of Being: Letters*. Edited by Sally Fitzgerald, Farrar, Straus and Giroux, 1979.

_____. "An Interview with Flannery O'Connor." Interviewed by Gerard E. Sherry. *Conversations with Flannery O'Connor*. Edited by Rosemary M. Magee. UP of Mississippi, 1987, pp. 97-102.

_____. *Mystery and Manners: Occasional Prose*. Edited by Sally Fitzgerald and Robert Fitzgerald, Farrar, Straus and Giroux, 1969.

_____. "To John Crowe Ransom." 12 Jan. 1955, *Flannery O'Connor Bulletin*, vol. 23, 1994-95, pp. 181-82.

_____, and Caroline Gordon. *The Letters of Flannery O'Connor and Caroline Gordon.* Edited by Christine Flanagan, U of Georgia P, 2018.

O'Neil, Rosemary. "Toni Morrison Talks about Fiction's Depiction of Race." *The Chicago Maroon,* 3 June 1997. www.en.utexas.edu/amlit/amlitprivate/texts/morrison2.html.

"Overview." *Benny Andrews Estate.* www.bennyandrews.com/overview.

Pugh, Tison. "Chaucer's Rape, Southern Racism, and the Pedagogical Ethics of Authorial Malfeasance." *College English,* vol. 67, no. 6, 2005, pp. 569-86.

Ransom, John Crowe. "To Flannery O'Connor." 10 Jan. 1955. *Flannery O'Connor Bulletin,* vol. 23, 1994-95, p. 180.

Robertson, Allen. "The 'N...' Word." *Dance Consortium.* www.danceconsortium.com/features/article/the-n-word-by-allen-robertson.

Schultz, Bruce. "Collection Pulled from Reading List." *The Advocate* [Baton Rouge, LA], 26 Aug. 2000, p. 3B. *Newsbank.*

Shorter, Donald, Jr. Personal interview. 16 Nov. 2018.

Tenabe, Gabriel. "Andrews, Benny: American Painter." *St. James Guide to Black Artists.* Edited by Thomas Riggs, St. James, 1997, pp. 14-17.

Twain, Mark. *Adventures of Huckleberry Finn.* Edited by Gregg Camfield, Bedford, 2008.

Walker, Alice. "Convergence: The Duped Shall Enter Last: But They Shall Enter." *Flannery O'Connor Review,* vol. 12, 2014, pp. 3-12.

_____. *In Search of Our Mothers' Gardens.* Harcourt, Brace, 1983.

Warren, Nagueyalti. "Introduction to Alice Walker's 'Convergence.'" *Flannery O'Connor Review,* vol. 12, 2014, pp. 1-2.

Williams, Melvin G. "Black and White: A Study in Flannery O'Connor's Characters." *Black American Literature Forum,* vol. 10, no. 4, 1976, pp. 130-32.

Wood, Ralph C. "Where is the Voice Coming From? Flannery O'Connor on Race." *The Flannery O'Connor Bulletin,* vol, 22, 1993-94, pp. 90-118.

CRITICAL
READINGS

The Coming Censorship of Fiction

Basil Tozer et al.

Editor's Note: One of the most interesting debates about censorship in the early twentieth century was provoked by a 1908 article by Basil Tozer. Tozer warned that the increase of sexually suggestive (or even explicit) fiction might make it likely that an official censor of fiction would be appointed in Britain. Such a censor already existed for drama. Tozer's essay prompted a number of replies by both British and American writers, a sampling of which follows his essay (reprinted below). Especially interesting is the emphasis many of the writers give to the roles and motives of women in writing so-called "Fleshly Fiction."

Tozer's Essay: The Coming Censorship of Fiction

Though it seems but yesterday, it must have been quite twenty years ago that a book from Ouida's pen used to be deemed *ipso facto* an unclean thing by the great body of the public that borrows its novels from the lending-libraries.[1] At that time there were mothers who would take precautions to prevent, or try to prevent, their daughters from reading Ouida's novels, just as there were daughters who kept Ouida's works well out of sight of their mothers. Some fathers, too, looked askance at the yellow covers with the Ouida trademark, and I well remember an elderly man of great integrity but narrow views who caused his pretty grandchild considerable pain by snatching *Moths* out of her hands and burning it before her eyes. Then there were contemporaries of Ouida's who followed in her wake, some few even who stepped in where Ouida with her true sense of artistic perspective would not have thought of treading. Their books were of course banned too by certain strait-laced people of those days who pretended to discover "impropriety" in books that none but an out-and-out Mrs. Grundy would have censored,[2] and that emphatically no man or woman of the world—I mean by that no man or woman of intelligence and devoid of hypocrisy and cant—could by any possibility have objected to. Twenty years ago! In face of the extraordinary change that has taken place within the last few years in the tone of a great deal of our lending-library fiction, the thought is as strange as the reflection that a century ago a lad was strung up on a gibbet for robbing the Brighton *Mail* of half a guinea.

When, two years ago, I had the temerity, in an article headed "The Increasing Popularity of the Erotic Novel," published in the *Monthly* Review, openly to draw attention to the change for the worse that was coming over modern novels of a particular class, a section of the newspaper Press at once cried out that the statements made were false in every detail. But soon other writers took the matter up, among them no less distinguished a philosopher than Dr. William Barry, whose anonymous article, "The Fleshly School of Fiction," published in the *Bookman* of October last, created a profound impression and was quoted throughout England, also on the Continent and in America. By some his bold assertions were warmly upheld. By others they were angrily condemned. As an outcome of the controversy that followed—for a time it almost resembled an agitation—we find in the Preface to The Literary Year-Book for 1908 the guarded statement that "the *Bookman*'s campaign against 'The Fleshly School' has elicited, among some welcome protests, a few slightly interested opinions, and on the whole it must be said that the tone of some new novels remains objectionable."

The enormous financial success that has resulted from the circulation of the "fleshly" books referred to, books devoid of literary merit but made attractive to a great body of the general reading public by certain unveiled descriptions which they contain, has led to the writing of a vast amount of filthy fiction by persons, many of them obviously women, who until now had never tried to write anything for publication. Through the courtesy of two publishing houses of good standing I have been afforded the privilege (sic) of examining a number of manuscripts of this description that have quite recently been submitted to them. In almost every case it becomes obvious that the writers have been "inspired" to produce the illiterate and disgusting stories referred to, mainly through their having thoroughly saturated their thoughts with the garbage of the same sort—only less so—that was published early in last year. They have apparently argued thus: "There is nothing clever, or extraordinarily attractive, in these books; therefore they must have sold as largely as they have done only because of their plain-spokenness. I believe I could write stuff like that myself. Anyway I will try. And I will go one better than even these people. And presently I shall be rich beyond the dreams of avarice!" And with that they have sat down and set to work.

Unfortunately for these people, though fortunately for the reading public, only a small proportion of our publishers are willing to debase their calling, and to bring their firms into disrepute with the body of the public that is right-minded, by placing upon the book market meretricious filth of the sort referred to. The would-be authors who at present are making the round of the publishing houses with prurient manuscripts to sell, seem not to be aware of this. A remarkable trait in some of these unhealthy-minded writers is their extraordinary self-assurance—in several cases it amounts almost to effrontery. Thus a young man who recently sent to a well-known publishing house one of the coarse productions that publishers of fiction are growing accustomed to receiving frequently, had the self-assurance to compare his work with that of two of the most distinguished of our modern novelists, adding that in his opinion "the descriptive passages in those men's books" were at least as plain-spoken as his. As rational would it be to compare the suggestive photographs that are sold secretly in all large cities, and almost openly in such places as Port Said, with the undraped figure of the Venus of Medici. Yet another writer of the modern fleshly school contrasts her unpublished stories with the masterpieces of Loti and de Maupassant, unable apparently to realise that the fleshly element—if I may so describe it—in the works of our great masters of French and of English literature is in most cases incidental to the narrative, and not its *raison d'être* [reason for being or existing].

All that, however, is in a sense by-the-way. The question we have now to face is, What has the future in store for English novelists, and for the scores of men and women who earn a livelihood by producing fiction of a lower grade than novels, if presently they find themselves securely muzzled by a censor chosen and appointed as our existing censor of plays is chosen? It is easy to smile incredulously at the suggestion and say that a censor of fiction never will be appointed.

Men and women laughed outright when it was first suggested that the office of censor of plays might one day be created. How inimical to the interests of the reading public, not to mention the rank and file of novelists, the appointment of a censor of fiction would be, is almost too obvious to call for comment. Judging, indeed, by the example set by our censor of plays, the probability is that many admirable works of fiction would be condemned unjustly owing solely to the censor's inability to discern the difference between a powerfully-written story true to life, and one with nothing to "recommend" it but its undisguised or its thinly-veiled eroticism. Indeed the appointment of an official censor with power to forbid, wholly upon his own responsibility, the publication of any work of fiction to which he might take exception, would come near to being a calamity. For what would happen if such a man should chance to be a person exceptionally ignorant of letters, or unduly biased in one direction or several directions, or abnormally strait-laced? The ably-written moral story with a sexual problem wrapped up in its pages might be banned simply to satisfy some favourite whim. The moral story of illicit love probably would be suppressed on the ground of its being too plain-spoken in parts of its dialogue, or in some of its descriptive passages. Novelists with a true knowledge of human nature, with facility to express themselves, and with the gift to paint in words living and vivid pictures for the gratification of thousands of men and women of intellect and culture the world over, would be compelled to abandon their avocation—would be to all intents muzzled into silence.

All this, I maintain again, may come about, and, if it does, whom shall we have to blame? Only the handful of writers who within the past year or two have been launching upon the book-market works of fiction—they cannot rightly be termed novels—that grow steadily filthier with every new book they write. One could almost think this handful of writers congratulated itself each time one of its members succeeded in getting placed upon the market a story a little coarser than any that had preceded it, and that then and there the remaining members set to work to try to write a book obscener still. If only such books had merit in addition to their eroticism, as so many of the French novels have, one might be tempted to look—wrongly, no doubt—with greater tolerance upon their pruriency. But of the books referred to that have been published of late years, hardly one has the semi-redeeming qualification of literary style or merit. Can one feel surprise, then, at the outcry that is being raised by a body of our leading men of letters at the degradation of the modern novel by the writers of the fleshly school?

Though this question has been commented upon more than once in some of our newspapers, all that has been written, even about the actual spread of eroticism, is infinitesimal by comparison with what has been said, and is still being said, by thinking people throughout the country, and by the feeling of indignation and disgust that has been aroused. Some months ago the Bishop of Norwich referred in one of his sermons to the growth of eroticism in the modern novel of a particular class, but the majority of those who feel most strongly upon the subject are impotent to interfere. Many thousands of persons scattered throughout the country realise that something ought to be done to prevent the little clique of writers referred to, and their unintelligent imitators, from further prostituting English literature, and apparently the bulk of them wish sincerely that something could be done to stop it. There, for the moment, the matter rests, but it cannot rest for long. Let a few score more of the fleshly narratives be launched upon the book market, and sold in their tens of thousands, and without excitement, or any sort of preliminary demonstration, we shall find ourselves saddled with a censor of fiction who, rest assured, will quickly shut down not merely the fiction that is admittedly filthy, but in addition a vast amount of excellent work that most certainly ought to be published. Then, and only then—when, of course, it will be too late to enter a protest that will mend matters—our British novelists will rise up in arms and metaphorically rend those among their colleagues who will have been directly to blame for the introduction of this unjust muzzling order.

That the foregoing prognostication will be derided by some publishers of novels, by some novel-writers, and by plenty of novel-readers, I know full well. All I ask, then, of the sceptics and the scoffers is that they keep well in mind the statements just set down, and note carefully what transpires within the next few years. For that the output of fleshly books will continue, and perhaps increase, is probable. Quixotic indeed would it be to imagine that so valuable an asset as a book that must run through edition after edition, and that consequently can be deemed even before publication to be almost a gilt-edged security, is likely to be kept off the market because a few objectors openly expound views and theories contrary to general opinion. Let it also be remembered, however, that the instalment of a censor of fiction must affect adversely not writers only. For the creation of such an office will hit many publishers a hard blow. It will hit the booksellers too. It will hit also the lending libraries. And it will hit, though less severely, what are called the "popular" magazines, while some of the daily journals, especially those provincial papers that owe their circulation in a measure to the popularity of their serial stories, will feel the touch of the censor's claw.

As a natural result of the reign of a literary censor, indeed as the only result possible, the book-market will be flooded with stories that will be neither flesh nor fowl,—stories invertebrate, cold and flaccid. The late Sir Walter Besant told me once that he had just received a letter from a correspondent who expressed extreme indignation at his, Sir Walter's, having made a male character in one of his stories kiss a woman to whom he was in no way related, and to whom he was neither married nor affianced. "Until now," the letter ran, "I have thought your books quite safe to give to my daughter to read, but in future I shall not be able to put a book of yours into her hands until I have read it myself." Probably there are thousands of men and women who think as that man thought. What would the condition of English literature be with such a man as censor? Only recently some of Sir Walter Scott's classics were banned on the ground of their "impropriety" by a committee of local provincial magnates appointed to select volumes for a certain public library. With that precedent before us nothing in the way of prudery seems impossible. Certainly a heroine moulded on the lines of Mr. Thomas Hardy's beautiful Tess would be blue-pencilled, as they say on the Turf, "from start to finish." Mr. Eden Phillpotts would never be allowed to give us another *Secret Woman*, for that memorable scene in the bracken would have made the censor blush. In future the monks of the Order of Robert Hichens would be compelled by the censor to refrain from pirouetting with pretty girls on the parched plains of Egypt or in any other of Allah's gardens. Even Mrs. "Malet" would be forced to strangle her art and to come up, or rather sink down, into a line upon the level of the commonplace, for though another legless lad might manage to crawl unchecked past the censor, most assuredly another woman as seductive as the *houri* who in the small hours enticed poor Sir Richard Calmady to his fate, would be stamped out of existence on the spot.

There are, as already implied, many admirable modern works of fiction that no right-minded man or woman not hide-bound by senseless scruples, or by alleged religious prejudice, or by the grotesque teachings of a Mrs. Grundy who should have been relegated to her grave long ago, can well object to. The volumes to which reference has just been made are among them. Other works of the sort are in preparation as I write, and surely all who are able to appreciate human, powerful and well-written stories—"evenly-balanced" stories, as some of the reviewers term them—must look forward to reading such books as soon as they appear. Is it worth while, then, when books of this kind are to be had, to rot away the intelligence of a great body of the reading public, especially of boys and girls in the most impressionable period of their existence, by saturating their minds with a train of thought made up of descriptions of filthy scenes, filthy acts, and a dialogue of double entendre, and in doing so run a grave risk of presently checking abruptly the output of any novels apart from stories that will be colourless, insipid, and mawkish—stories, in short, that will be wholly devoid of any sort of human emotion? All who live with their eyes open, and are able to look ahead, must admit that the writers, publishers and booksellers who together are deliberately prostituting the English novel, are wittingly or unwittingly imperilling their own future prosperity.

A Response in *The New York Evening Post*, April 14, 1908

THE INDECENT NOVEL. In the April number of the *National Review*, Mr. Basil Tozer writes on "The Coming Censorship of Fiction." It is his belief that, unless something is done to check the rising tide of prurient authorship, the Government will step in and appoint a censor of novels whose undiscriminating axe will fall alike on the just and the unjust, the work of the master who deals in realities and the work of the imitator who appeals to debased appetites. Is such a result chimerical? the writer asks. And he replies: "It is easy to smile incredulously at the suggestion, and say that a censor of fiction will never be appointed. Men and women laughed outright when it was first suggested that the office of censor of plays might one day he created." How stern a reality the censor of plays is now in England we have all recently been learning. Petitions against him have been handed in by the most prominent writers for the stage, which he has been accused both of stifling and corrupting. What would happen in the realm of fiction under a similar official? Mr. Tozer foresees a dismal future.

> Only recently some of Sir Walter Scott's classics were banned, on the ground of their "impropriety," by a committee of local provincial magnates appointed to select volumes for a certain public library. With that precedent before us nothing in the way of prudery seems impossible. Certainly a heroine moulded on the lines of Mr. Thomas Hardy's beautiful Tess could be blue-pencilled, as they say on the turf, "from start to finish." Mr. Eden Phillpotts would never be allowed to give us another "Secret Woman," that memorable scene in the bracken would have made the censor blush. In future the monks of the Order of Robert Hichens would be compelled by the censor to refrain from pirouetting with pretty girls on the parched plains of Egypt or in any other of Allah's gardens. The sins of the cheap eroticist shall be visited on their own generation.

It is all well enough to point out that there is a rising tide of indecent fiction. But, in the absence of an official censor, where are the means to sweep it back? Mrs. Partington [a fictional woman who tried to sweep back the Atlantic Ocean with a broom], with her discriminating mop, would find it impossible. Mrs. Grundy might. But her triumph, as we have indicated, would mean a general whelming back of the narrative flood, which would send adrift the good novels with the bad. Mr. Tozer has heightened the difficulty of his own task by making the limits of his toleration so broad. How far would general opinion go with him? Thomas Hardy, of course. Eden Phillpotts, yes. Robert Hichens—well, yes. Lucas Malet—um-m—yes. But that, after all, is laying down a standard of graduated artistry which it would be very hard to enforce in practice. Where shall we stop? For from Thomas Hardy to Eden Phillpotts the descent may be as sharp as from the last name in our list of imprimaturs to the first on our *Index Liborum Prohibitorum* [index of prohibited books]. With the very low forms of squalid novel-writing, there can be no question. That stands under the censorship of the police and the self-respect of the reputable publisher. The problem really resolves itself into the necessity of passing decision on individual cases. Censorship of some kind is, of course, always being exercised and in the absence of a public functionary, time, which is, after all, the great healer and sanitarian, will repress the unhealthy growth. On the whole, we cannot quite share our writer's trepidation over the mediocre and indecent novel. We do not take its popularity as indicative even of a peculiarly intense debasement of taste in the public, or of a peculiarly vicious viewpoint and philosophy on the part of the purveyors of this sort of fiction. Behind the literary manufacture of the suggestive and the nasty is not ethical anarchy, but our very old friend the spirit of imitation.

A large proportion of the literature of modified lubricity, for instance, is written by women. We have no doubt that shy maiden ladies in brooding villages on the banks of the upper Thames turn out this sort of trash with the abandon that always characterizes the author who writes on what he knows nothing about. In other words, it is precisely because Thomas Hardy wrote "Tess" and "Jude" that authors less gifted write stories of the same kind, less masterful, but such as Mr. Tozer would tolerate, and other authors still less gifted are turning out such stuff as Mr. Tozer's evil dreams are made on. Were this the age of Dickens and Thackeray, these same ladies would be writing three-volume novels of sentimental melodrama and studies of manners. So it comes down to a question of professionalism. Low-grade authors try to do what real artists have succeeded in doing. The low-grade eroticism of the cheap novel is but the reflection of love in the high places of fiction. The predominant role played by women writers may be explained by their better-proved mimetic qualities.

Ability to imitate alone, however, is not enough to explain our coarser type of realistic novel. There has been also what we may describe as the influence of sociological forces that are now working themselves out in Europe and to a less extent among us. Specifically, there is woman's emancipation. "Feminism" has brought with it a bolder discussion of the problems of sex. In Germany, the most ruthless realists are the women writers, simply because in revolt against gross political and social inequality, they have swung wildly in the other direction of sexual anarchism. In England, politics have contributed. Statesmen and scientists speak so freely of "state endowment for motherhood," of "mating" for the "breeding" of future efficient citizens, of time-limits for marriages, of what not, that speech in general has become bolder and "advanced" ideas do not hesitate to proclaim themselves in the market-place. The effect on the poor, mimetic hack-novelist is obvious.

A Response in *The Montgomery Advertiser*, April 21, 1908

SUGGESTED CENSORSHIP. A writer in one of the late magazines calls attention to what he styles "The Coming Censorship of Fiction." He takes the position that there is a constant increase in the output of indecent novels, and that unless the rising tide of prurient fiction is checked the government will be compelled to take a hand, in the suppression of this kind of authorship, or at least preventing such books from going through the mails.

Perhaps this is true but where is the blame for it? Writers of such books do not work for glory or fame or notoriety, but for money. It seems to be something of a going and coming proposition. As long as readers want such books they will be written and published, and as long as they are published there will be purchasers of a certain type. The public has a somewhat confirmed habit of getting what it wants and will pay for. If no such books were written they would not be read, we may say, but on the other hand if there were no readers for them they would not be written, and thus the problem shifts back and forth. But [if we] suppose such a censorship is established[,] where shall it begin, and where shall it end?

Shall nothing be condemned and suppressed except the cheap fiction? Or shall the pruning-knife be applied to all printed matter that is not clean and decent? If there is to be an impartial weeding out and suppression of all printed matter that is not unobjectionable it might be found both proper and necessary. In the interests of fairness and impartiality it might be necessary to strike at higher game than the dime novel nuisance. If strict and impartial justice should mark the work of the censors some of the time-honored English classics might suffer. For these old classics lack very much of being faultless in this respect. Shakespeare's "Venus and Adonis" is not a work that careful parents would select for their children to read, and there are many passages in his dramatic works which need to be blue-penciled before being read in the parlor. Edmund Spenser's "Faerie Queen" abounds in indecency all the way through, though Spenser was one of England's great poets and this was one of his greatest works. When we come to Chaucer it is difficult to speak respectfully, though he was another English poet of renown. Most of his poems are below the strict end of decency, while his "Canterbury Tales" exude filth and foulness from every stanza. We hardly think that any man of judgment and good taste would select that book for family reading, or that it would be selected as a book to read from to a mixed audience. And so we might go on and designate other books of famous authors—books to be found in all public libraries and which go through the mails and are sold and distributed without question. Shall the cheap indecent novels and tales be condemned and suppressed while the equally foul classics go unquestioned? That doesn't look exactly like a fair deal, as we view it. It may be argued that these cheap works are more hurtful to the general public than are the productions of the great writers of the past, and doubtless that is true to a certain extent. Cheap fiction is more generally bought and read by the general public, especially the young, than are the more expensive and pretentious books and for that reason, if no other, they are more demoralising, and ought to be kept out of circulation. The main difficulty we see in the exercise of such censorship would be to know where to draw the line between that which is proper and that which is indecent. It would require a nice sense of justice and fairness to distinguish between the two, and perhaps no two readers would agree in all cases. Still it might be done, and all indecent literature be suppressed, but we insist that if this is to be done some of the English classics will be in great danger.

A Response in *Current Opinion*, June 1908

"THE COMING CENSORSHIP OF FICTION." There is a very real danger, in the opinion of Basil Tozer, an English magazine writer, that unless the rising tide of prurient novels is stemmed, a censorship of fiction will be established. "It is easy to smile incredulously at the suggestion," he remarks, "and say that a censor of fiction never will be appointed. Men and women laughed outright when it was first suggested that the office of censor of plays might one day be created." But such an office *has* now existed in England for several years, and its activities have proved so mischievous that leading English authors and dramatists not long ago signed petitions demanding its abolition. Mr. Tozer is, of course, thinking primarily of England when he prophesies a censorship of fiction; but, in view of the fact that one of the "best sellers" in the American book world during the past winter has been a peculiarly frank erotic novel, his remarks may be felt to be equally applicable to this country. [Then quotes extensively from Tozer's article and from the response published in *The New York Post*.]

A Response by James Marchant, September 1908
THE CENSORSHIP OF LOW-GRADE LITERATURE AND
ILLUSTRATIONS
BY JAMES MARCHANT
(Director of The National Social Purity Crusade)

The title of this paper has been chosen by the Council of this Congress. A censor of newspapers, novels, illustrations, picture postcards would surely be a superman. But superman or not, a censor is in part well-nigh inevitable. Within the last ten, nay, five years things have become steadily worse. Critics like Dr. Barry have uttered stirring warning cries. Recently Mr. Basil Tozer, who has had access to many MSS. which have been submitted to two of the leading publishers, has asserted: "The enormous financial success that has resulted from the circulation of the filthy books referred to, books devoid of literary merit, but made attractive to a great body of the general reading public by certain unveiled descriptions which they contain, had led to the writing of a vast amount of filthy fiction by persons obviously women. Let a few score more be launched upon the book market, and without any excitement we shall be saddled with a censor of fiction."

There are an increasing number of novels which librarians who have regard for public morals keep under the counters, but which are unhappily in constant demand. There are from ten to fifteen periodicals, with a weekly circulation amounting to nearly half a million, which must be unhesitatingly described as dangerous to morals. Some of them are illustrated, and in the case of at least one of them, having an English circulation of over one hundred thousand and a considerable circulation (as I learn from missionaries whose work is hindered by them) in the Colonies, which can, it is said, be purchased at any bookstall in the world—the illustrations have but one object in view—and appeal to the beast in man. Of scandalous postcards, sold at the shops which make a speciality in nasty things, there is almost no limit. The results, both at home and in France, Germany and Italy, of the unfettered circulation of these things, is seen in juvenile crime and depravity. It is to be hoped that all this does not really mean that our social life is decadent. But we may well raise the question and hesitate about the answer. What is the remedy? At present we mainly rely upon the publishers who, be it said to their credit, as a body will not lower the moral status of their output. May they be fully recompensed and shut the door closer! The Publishers' Association ought surely to turn its serious attention to the checking of those few publishers who have already fatally lowered the standard. That would be one of the best forms of censorship. The Newsagents' Federation, formed in June of this year, with Mr. D. J. Shackleton, M.P., as Hon. President, is, I know from inside knowledge, gravely concerned about the circulation of noxious periodicals and is determined to check it. I believe, under the wise and strong guidance of Mr. Wynford Brierley, Editor of the National Newsagent, and organising secretary of this Conference, it can do much. The Postcard Association now being formed, and promoted by the excellent firm of Raphael Tuck, may follow the lead and bring pressure to bear upon the vendors of suggestive rubbish. In these directions there is hope for the future. Moral censorship of this kind is infinitely to be preferred to State censorship.

But there will unfortunately remain those who will not yield to moral force. Can these be dealt with by the police? I have ample reasons for knowing that many of these doubtful papers are read every week by the police, and often submitted to their solicitors, who would prosecute if they were sure of a conviction. In the present state of public opinion they are more than doubtful, and the devil has the advantage. It seems that the law needs strengthening in the direction of more clearly defining what is indecent. But that may not be practical. We must await the report of the present inter-Departmental Committee on indecent advertisements. But the ultimate test, when all is said and done, must be what the public tolerates. The lasting and effective censorship is public opinion. A State censor may be appointed to do for literature what is now done for plays. That censor, so far as concerns the rubbish of the kind we are contemplating, might very well be the new public prosecutor. That would be better than the present state of affairs. The police, after all, have enough to do without watching doubtful prints and the vicious tendencies of erratic novels. But a general censor of literature would be a calamity. And it is to be hoped that the Institute of Journalists, the Newsagents' Federation, the Publishers' Association, and similar organisations, the teachers in our schools, parents and librarians, the churches, and men's organisations and unions, will combine to make unwholesome literature distasteful and impossible. The wise words of Dr. Barry point the moral of the lesson and the road to purity in literature. "The heart of this people needs to be changed, its dream of soft living dissipated, the smoke swept from before its eyes, that it may see, repent, literally thinking new thoughts which shall be the old gospel, applied to our own times. There is little token of such a repentance. Until it comes, he that is filthy will be filthy still, the courtesan will be in honour and her Book of Hours will consist of those pleasant stones where flowers of evil are planted and death gathers the spoil. Grapes will not grow from thorns, nor figs from thistles, and unless English men and women keep their hearts pure, it is hopeless to expect their literature will be clean."

A Response by "Quill" in *The Northern Whig*, April 11, 1908

THE SUPPRESSION OF BAD BOOKS (By Quill.) Mr. Basil Tozer contributes to the April number of the *National Review* an article on "The Coming Censorship of Fiction," in which he elaborates the thesis with reference to the number of objectionable novels that are being published that public opinion will eventually demand the institution of a censor to examine and license books previous their publication in the way that plays are licensed by the dramatic censor. The argument is that the issue of demoralising books will become so intolerable that nothing short of drastic supervision of this kind will meet the case. I am not at all sure that Mr. Tozer is right. I do not doubt that books of the objectionable character referred to are being written and published, but if I were to judge from my own experience I should say that he and other writers who have been making outcry recently about this subject somewhat exaggerate the evil. But let me confess at once that my experience is limited. There are so many first-rate novels to read that I studiously avoid those which are second-rate. I do so for the simple reason that so long as one can get a hold of good novels it is a pure waste of time to read those that do not attain the highest level of excellence. For my sins I have often been compelled in the course of my occupation as a reviewer to do so, but that is another story. If you ask me whether you should read the novels of Hall Caine or Marie Corelli my reply is—"by all means, but not until you have first read the novels of Fielding, Smollett, Scott, Dickens, Thackeray, Jane Austen, George Eliot, Charlotte Bronte, Hawthorne, Meredith, Hardy, and many another besides. When you have read every novel in English that is better than Hall Caine's and Miss Corelli's—the list is not a short one, mind you— if you have the time left, and I don't think you will have much, you can take "The Christian" and "The Master Christian." It will be seen therefore that I am in no position to speak with authority as to whether the sex novel of the objectionable kind is on the increase or not. I accept, however, the accounts of those who say that it is, and I regret the fact on the double ground that these novels are injurious to morals, and that they are bad art. We used to hear a great deal at one time about art for art's sake. This is the formula which was used to convey what in my belief is the thoroughly unsound doctrine that art and morality have nothing to do with each other. So far from their having nothing to do with each other they are indissoluble. Morality is concerned with conduct, which we have it on Matthew Arnold's authority that conduct is three-fourths of life, and is it not in life that all art has its theme and its inspiration? A prurient novel is an evil thing morally, but it is also an evil thing artistically. The question remains how a bad book is to be kept from getting into circulation. It is not a new question, for in one form or another it has been subject of debate from oldest times. It is difficult because there are so many degrees of badness, and it does not apply to books alone, but to every art form and to every achievement of human activity that professes to be artistic. There are books which all decent people are agreed should not be touched with a pair of tongs, and there are pictures which are an abomination. There is no difficulty in dealing with the worst books. They come under the purview of the police, and with them the police are quite capable of dealing; but what are we to do with the suggestive books and the suggestive pictures, of which the immorality lies rather in their tendency than in their actual expression? The critic condemns them, but in no case would it be possible to secure their condemnation from a court of law. In some of them the immorality is so cloaked that they even pass muster as being highly moral. Are we call in a censor to put these things down? Mr. Tozer thinks that if the reprehensible output continues on the present scale we shall have no alternative but to do so. To him it is a very unpleasant prospect, as it is to me, for despotism, however benevolent, is to be deprecated. The real objection to censorship is that the man has not been born to whom such powers can be safely entrusted. There is no form of dictatorship so objectionable as that which presumes to dictate in matters of taste. The censor of literature will of necessity be bound to adopt a set of arbitrary rules, and under these rules no doubt much bad, but also some good, literature will be condemned. "Judging," Mr. Tozer says, "by the example set by the censor of plays, the probability is that many admirable works of fiction would be condemned unjustly, owing to the censor's inability to discern the difference between a powerfully written story true to life and one with nothing to recommend it but its undisguised or its thinly-veiled eroticism." The vagaries of public bodies which resort to the censorship of the fiction which is to be supplied in free libraries constitute an "awful example" in this respect. Have we not read of the London Council Council [sic] placing under the ban the works of Sir Walter Scott, of Jane Austen, of George Eliot, and of Charlotte Bronte? As Mr. Tozer says, "With that precedent before nothing the way of prudery seems impossible. Certainly," he adds, a heroine moulded on the lines of Mr. Thomas Hardy's beautiful Tess would be blue-pencilled, as they say on the turf, from start finish." It is not in the subject matter of a book but in the manner in which it is treated that the possibilities of immoral tendency lie. I think Mr. Tozer is quite right when says that Hardy's Tess would be censured under any set canons relating to subject matter; nevertheless *Tess* is one of the greatest novels in the language. But, as we are not to have a censorship, how are we to suppress bad books? Mr. Tozer appeals to authors to cease writing and to publishers to cease publishing them. That is well enough, but nothing effectual can be done until we get the public to cease reading them. The way to suppress bad books is to educate the public to loathe them. Repressive measures are apt to intensify rather than lessen the evil against which they are directed. Let it be given out that the sale of any book should be prohibited, and the sales of it will at once go up immensely. Men and women still retain their hankering after forbidden fruit. The best corrective—the only effectual corrective—to the reading of bad books is to engender taste for the excellent. No man who has been nurtured in the best fiction can ever take pleasure in the inferior, the tawdry, the sloppy sentimental, and the prurient. You cannot proscribe immoral books by Act of Parliament. Still less can you proscribe those which are merely worthless. When it does not pay to produce the second rate it will not be produced, and there will be no need for a censor. It may said that this is an ideal state of matters from which we are far enough off. No doubt that is so, but all our boasted education has indeed gone for nothing if we are not nearer than we once were.

Notes

1. The pseudonym of the English novelist Maria Louise Ramé (1839-1908).

2. A "a narrow-minded, conventional person who is extremely critical of any breach of propriety" (dictionary.com).

Works Cited

Caine, Sir Thomas Henry Hall. *The Christian*. Appleton, 1896.

Correlli, Marie. *The Master Christian*. Bernhard Tauchnitz, 1908.

"The Coming Censorship of Fiction." *Current Opinion*, vo. 44, no. 6, June 1908, pp. 620-21.

Hardy, Thomas. *Jude the Obscure*. Harper and Brothers, 1898.

_____. *Tess of the D'Urbervilles: A Pure Woman Faithfully Presented*. 3 vols. 1891 by McIlvaine & Co., 1891.

Hichens, Robert. *The Garden of Allah*. 2 vols. Methuen, 1904.

Malet, Lucas [pseudonym of Mary St Leger Kingsley]. *The History of Sir Roger Calmady: A Romance*. 2 vols. Methuen, 1901.

Man of Letters, A. [William Barry]. "The Fleshly School of Fiction: A Protest Against the Degradation of the Modern Novel." *The Bookman*, Oct. 1907, pp. 25-27.

Marchant, James. "The Censorship of Low-Grade Literature and Illustrations." Papers on Moral Education: Communicated to the First International Moral Education Congress Held at the University of London September 25-29, 1908, edited by Gustav Spiller. 2nd ed. David Nutt, 1909, pp. 214-16.

Phillpotts, Eden. *The Secret Woman*. Macmillan, 1905.

"Preface." *The Literary Year-Book 1908*. Routledge, 1908, pp. 3-8, esp. p. 7.

Ouida. *Moths*. 1880. Chatto & Windus, 1885.

Quill. "The Suppression of Bad Books." *The Northern Whig*, 11 Apr. 1908, p. 10. https://www.britishnewspaperarchive.co.uk/viewer/bl/0000434/19080411/221/0010. Accessed 10 Feb. 2019.

"Suggested Censorship." *The Montgomery Advertiser*, 21 Apr. 1908, p. 4, https://www.newspapers.com/clip/28195895/the_montgomery_advertiser/. Accessed 10 Feb. 2019.

Tozer, Basil. "The Coming Censorship of Fiction." *The National Review*, vol. 51, Apr. 1908, pp. 236-42.

_____. "The Increasing Popularity of the Erotic Novel." *The Monthly Review*, vol. 20, Sep. 1905, pp. 53-59.

"Fighting Race Calumny": Efforts to Censor *The Birth of a Nation*

C. E. Bentley, Jane Addams, and Mary Childs Nerney

Editors' Note: D. W. Griffith's famous 1915 silent film *The Birth of a Nation*, based on the novel *The Clansman* by Thomas Dixon, is often considered a landmark in the history of American cinema. But it is also widely regarded as an exceptionally racist movie—one that actually glorifies the Ku Klux Klan. Endorsed by President Woodrow Wilson, it was an enormously popular film and was one of the biggest of any "big-budget productions" during the early days of American moviemaking. Efforts to ban or censor the film, particularly by the newly formed National Association for the Advancement of Colored People (NAACP), were instant and energetic. The pieces below consist of (1) a brief letter by Mary Childs Nerney of the NAACP; (2) a lengthy article concerning Jane Addams, the famous civil rights advocate; and (3) two lengthy articles (titled "Fighting Race Calumny") about the organization's efforts written by C. E. Bentley, the group's national treasurer and published in the May and June 1915 issues of *The Crisis*, the organization's journal. All three documents provide intriguing insights into important issues. Bentley's articles, which are reprinted last, are especially interesting because of their copious detail.

Mary Childs Nerney's Letter
April 17, 1915
Mr. George Packard
1522 First National Bank Bldg.,
Chicago, Ill.
My dear Mr. Packard:
I am utterly disgusted with the situation in regard to "The Birth of a Nation." As you will read in the next number of the *Crisis,* we have fought it at every possible point. In spite of the promise of the Mayor to cut out the two objectionable scenes in the second part, which show a white girl committing suicide to escape from a Negro pursuer, and a mulatto politician trying to force marriage upon the

daughter of his white benefactor, these two scenes still form the motif of the really unimportant incidents, of which I enclose a list. I have seen the thing four times and am positive that nothing more will be done about it. Jane Addams saw it when it was in its worst form in New York. I know of no one else from Chicago who saw it. I enclose Miss Addams' opinion.

When we took the thing before the Police Magistrate he told us that he could do nothing about it unless it led to a breach of the peace. Some kind of demonstration began in the Liberty Theatre Wednesday night but the colored people took absolutely no part in it, and the only man arrested was a white man. This, of course, is exactly what Littleton, counsel for the producer, Griffith, held in the Magistrates' Court when we have our hearing and claimed that it might lead to a breach of the peace.

Frankly, I do not think you can do one single thing. It has been to me a most liberal education and I purposely am through. The harm it is doing the colored people cannot be estimated. I hear echoes of it wherever I go and have no doubt that this was in the mind of the people who are producing it. Their profits here are something like $14,000 a day and their expenses about $400. I have ceased to worry about it, and if I seem disinterested, kindly remember that we have put six weeks of constant effort of this thing and have gotten nowhere.

Sincerely yours,

Mary Childs Nerney, Secretary.

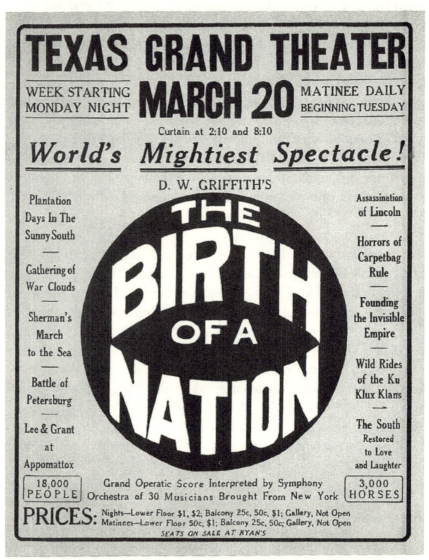

A reproduction of the advertisement which appeared daily in the El Paso Herald *during the week preceding the movie's run at the Texas Grand Theater in March, 1916.*

Source: Wikipedia.

An Interview with Jane Addams

This interview, published in the *New York Evening Post* on March 13, 1915, appeared under the following headline: "Jane Addams Condemns Race Prejudice Film / Calls It 'Pernicious Caricature of Negro Race.' / Producer seems to have gathered most vicious and grotesque individuals to show them as representatives of entire race, says head of Hull House after seeing 'The Birth of a Nation' moving picture drama." The article itself read as follows.

"Pernicious caricature of the negro [sic] race," is the way in which Miss Jane Addams of Hull House, Chicago, expressed her opinion to-day of the motion-picture drama "The Birth of a Nation," now being shown in New York, in which is told a story of Reconstruction days and Ku Klux Klan violence in the South following the Civil War. After having seen the film, Miss Adams softened no terms in her condemnation of it.

"The producer seems to have followed the principle of gathering the most vicious and grotesque individuals he could find among colored people, and showing them as representatives of the truth about the entire race," she said in describing her impressions of the play. "It is both unjust and untrue. The same method could be followed to smirch the reputation of any race. For instance, it would be easy enough to go about the slums of a city and bring together some of the criminals and degenerates and take pictures of them purporting to show the character of the white race. It would no more be the truth about the white race than this is about the black.

An Anachronism

"One of the most unfortunate things about this film is that it appeals to race prejudice upon the basis of conditions of half a century ago, which have nothing to do with the facts we have to consider to-day. Even then it does not tell the whole truth. It is claimed that the play is historical: but history is easy to misuse. It is undoubtedly true that some of the elements of the plot are based on actual events, but they are only a part of the picture. You can use history to demonstrate anything, when you take certain of its facts and emphasize them to the exclusion of the rest.

"Nobody denies that in the haste and confusion of the period after the Civil War the men in control of politics did very tyrannical and shortsighted things; and made a great many mistakes. The carpet-baggers from the North, who went in and influenced the negroes against the interests of the whites, unquestionably did a great deal of harm; but to present the tendency they represented as the only one is as unfair to the North as to claim that all Southerners wanted to oppress the negroes would be to the South. Then the film shows a ridiculous scene in a Southern Legislature, to which the election of a majority of negroes has been obtained by defrauding whites of their votes. Negro legislators are shown taking off their shoes at their desks, drinking whiskey from flasks while making speeches, acting in all sorts of uncouth ways. It is laughably false to the whole truth.

"Then there is the impression that is created of the Ku Klux-Klan—perfectly ridiculous. The Klan takes the place of the melodrama hero, always doing the noble thing and rescuing the heroine in distress. There are the revolting scenes of the pursuit of one white girl, which rouse feeling against the negro; and then there follows a second similar scene of attempted forced marriage between a powerful mulatto politician—there may have been such vicious individuals as this man is shown to be, but they were certainly exceptions—and a white girl. Of course, the Klan breaks in just in time to prevent the success of the design. At every turn the Klan is made to appeal to the enthusiasm of the spectator as the heroic defender of a victimized people. None of the outrageous, vicious, misguided outrages, which it certainly committed, are shown. I am not interested in loading blame for those outrages on the men who made up the Klan. It was natural that in the heat of the times they made mistakes, just as did the men of the North. I am simply contending that what this play tells of it is not the whole truth.

The Part of the Klan
"Of course the spectators applaud the Klan. It is not shown to them except to stir their sympathy. Of course they applaud slights and contempt for the negroes; they are shown only as despicable brutes.

"It is certainly to be hoped that such a film can be suppressed. As an appeal to race prejudice, it is full of danger."

"Do you recall any portions of the play that you found particularly objectionable?" Miss Addams was asked.

"No, it was rather the whole tone of the second part," was the reply. "Of course, there are the unpleasant episodes in which white girls figure; but the evil is rather in the dominant attitude of mind toward the negro. As I have said, it seems to me an attempt to make him appear worse than childish, and brutal and vicious—actually grotesque and primitive and contemptible."

"How far did you observe that this attitude of mind influenced the spectators?"

"It is hard to tell, of course. Certainly I felt that they were made to feel a prejudice against negroes; some showed approval in applause when the hero refuses to shake hands with the mulatto politician, and they were roused to the point of clapping enthusiastically, before the end of the pictures, whenever the Ku Klux Klan appeared. That was the noticeable thing about the play—the success of the glorification of the activities of the Ku Klux Klan, contrasted with the base and elemental character of the negroes misrepresented in the ludicrously perverted scenes of plantation life. The production is the most subtle form of untruth—a half-truth."

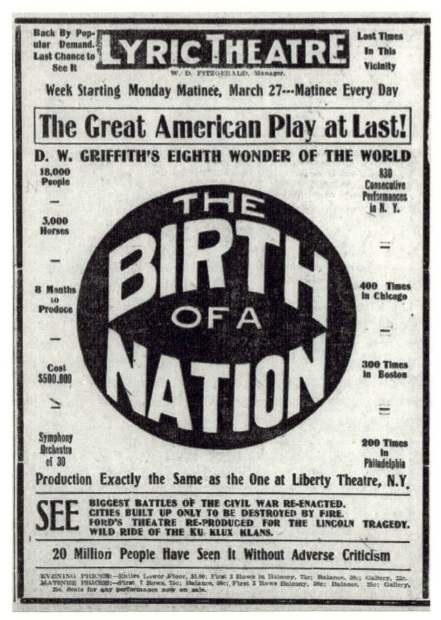

Early newspaper advertisement for the film. Source: Wikipedia.

"Fighting Race Calumny"

This was the original title of the two articles published in the May and June 1915 issues of *The Crisis*. The texts of the articles themselves are as follows.

AN INSTANCE OF THE WAY THE N.A.A.C.P. WORKS
THE CHRONOLOGICAL RECORD OF THE FIGHT AGAINST
THE "CLANSMAN" IN MOVING PICTURES

February 12-26:

We are advised by our Los Angeles Branch that "The Birth of a Nation," a picture play founded on Dixon's "Clansman," is running in that city and that the branch has been unable to suppress the play because it has the approval of the National Board of Censorship, located in New York.

Advance announcement of this performance in New York appears in the local press.

We go to the office of the Board of Censorship and request:

The names of the committee who approved the picture so that we may ascertain its character from someone who has seen it; the names and addresses of the National Board of Censorship; a list of the cities where the film has been released; the possibility of arranging for an advance performance when the film could be reviewed by the entire Board of Censorship and a committee from our Association.

We appeal to the Chairman of the National Board of Censorship, Mr. Frederic C. Howe, for an advance performance and it is arranged.

February 27:

We write a letter to the members of the National Board of Censorship stating our position in regard to the picture.

The National Board of Censorship and a committee from our Association are invited to attend the advance performance on March 1. We were at first promised twelve tickets; later the number is cut to two by the office of the Board of Censorship and *colored people are excluded.*

March 1:

The National Board of Censorship meet after the performance and (according to their Chairman, Dr. Howe), disapprove certain incidents in the first section of the film and practically the entire second part. No communication in regard to this action is sent from the office of the Board of Censorship to the N.A.A.C.P.

March 3:

The owner and producer of the film are summoned by the N.A.A.C.P. to the Police Court on the grounds that they are maintaining a public nuisance and endangering the public peace. They are represented by Martin W. Littleton. Chief Magistrate McAdoo rules that it is not within his jurisdiction to stop the performance unless it actually leads to a breach of the peace.

March 8:

We write for a statement of the disapproval of the play by the Board of Censorship. We do not get it. We request all our members in New York and vicinity to write letters of protest to the press.

March 9:

We again write to the Board of Censorship for a statement of their disapproval of the film and also request a copy of the statement of release which is being sent to other cities, and a list of the states where bills for public censors are pending.

We are advised by a member of the Board of Censorship that the action of the Board on March 1 in disapproving the film was not official. No communication on the subject comes from the office of the Board.

March 10:

Prominent members of our Association, Mr. Jacob H. Schiff, Miss Jane Addams, Dr. Jacques Loeb, Miss Lillian D. Wald, as well as several prominent white Southerners, see the play. All agree in condemning it.

March 10:
The National Association brings criminal proceedings against Aitken and Griffith, owner and producer of the film, and retains James W. Osborne as attorney.

March 11:
We send a letter to the moving picture trade calling their attention to the action of Aitken and Griffith in producing this play after it has been disapproved by the National Board of Censorship.

March 12:
We appeal to the Commissioner of Licenses to stop the performance under that section of the penal code which applies to public nuisances.

We are advised that the Board of Censorship is seeing the play in its revised form. We attend the same performance and find that only slight changes have been made.

March 13:
Miss Jane Addams who has witnessed the play at our request, gives an exclusive interview condemning it to the *Evening Post*, which is sent out by the National Association to the press of the country. None of the New York papers carried this except the *Post* which, we understand, is the only paper in New York that has refused the advertising for "The Birth of a Nation."

March 15:
We are officially advised by the office of the National Board of Censorship that the film has been approved by the Board. Some of the members present tell us that the producer was even cheered when he came into the room.

March 16:
We are asked by the Board of Censorship to retract our letter sent to the moving picture trade. We do not.

We request of the Board of Censorship the addresses of their committees and again ask for a list of the cities where the film has been released and a list of states where bills for public censors are pending. We do not get this information.

March 19:
We write the Mayor requesting him to use his authority to suppress the play as an offense against public decency and as endangering public morals; also on the ground that the effect of the picture is likely to lead to a breach of the peace.

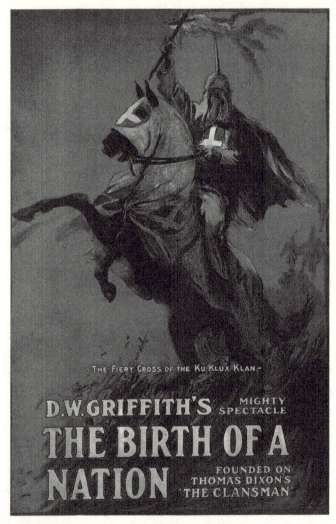

Early newspaper advertisement for the film. Source: Wikipedia.

March 23:
A review of the play in the *New Republic* for March 20 published under the title "Brotherly Love," is mailed by the N.A.A.C.P. for editorial comment to five hundred newspapers.

March 24:
The New York press breaks its silence by publishing the "story" of the split on the Board of Censorship over the vote on this film.

March 26:
We are advised by the Mayor that he will receive a delegation from our Association. We invite all churches, clubs, and organizations interested, in New York and vicinity, to unite with us in appearing at this hearing.

March 27:
We attempt to arrange a procession to the Mayor's office. License is refused on the ground that it might lead to a breach of the peace.

March 29:
The National American Woman Suffrage Association refuses to co-operate with the National Board of Censorship in working against the bill for a public censor pending in Pennsylvania, because of the action of the Board on this play.

March 30:
Hearing before the Mayor with following speakers: Dr. Frederic C. Howe, Chairman of the National Board of Censorship; Dr. William H. Brooks, Pastor of St. Mark's M. E. Church; Dr. W. E. B. Du Bois, Editor of *The Crisis*; Dr. Stephen S. Wise, Rabbi of the Free Synagogue; Mr. Fred R. Moore, Editor of the *New York Age*; Mr. George E. Wibecan, President of the Brooklyn Citizens' Club; and Mr. Oswald Garrison Villard, President of the New York *Evening Post* Company, and Vice President of the N.A.A.C.P.

The following organizations were represented: The colored and white ministry of Greater New York, the Citizens' Club of

Brooklyn, the Committee of One Hundred of Hudson County, N.J., the National League of Urban Conditions Among Negroes, the United Civic League, the Columbus Hill Civic League, and the Northeastern Federation of Women's Clubs.

The Mayor told the delegation which overflowed the Council Chamber that he had seen the film and that he agreed with all that had been said about it. He felt that it might perhaps incite to breaches of the peace and had already so advised the management of the theatre and the owners of the film; the latter had consented to cut out the two scenes which had been particularly objected to and the play would be produced in that form for the first time that night. This, the mayor was careful to say, had been done without any attempt on his part to exercise any power he might be given by statute. The breadth and force of such powers were in doubt, he said, but if it was found necessary to take the matter up again he would take such steps as were authorized by law.

March 31:
We adjourn our legal case with the idea of discontinuing it if the changes promised by the Mayor are made in the film.

April 1:
We see the play in its second revised form and find again that only unimportant changes have been made and that the two particularly objectionable scenes still remain the motif of the second part.

We again appeal to the Mayor calling his attention to the fact that these scenes which he promised the delegation should be eliminated have not been cut out.

April 2:
Miss Rosalie Jonas, a native of New Orleans, with other prominent Suffragists in New York, file protest with the Mayor against the play.

We are advised by the Mayor that he has been assured by the producers of the film that they will meet his wishes in the matter of elision.

(To be continued, and we trust concluded, in our next [issue].*)*

Part II

We gave last month a chronology of the fight of the National Association for the Advancement of Colored People against Tom Dixon's latest libel. This is a continuation of that narrative.

"The Birth of a Nation" is now being shown in New York, Boston, Los Angeles, San Francisco, and is booked for Chicago for the summer. In each place our branches have protested. In Los Angeles they got no results. In San Francisco a few objectionable scenes were eliminated.

In Des Moines, Iowa, the play cannot be presented because of the fact that Mr. S. Joe Brown some years ago introduced an ordinance which was passed prohibiting plays arousing race feeling.

In Ohio, Cleveland and Toledo branches and other agencies co-operating, kept out the play, "The New Governor," and think they can keep this out of the State.

The center of the fight has been Boston.

April 6:

The film interests attack *The Crisis* as an "incendiary" publication. They explain Jane Addams' criticism by declaring that she saw only half the film, which is absolutely false; and they declare that the film had the endorsement of the President of the United States, George Foster Peabody, Senator Jones of Washington and others.

April 9:

A hearing was held before Mayor Curley. Many prominent persons took part. A letter to us saying: "When the hearing was over a little bout occurred between Moorfield Storey and Griffith. It seems in the Boston papers that Griffith had promised Mr. Storey $10,000 for any Charity he would name if he could find a single incident in the play that was not historic. Mr. Storey asked Mr. Griffith if it was historic that a colored lieutenant governor had locked a white girl into a room in the Capitol and demanded a forced marriage in South Carolina? Mr. Griffith only answered, 'Come and see the play' and held out his hand to Mr. Storey. Mr. Storey drew back and said, 'No sir,' refusing to shake hands with him."

April 15:

George Foster Peabody, in a public letter, calls the film "unfair to the Negro and to the white equally and a travesty on sound peace principles." Senator Jones writes: "I never endorsed it," and continues, "the character of the second part of the play became evident before it began and I did not stay to see it." The Rector of Trinity Church, Boston, calls the film "untrue and unjust." Persons unconnected with this organization threw rotten eggs at the screen in New York City.

April 17:

A new feature is added to the film in Boston "portraying the advance of Negro life." A prominent New York lawyer informs us that this was done at the suggestion of Mr. Booker T. Washington. Colored citizens of Boston are refused tickets to the first exhibition of the film. The colored people persist in demanding tickets and eleven of them are arrested including Mr. W. M. Trotter, editor of the *Guardian*, and the Rev. Aaron Puller. All were discharged except the two mentioned.

April 19:

Great protest meeting in Faneuil Hall presided over by Frank B. Sanborn. Governor Walsh of Massachusetts promised to advocate a law which will enable such films to be suppressed.

April 20:

The state police of Massachusetts refuse to permit "The Birth of a Nation" to be exhibited on Sunday.

The Massachusetts court orders elimination of the rape scene in the film. Large hearing before the legislature.

April 28:

Mrs. Carter H. Harrison, wife of the former mayor of Chicago, denies that she ever approved the film. "It is the most awful thing I have seen. It would arouse racial feeling. I am a southerner and you naturally would expect me to oppose such pictures as this."

April 29:
Clergymen representing six Protestant denominations protest against the film.

April 30:
The secretary to the President of the United States replying to W. H. Lewis, of Boston, and to Bishop Walters, writes: "Replying to your recent letter and enclosures, I beg to say that it is true that 'The Birth of a Nation' was produced [i.e., shown] before the President and his family at the White House, but the President was entirely unaware of the character of the play before it was presented and has at no time expressed his approbation of it. Its exhibition at the White House was a courtesy extended to an old acquaintance."

A committee of the Massachusetts legislature reports a bill which is a compromise between several proposals. This bill places unlimited powers of censorship in the hands of the Mayor, the police commissioner and the chief justice of the municipal court. This bill has passed the lower House and is before the Senate.

May 2:
Mass meeting of 2,500 persons at Tremont Temple to protest against the film. Ex-President Eliot, Dr. S. M. Crothers, Dr. F. M. Rowley, Miss Adelene Moffat and Mr. Ralph Cobleigh were among the speakers. A mass meeting was also held on Boston Common. Mr. Cobleigh declared that Dixon had told him that the object of the film was the ultimate deportation of 10,000,000 Negroes from the United States, and the repeal of the war amendments. President Eliot said that this proposal was "inconceivable and monstrous" and "an abominable outrage." He continued: "A more dangerously false doctrine taught by the play is that the Ku-Klux-Klan was on the whole a righteous and necessary society for the defence of Southern white men against black Legislatures led by Northern white men. This is the same sort of argument being used by the Germans to-day, that a contract may be destroyed as a military necessity. Undoubtedly, grievous conditions existed in the South, but they did not justify the utter lawlessness and atrocities which marked the trail of the

Ku-Klux. There can be no worse teaching, no more mischievous doctrine than this, that lawlessness is justified when necessary."

May 5:
The Rev. A. W. Puller was discharged by the court while Mr. Trotter was fined for assault on a policeman, but entered an appeal. The judge blamed the ticket seller chiefly for the disturbance.

May 15:
Telegram from the Chicago Branch, N.A A.C.P.: *Mayor Thompson has unqualifiedly refused license to the photo-play "Birth of a Nation."*
C. E. Bentley, Treasurer, N.A.A.C.P.

Works Cited

Addams, Jane. "Jane Addams Condemns Pernicious Race Film." *New York Evening Post*, 13 Mar. 1915, p. 58.

Bentley, C. E. "Fighting Race Calumny." *The Crisis*, May 1915, pp. 40-42.

_____. "Fighting Race Calumny Part II." *The Crisis*, June 1915, pp. 87-88.

Nerney, Mary Childs. "Letter to George Packard." *NAACP Records,* Manuscript Division, Library of Congress.

"Hidden Things": Self-Censorship in the Poetry and Career of Constantine Cavafy_____

Robert C. Evans

> Hidden Things
> From all that I've said and all that I have done,
> don't seek to find out who I was.
> Certain impediments stood in the way,
> transforming my actions and my manner of life.
> Certain impediments stood in the way,
> and often checked me on the verge of speech.
> In my least noticed acts, in the most veiled
> of my writings—only there will you understand me.
> But maybe, in the end, it isn't worth
> so much thought and effort to find me out.
> Later, in a more perfect society,
> someone made like me
> is sure to come forward and act freely. (McKinsey 92)

Constantine Cavafy (1863-1933) is widely regarded as perhaps the greatest of modern Greek poets and also as one of the most significant poets of the entire modern era. His small body of work has been translated into English astonishingly often: the Library of Congress catalog lists thirty different translations published between 1968 and 2015, and even more translations (as yet uncataloged by the LoC) have appeared since then. Cavafy has also been the subject of numerous articles and various books, and he was even the focus of a 1996 Hollywood-style biographical film (rather than a simple academic documentary). YouTube is full of videos about Cavafy (including both amateur and professional performances of his poems, academic lectures and discussions, and a whole series of readings, by Sean Connery, of a Cavafy poem set to music by the famed composer Vangelis). Photographers and artists have based various works on Cavafy's texts, and interest in him in countries beyond Greece continues to grow, with no sign of abating.

Why all this intense attention to a poet who lived an obscure life, published few works, and left no autobiography? The most obvious and most important answer is that his poems are often unusually powerful. They are, somehow, understated but vivid, subtle but strikingly memorable. But another explanation of Cavafy's popularity is that he is, perhaps, the most talented gay poet of his or any other recent generation. He wrote about homoerotic desire during a time when it was not only scandalous but also dangerous to do so. And he wrote in ways that seem to avoid many pitfalls that frequently cripple erotic verse. These include crudity, banality, sentimentality, extravagance, and/or preciousness—traits that often damage, for instance, the work of many of the so-called Uranian poets who wrote in late-nineteenth and early twentieth-century England. One only has to compare and contrast Cavafy's writings with the work of, say, A. C. Swinburne to appreciate the Greek poet's impressive achievement.[1]

But Cavafy, of course, could never run the risk of writing as freely or publicly as he might have wished. Nor could he have run the even greater risk of openly publishing or loudly advertising his homoerotic poetry. His poems were typically circulated in small private editions passed around among friends. He never made money as a poet (supporting himself, instead, by working a tedious job as a government bureaucrat). And he wrote during a time when gay poets sometimes either came to tragic ends (think, for instance, of Hart Crane or Federico García Lorca) or lived lives of relatively silent misery. As a writer, Cavafy had to exercise great caution and wary self-censorship. As a man, he also had to live in real fear of what might happen to him if his sexual orientation ever became too widely known. In 1902, for instance, he jotted an unduly harsh note to himself that reads as follows:

> I know that I am cowardly, and am unable to act. Therefore I confine myself to words. But I don't think that my words are without purpose. Someone else will act. But my many words—the words of a coward—will make it easier for that person to act. My words clear the ground. (qtd. in McKinsey 19)

Three years later, in 1905, Cavafy again wrote (apparently) about the ways the restrictive morals of his time had affected his life, his creativity, and his entire career:

> The miserable laws of society—having nothing to do with health, nor the result of reasoned judgment—have diminished my work. They've hobbled my means of expression, hindered my ability to move and enlighten others who are made like me. . . . So, what am I to do? Artistically, I never had a chance. And I shall go on being an object of speculation; and shall be understood most fully by what I have disavowed. (qtd. in McKinsey 66)

One of the great ironies of Cavafy's life is that the very forces that constrained his creativity also enhanced it. Like the great Russian composer Dmitri Shostakovich, Cavafy often did his best work when faced with the greatest restrictions and threats. In both cases, real suffering led to great art. Both men might have been happier human beings if they had lived in freer times and places, but one wonders if they would have been as intensely imaginative and creative if their lives had been easier. Both men had to police themselves to avoid being policed (or ostracized, or imprisoned, or perhaps even killed) by others. Both not only had to fear external censorship but also had to practice self-censorship. And in both cases, the restrictions on their personal freedom may ultimately have contributed to the effectiveness of their art. One of my purposes in this essay is to survey various early poems in which Cavafy deals with issues of censorship and self-censorship. In citing these poems, I will quote from Daniel Mendelsohn's superb translations.

Cavafy's Self-Censorship: A Preliminary Overview

Both the theme and the effects of censorship and of self-censorship can be seen not only in particular phrases and lines by Cavafy but also in entire texts. An early published poem entitled "Finished," for instance, begins with the following lines (although there is no reason to assume that they have any specific sexual relevance):

Deep in fear and in suspicion,
with flustered minds and terrified eyes,
we wear ourselves out figuring how
we might avoid the certain
danger that threatens us so terribly. (9)

Similarly, a poem entitled "As Much As You Can" begins by raising the possibility that an unnamed "you . . . cannot make your life the way you want it" (15). "Orophernes" mentions "the exquisite nights of Ionia / when fearlessly, and completely as a Greek, / he came to know pleasure utterly." Although it is unclear why Orophernes should previously have feared knowing "pleasure utterly," or what kind of pleasure, specifically, is meant (23), at the end of the poem his own physical beauty is emphasized (25). A poem tellingly entitled "Dangerous" is far more intriguing in this respect. Daniel Mendelsohn calls it "the first of [Cavafy's] poems that situated homoerotic content in an ancient setting" (xxxiv). Most of it is spoken by a fictional character named Myrtius, who lived, supposedly, during the fourth century A.D.:

Strengthened by contemplation and study,
I will not fear my passions like a coward.
My body I will give to pleasures,
to diversions that I've dreamed of,
to the most daring erotic desires,
to the lustful impulses of my blood,
without any fear at all, for whenever I will—
and I will have the will, strengthened
as I'll be with contemplation and study—
at the crucial moments I'll recover
my spirit as it was before: ascetic. (37)

This is a witty and ironic poem: the speaker, trained as a kind of Puritan, plans to indulge himself in pleasure because he is sure that after doing so he can regain control of himself thanks to his Puritan training. One suspects that Cavafy is less sure of this ability than Myrtius is; the joke may be on the speaker. In any case, the idea

---

of fearing one's passions—or at least the fear of openly expressing them—is a common theme in Cavafy's poetry.

As one moves through Mendelsohn's edition of the complete poems, the erotic aspects of Cavafy's writing become increasingly explicit. One poem, "Chandelier," for instance, describes the setting of a heated erotic encounter and ends by noting that

> In the small room, which has been set
> aglow by the chandelier's powerful flames,
> the light that appears is no ordinary light.
> The pleasure of this heat has not been fashioned
> for bodies that too easily take fright. (54)

Those last two lines, in particular, along with other details, imply a kind of eroticism often tinged with apprehension and with the need to hide. In "Since Nine—," for instance, the speaker recalls the days of his youth—recollections that have "reminded [him] / of *shuttered* perfumed rooms / and of pleasure spent—what *wanton* pleasure!" (55; my italics). The references to "shuttered" rooms and "wanton" pleasure typify Cavafy's phrasing: eroticism in his poems can rarely be openly displayed and often smacks of the unusual or of the "sexually lawless or unrestrained" (dictionary.com definition of *wanton*). Perhaps such passion seems wanton precisely because it usually has had to be repressed, suppressed, or hidden: it gradually builds up, so that when it is suddenly released the release seems uninhibited (if still carefully kept secret).[2]

In "One of Their Gods," some inhabitants of an ancient town realize that an extraordinarily beautiful young man who walks among them must in fact be "one of their gods." Yet even this powerful god, ironically, must be circumspect in pursuing his "suspect diversions":

> . . . as he disappeared beneath the arcades,
> among the shadows and the evening lights,
> making his way to the neighborhood that comes alive
> only at night—that life of revels and debauch,
> of every known intoxication and lust—
> they'd wonder which of Them he really was

and for which of his suspect diversions
he'd come down to walk Seleucia's streets
from his Venerable, Sacrosanct Abode. (65)

This passage implies that even the gods cannot resist the temptations—but also, it would seem, the risks—of illicit passions. Even gods must behave warily in such circumstances, either for fear of being censured by other gods (unlikely) or from fear of being manhandled and abused by ignorant humans. Apparently, however, even the gods decide that some "suspect diversions" are worth potential dangers.

After a certain point in the Mendelsohn edition, references to passions that must be hidden become increasingly common. In "I've Gazed So Much—," the speaker recalls beautiful "Faces of love" now merely remembered but at one time "*secretly* encountered" in "the nights of my youth" (75; italics mine). In a text entitled "In the Street," the speaker describes a handsome youth who "aimlessly . . . ambles down the street, / as if still hypnotized by the *illicit* pleasure, / by the *very* illicit pleasure he has had" (76; italics mine). "Passage" describes a youth who, when much younger, "*timidly*" had to restrain the kind of "*outlaw* sensual abandon" to which he now gives free rein (78; italics mine). In "To Stay," the speaker recounts an intense but secretive encounter:

The *vigilant* servant was sleeping by the door.

No one would have seen us. But
we were so on fire for each other
that *caution* was beyond us anyway. (88; italics mine)

Again and again, Cavafy's speakers use words that imply the need for secrecy, discretion, and circumspection. Eroticism is rarely if ever truly private in a Cavafy poem; the need to worry about discovery is always in the backs of lovers' minds, and in fact this kind of fear may even intensify the passion they feel. A different way of saying this is that eroticism in Cavafy's poetry must almost always be *completely private*; it must be indulged in only behind closed doors, in disreputable parts of town, in places where the lovers cannot be seen or recognized. Cavafy is the poet of the homosexual closet, and yet his poetry is also, paradoxically, poetry that often describes what happens behind closed doors. He had to censor himself, but some of his greatest works are precisely about the need for self-censorship. Eroticism in his poetry must be private, but for that very reason it is always tinged with worries about what others might think. The private is always tinged with social awareness and apprehension.

Ancient and Modern Settings

Although most of the poems implying wanton and therefore hidden passions are set in modern times, occasionally Cavafy focuses on handsome young men from centuries ago who also had to exercise the same kind of discretion. "From the School of the Renowned Philosopher," for instance, describes a youth whom fortune had blessed with a "form of highest comeliness" but who had become "an habitué / of the depraved houses of Alexandria, / of every *secret* den of debauchery" (109; my italics). A similar work—"In the Taverns"—also seems set in classical times. It describes one handsome youth who has been abandoned by another such person who, in turn, has been seduced by yet another man who could offer him a luxurious home. Cast adrift, the poem's speaker avows that "In the public houses and the lowest dives / of Beirut I wallow. In low debauchery / I spend my sordid hours" (134; spacing Cavafy's). Another poem set in the past—"Theater of Sidon (400 A.D.)"—takes place in the early days of Christianity, a fact that helps explain its highly particular tone:

> I now and then compose,   in the language of the Greeks,
> *exceedingly daring* verses,   which I circulate
> *very secretly*, of course—   gods! *they mustn't be seen*
> by *those who prate about morals*,   those who wear gray clothes—
> verses about a pleasure   that is select, that moves
> toward a barren love   of which *the world disapproves*. (118; spacing
> Cavafy's; my italics)

Here one senses a young man not simply caught in a specific set of common censorious circumstances but also trapped by a massive, engulfing cultural transformation—one in which a whole new set of moral and religious assumptions were making homoeroticism seem a "barren love" (in more senses than one) because it was censured by an entirely new and whole "world." Cavafy himself was living in the aftermath of that major cultural change: he was having to try to survive in the new culture the Christians had established. And so his poems sometimes—as in this one—look back to the era when an earlier freedom was finally and utterly lost (or so it seemed in Cavafy's day).[3]

More typically, however, Cavafy implies modern settings, as "In Despair," in which a young man laments a lost lover for whom the pressures of both social disdain and self-contempt had simply become too great:

> The other wished—he said—   he wished to *save himself*
> from that *stigmatized*   pleasure, so unwholesome;
> from that *stigmatized*   pleasure, in its *shame.*
> There was still time, he said—   time to *save himself.*
>
>   (115; spacing Cavafy's; my italics)

Here the young man seems to have internalized the social prejudice that homoeroticism is "unwholesome": he feels the force not only of external social pressures but of internal self-contempt. The former, in fact, may contribute to the latter. In any case, the poem's speaker feels triply isolated: subject to social disdain, he has not only been abandoned by the "other" but now feels pressured, by the example of that "other," to feel self-disdain.[4]

Occasionally Cavafy's young men reject these kinds of pressures, but they can usually only do so internally, in their own minds and feelings, rather than in any explicitly or socially defiant way. "He Came to Read—," for instance, concludes as follows: "To his flesh, which is beauty entire, / the fever of desire has come; / without *foolish shame* about the form of its enjoyment...." (121; my italics). But the speaker of this poem is, apparently, and despite his desire, entirely alone. Whatever "form of ... enjoyment" he intends to pursue will almost certainly be hidden in one way or another. Speakers like this can reject society's foolishness, but they can never do so openly, in any explicit kind of challenge. Even their defiance can only be internal. Paradoxically, of course, by writing about such figures, Cavafy himself engages in a more open kind of defiance. But then, to tighten the paradox even further, even his defiance can only be open in a very limited kind of way. Self-censorship affects both the speakers and the poet who created them.

At times, however, Cavafy's speakers almost assume that disaster will someday strike—indeed, *must* strike. Caution can never be completely foolproof; exposure sometimes seems inevitable. "The 25th Year of His Life," for instance, describes a young man haunted by an earlier chance encounter with another youth, one whom the first young man cannot put out of his mind and whom he compulsively seeks but cannot find again. The poem concludes:

Not to *betray* himself: this is what he strives for, of course.
But sometimes he's almost indifferent.—
Besides, he knows what he's *exposing himself to*,
he's made up his mind. It's not unlikely that the life he's living
will lead him to some *devastating scandal*. (127; my italics)

The risk this young man runs is not the risk of mere minor embarrassment; it is the risk of "devastating scandal," potentially life-altering if not in fact life-destroying. This is one reason Cavafy's poems are often set in cities. Cities were large, populous, and often anonymous. They had neighborhoods where one's own acquaintances often never ventured—"disreputable" places where one might visit secretly, carefully, with less chance of being recognized by people one knew. Cities were especially attractive, therefore, to people from small villages; they offered villagers the kind of freedom and anonymity they could never hope to enjoy at home. This fact is emphasized in a poem entitled "In the Boring Village," where a young man "sick with desire" and "carnal yearning" must try to content himself with waiting

for another two or three months to pass,
for another two or three months till business tapers off,
so he can make for the city and throw himself
straight into its bustle and amusements . . . . (129)

In the meantime, he must censor and police himself, back in the "boring village."

This kind of self-censorship, of course, takes place everywhere in Cavafy's world and works. In "Impossible Things," for instance, the speaker, alluding to Keats, observes that "A poet has said: 'The loveliest / music is the one that cannot be played.' / And I, I daresay that by far the best life / is the one that cannot be lived" (294). "Best" in what senses, however? The most beautiful? The most imaginative? The least imperfect *because* the most merely imagined? The speaker doesn't explicitly say, but surely there is also some irony in the fact that perfection cannot actually be "finished" or "brought to completion" or "thoroughly performed"—standard root meanings of the verb "to be perfected." This sort of paradox runs throughout Cavafy's homoerotic writings: the "best life" is indeed the *love* "that cannot be lived."

Poems Set in 1903
Several poems dated "1903" reflect (or, in one case, suppress) the vacillations, mixed feelings, and ambiguities of their speakers' situations. Thus "Strengthening (1903)" opens on a note of defiance: "Whoever longs to make his spirit stronger / should leave behind respect and obedience" (310). And this same defiant note continues throughout the rest of the text, which ends with these four lines:

Many things will he be taught by pleasures.
He will never fear the destructive act;
half the house must be demolished.
Thus will he grow virtuously into knowledge. (310)

This is one of the few poems by Cavafy that actually sounds didactic and, for that reason, uncharacteristically simplistic. It isn't surprising that these lines are in the future tense, or that the first two lines are

---

in the imperative mood: we are told what a person "should" do and "will" do, not what he actually does or (more significantly) *can* or *cannot* do. There is a note of false bravado in this poem, as if the speaker is ignoring the actual realities of his situation. Far more typical—and typically complex—is the next poem, "September of 1903." This poem, in fact, *almost* sounds like a response to the one that immediately precedes it. It opens with these lines:

> At least let me be deceived by delusions, now,
> so that I might not feel my empty life.
>
> And I was so close so many times.
> And how I froze, and how I was afraid;
> why should I remain with lips shut tight;
> while within me weeps my empty life,
> and my longings wear their mourning black. (311)

As the rest of the poem makes clear, the context here is explicitly erotic: the speaker regrets not having acted on his sexual impulses on those occasions when he had, perhaps, the chance or at least the temptation to do so. His emphasis here is not on what he *should* do or *will* do but on what he actually, in fact, *failed* to do. And he failed, one guesses, not because of any lack of desire on his part (in fact, just the opposite) but because of the felt need to restrain, suppress, and disguise such desire—to censor not just his words but also his feelings and behavior. If the speaker of "Strengthening (1903)" sounds falsely brave, the speaker of the present poem sounds convincingly stymied and frustrated. He resembles (especially in those perhaps overly sentimental, self-pitying final two lines) a bit like T. S. Eliot's J. Alfred Prufrock.

Far more completely successful (partly because it is rooted in such specific imagery) is the very next poem, "December 1903":

> Even though I may not speak about my love—
> I may not talk about your hair, or your lips, or your eyes;
> still, your face, which I keep inside my soul;
> the sound of your voice, which I keep inside my mind;

the September days that dawn within my dreams:
my words and phrases take their shape and color from these,
whatever subject I may touch upon, whatever idea I may be speaking
of. (312)

One assumes that here, as so often, the speaker is *recalling* a lover rather than actually, really speaking or writing to that person in the here and now. The direct address, therefore, can only really be self-address; the speaker isn't really talking to someone else but merely to himself (but also to us). And, to make matters even more complicated and painful, he cannot speak very freely to many other people, in his own day, even if he wanted to. If Cavafy had tried to widely publish poems like this, he would have had to be very discreet, very ambiguous, very deliberately unclear. He would have had to hide the precise nature of his love, as in a sense he does here by failing to make the gender of the other person explicitly obvious and/or by failing to describe explicitly any particular erotic behavior. As he says in the opening line, "I may not speak about my love." But it is, ironically, in this very line (and in the next one) that he actually speaks most clearly by announcing that he *cannot* speak clearly. By referring indirectly to the so-called love that dare not speak its name, he in fact *does* speak—or at least strongly imply—that name. It is this sort of complexity that makes a poem such as this one so much more intriguing and successful than an unconvincing text such as "Strengthening (1903)." Fortunately, Cavafy's failures are few and far between. It is, often, precisely his need to censor himself that makes so many of his poems so complex, intriguing, and successful.

Conclusion
Typical of the latter sort of poem is one entitled "On the Stairs":

As I was going down the shameful stair,
you came in the door, and for a moment
I saw your unfamiliar face and you saw me.
Then I hid so you wouldn't see me again, and you
passed by quickly as you hid your face,
and stole inside the shameful house

where you likely found no pleasure, just as I found none.

And yet the love you wanted, I had to give you;
the love I wanted—your eyes told me so,
tired and suspicious—you had it to give me.
Our bodies sensed and sought each other out;
our blood and skin understood.

But we hid from each other, we two, terrified.

This is, in many ways, a splendid poem and one that is characteristic of Cavafy at his best. By presenting himself so honestly in this text, the speaker earns our respect even when he initially seems ashamed of himself. The "shameful stair," we sense, is not a stair he would freely have chosen to use if other stairs—other paths—had been freely open to him. The mere fact that he considers the stair "shameful" implies his injured sense of self-respect, his frustration at having to behave in ways he considers undignified and demeaning. But his dilemma is not merely his own; it is also the dilemma of other people (like the unnamed stranger here): both would rather not be where they are; both would rather not have to settle merely for sexual release; both desire something deeper, richer, more meaningful. But neither feels capable of freely seeking that something—or of openly offering it. And yet neither of them, apparently, feels any real pleasure in the mere, ephemeral, fleeting sexual pleasure they both seek (and perhaps pay for?).

Perhaps the most poignant line of the entire poem is this one: "And yet the love you wanted, I had to give you." It is love, not merely sex, that each one wants but that neither achieves. Also effective is the ambiguity of this phrase: "your eyes told me so, / tired and suspicious." *Whose* eyes were "tired and suspicious"? The stranger's, or the speaker's, or both?

Ironically, the two persons feel mutual desire, mutual longing for love, but also mutual terror. And it is the terror that finally dominates their thoughts, feelings, and behavior. Each of them must censor himself, even though both of them are capable, ideally, of mutual love. This is Cavafy at his complex best.

Many more such poems might easily be discussed (in fact, it is hard to think of many other poets, besides Cavafy, who wrote so well, so consistently, in such a relatively small body of work). But perhaps the best poem to end with here is the one with which this essay began, this time in Daniel Mendelsohn's translation:

Hidden (1908)

From all I did and from all I said
they shouldn't try to find out who I was.
An obstacle was there and it distorted
my actions and the way I lived my life.
An obstacle was there and it stopped me
on many occasions when I was going to speak.
The most unnoticed of my actions
and the most covert of all my writings:
from these alone will they come to know me.
But perhaps it's not worth squandering
so much care and trouble on puzzling me out.
Afterwards—in some more perfect society—
someone else who's fashioned like me
will surely appear and be free to do as he pleases. (319)

This is in many ways a very poignant poem. The speaker feels—perhaps even more than most human beings—that time is running out, that he has not lived entirely as he might have or might have hoped to do, and that the gift of life will soon be over. Many people feel, as the end of their life nears, that they did not use their time fully or wisely or profitably because they made mistaken choices. This speaker feels that because of external pressures he never really had a chance to live the kind of life he could have lived or been the kind of person he might have been. It is one thing to censor a book: that is bad enough. It is another to censor an entire human life—or the lives of entire groups of people. It is even worse when those people feel that they have had to censor themselves. By *censor* here, I do not mean simply censorship of speech or writing. I mean censorship of thoughts, feelings, behavior, and potential relationships. I mean depriving an entire life of freedom and, if not of happiness altogether, then of the kind of happiness a person might otherwise have sought. Cavafy is a poet who speaks to anyone who feels that his or her life might have been different, might have been better, might have been richer and more fulfilling, if he or she had not had to engage in a lifelong habit of self-censorship.

In Cavafy's case, that kind of censorship affected not just his existence but also his literary production. It affected what he could feel, think, write, and attempt to publish. It also, of course, affected what potential readers could potentially read. In a strange way, however, Cavafy's need to censor himself came into conflict with a deep desire to express himself—a desire he could never wholly censor or suppress. And from that conflict was born some of the richest, most complex, most subtle and suggesting poetry of the modern period. Like Shostakovich (although to a much lesser degree), Cavafy's art was born of suffering, and that is one of the factors that helped make it so profound and moving. His need to police himself contributed to the complexity and artistry of his poetry. And we, who have the good fortune to live in something closer to the "more perfect society" Cavafy himself never enjoyed, have the extra good fortune of having inherited his poems—the intriguing, thought-provoking, poignant records of a self-censored life.

Notes

1. For another illustrative contrast with Cavafy, see the poems by Philebus, Edmund John, and Cuthbert Wright in *Blue Boys*.

2. Sometimes Cavafy seems deliberately (if subtly) to contrast the ways others (or even the participants themselves) censoriously assess homoerotic behavior with the real, deeper potential of that behavior to express genuine affection. Thus, in "Days of 1901" the speaker refers early in the poem to a young man's many days of "*loose* living" only to conclude that sometimes this very same youth seems "a lad who—somewhat awkwardly—for the first time gives his *pure* body up to *love*" (143; my italics). The contrast between the first italicized word and the final two could hardly be greater. Here and in many other works, Cavafy suggests that gay men were capable of expressing genuine love through homoerotic passion. But he also

knew that often such passion was regarded by others (and sometimes even by the participants) as "common debauchery, so ruinous" (the last words of "Days of 1909, '10, and '11" [156]). Partly for this reason, the speakers of Cavafy's poems feel they must suppress their passions (as others do not) only to live to regret having done so. Thus, in "An Old Man," these lines appear: "He remembers the impulses he bridled; and how / much joy he sacrificed. His foolish caution, now, / is mocked by each lost opportunity" (183). Likewise, in "Che Fece … Il Gran Rifiuto," the person who denies himself and makes the grand refusal feels that "that [the word] No—so right—defeats him all his life" (189). Sometimes, however, the sense of having been defeated in life comes not from a speaker's own personal choice but from his sense of having been shut off and shut out by society, as in the opening lines of "Walls": "Walls without pity, without shame, without consideration / they've built around me enormous, towering walls" (191).

3.   For a hint of the kind of freedom Cavafy sometimes associated with the ancient past, see, for example, "Cimon Son of Learchus, 22 Years Old, Teacher of Greek Letters (in Cyrene)" (153).

4.   In "A Young Man, Skilled in the Art of the Word— in His 24th Year" (145), the young man of the title is totally obsessed with desire for another young man who allows the first youth access to his body without ever fully reciprocating his intense affection: "what's missing is the beautiful fulfillment / of love; what's missing is the fulfillment / which both of them must long for with the same intensity. // (They're not equally devoted to *abnormal* pleasure; not both of them. / He alone [the "Young Man" of the title] is utterly possessed by it.) (145; my italics).

Works Cited

Blue Boys: Poems by Philebus, Edmund John, and Cuthbert Wright. No editor listed. Gay Men's Press, 1990.

Cavafy, C. P. *Complete Poems*. Translated by Daniel Mendelsohn, Knopf, 2012.

McKinsey, Martin. *Clearing the Ground: C. P. Cavafy, Poetry and Prose*. Edited, translated, and with an Essay by Martin McKinsey, Laertes, 2015.

Banned, Bothered, and Bewildered: *Lady Chatterley's Lover*

Nicolas Tredell

D. H. Lawrence's last novel, *Lady Chatterley's Lover* (1928, 1929, 1960), is among the most famous banned books of the twentieth century, and it occupies an especially significant place in British cultural history. In his poem "Annus Mirabilis," Philip Larkin wryly observed that "[s]exual intercourse" started in 1963, "[b]etween the end of the *Chatterley* ban / And the Beatles' first LP" (90). The "*Chatterley* ban" on the publication of an unexpurgated UK edition of the novel was lifted as a result of the court case *Regina v. Penguin Books Limited* in 1960 in which a jury found unanimously—and jury verdicts had to be unanimous in British courts in those days—that the novel was not obscene, by what was then becoming the established legal criterion of "literary merit" (see Rolph 1961).

The end of the ban was seen as, in a familiar metaphor of the period, "opening the floodgates," for better and worse, to a much greater freedom of expression on page and stage in regard to the depiction of sexual activity and the words—including terms hitherto proscribed in public utterance—used to describe it. But, as Larkin's poem registers, it was seen as opening the floodgates to a much greater freedom of sexual behaviour as well as expression, as the beginning of what came to be called "the permissive society" and of the popularization of casual attitudes to sex of which Lawrence himself would have strongly disapproved. As Frank Kermode remarked, Lawrence's "success, such as it has been, would have depressed him: the times, on any view he could possibly have held of them, are still bad" (144). This would be even more so at this stage of the twenty-first century; but of course the twenty-first century can make reciprocal judgements on Lawrence. This essay will explore the controversies around the trial, especially with regard to the role of F. R. Leavis, the novel's "naughty" words, and its treatment of sexuality, and go on to consider its attitude to disability, its use of what we might today call *trolling*, its late Romanticism, and its ecological dimension.

Lawrence and Leavis

"The Trial of Lady Chatterley," as it was dubbed, was also especially significant because of the position Lawrence's work then occupied in English literary and academic life. Lawrence had died in 1930 and although his work had been famous—and notorious—in his lifetime, it was in the midtwentieth century, especially after World War II, that his critical standing rose to make him, for a time, one of the most eminent British novelists. His major backer was the literary critic F. R. Leavis—based in Cambridge, although, for much of his working life, without any permanent or high-level university post—whose influence in both universities and schools was unparalleled thanks to his critical insights, rhetorical power, and overall ideology, which gave the study of literature a unique and invaluable role in the promotion of a mature, healthy, life-affirming society.

Leavis constructed a "great tradition" of five English novelists whose work embodied these positive attitudes while engaging with human existence in its full complexity: Jane Austen, George Eliot, Henry James, Joseph Conrad, and D. H. Lawrence were "all distinguished by a vital capacity for experience, a kind of reverent openness before life, and a marked moral intensity" (*Great Tradition* 9). Only the last of these had a literary career that fell fully within the twentieth century. Leavis claimed that "Lawrence, in the English language, was the great genius of our time" (*Great Tradition* 23) and would later devote two books to him (*D. H. Lawrence: Novelist* and *Thought, Words and Creativity: Art and Thought in Lawrence*). This endorsement was crucial in making Lawrence the most significant novelist for generations of critics, university lecturers, and schoolteachers, though his books were still too scandalous to feature on school syllabi. A trial centered around his most notorious book was bound to focus the attention of these groups.

Indeed, the trial was a cross between a court case, a seminar series, a common room conversation, a lecture course, and a literary conference in which legal and critical discourses clashed and merged in fascinating ways. The key defense witnesses included a galaxy of literary and critical talent: the novelists E. M. Forster and Rebecca West and the poet C. Day-Lewis; the critics Joan Bennett, Graham Hough, and Raymond Williams from Cambridge University; Vivian de Sola Pinto from the University of Nottingham; Kenneth Muir from Liverpool University; and Richard Hoggart from the University of Leicester, whose *Uses of Literacy* (1957), strongly influenced by both Leavis and Lawrence, was one of the founding texts of modern cultural studies.

There was, however, one conspicuous absence—perhaps the most conspicuous—among the witnesses: Leavis himself. He could have performed very effectively in court; Raymond Williams remarked on his "extraordinary forensic skill" in a Cambridge English Faculty meeting (116), and his intellect, eloquence, and precision, as well as the charisma he carried with him, would have made his testimony formidable. In an essay in the *Spectator* ("The New Orthodoxy")—later collected as "The Orthodoxy of Enlightenment" in *Anna Karenina and Other Essays*—he argued that *Lady Chatterley's Lover* was "a bad novel" and the defense claims spurious; for example, the assertion that the novel was promarriage was wholly untrue.

Despite Leavis's dissent, the initial effect of the lifting of the *Chatterley* ban was to boost Lawrence's reputation and posthumous sales, making a wider range of his fiction available in paperback and chiming in with the concern with sexuality that he had helped to promote, even if he would have deplored some of its emphases. Lawrence could join other sixties figures—often, like him, dead or elderly white males—as a kind of guru, a guide to life, and especially to sexual activity. But as the sixties proceeded, there was at least one group who started to find his work oppressive: feminists.

As second-wave feminism movement emerged toward the end of the 1960s and developed in the 1970s, Lawrence came under attack, perhaps most notably from Kate Millett in *Sexual Politics* (1970). Although, or perhaps because, Lawrence's fiction had especially focused on passional experience in women—as indicated in the very titles of two of his novels, *Women in Love* (1920) and

Lady Chatterley's Lover itself—his particular way of focusing, his energetic, fluent, insistent, and sometimes hectoring style, and the gender and sexual ideology informing it, could seem overbearing, acknowledging female desire, to be sure, but trying to fit it into prescribed and rather vitalist heteronormative channels.

Partly because of this feminist critique, and partly for other reasons such as Leavis's own decline and the emergence of new young British novelists with different attitudes to sexuality who took for granted the freedoms the *Chatterley* case had helped to win, Lawrence's centrality increasingly diminished so that he could seem by the twenty-first century—even to those who had earlier seen him as crucial—marginal, eccentric and, in his attitudes to gender, power, and ethnicity, rather disagreeable: few people today would choose him as a guide to living. But in his day he broke new ground, not least, in *Lady Chatterley*, with its earthy vocabulary.

Impossible Words

The most immediately evident reason for the banning of *Lady Chatterley* was its use of what Lawrence himself, in a jaunty poem, called *impossible words*:

> They say I wrote a naughty book
> With perfectly awful things in it,
> putting in all the impossible words
> like b— and f— and sh—. ("My Naughty Book" 1, 491)

From the perspective of the second decade of the twenty-first century, these words no longer seem impossible but frequent (perhaps, for some, all too frequent), not only in novels but also in film and on TV, where what might be called the David Mamet school of scriptwriting, peppering dialogue with four-letter words in noun and adjectival form, is much in evidence. In the context of this essay, however, it is important to distinguish the way in which Lawrence in *Lady Chatterley's Lover* tries to use those words—not as dismissive insults, or phatic terms with no specific meaning that assist certain kinds of social interaction, but as words of power conveying an intense sexual vibrancy that should be cleansed of their obscene associations—what Leavis called "the hygienic undertaking" (*D. H. Lawrence* 70).

The paradox here is that, in a sense, the power of those words to convey such vibrancy depends, to a significant extent, on their being forbidden, not part of everyday discourse and dialogue as they are in the Mametian register. Once they become a standard element of demotic or indeed educated speech they lose the charge that comes from their forbiddenness, from the sense that to utter them is to break taboos. Ironically, the very freedom of expression with hitherto taboo words that *Lady Chatterley* exemplified and, once the ban was lifted in 1960, helped to disseminate, robbed the words of the power that Lawrence was trying to restore and enhance, turning them into banal and predictable features of quotidian life.

This move from the banned to the banal has also happened, to some extent, with Lawrence's treatment of sexuality. Another key reason for the long ban on the publication of the unexpurgated version of *Lady Chatterley* was its portrayal of the impulses and intimacies of desire, especially in its title character's adulterous relationship with her aristocratic husband's gamekeeper.

Sexuality

In Chapter 1 of the novel, speaking of the early sexual experiences with German youths of Connie Reid (later Lady Constance Chatterley) and her sister Hilda, the narrator—whose voice slips between that of his characters and a persona that much resembles Lawrence's in his other fictional and nonfictional works—says:

> [h]owever one might sentimentalize it, this sex business was one of the most ancient, sordid connexions and subjections. Poets who glorified it were mostly men. Women had always known there was something better, something higher. And now they knew it more definitely than ever. The beautiful pure freedom of a woman was infinitely more wonderful than any sexual love. The only unfortunate thing was that men lagged so far behind women in the matter. They insisted on the sex thing like dogs.
>
> And a woman had to yield. A man was like a child with his appetites. A woman had to yield him what he wanted, or like a child

he would probably turn nasty and flounce away and spoil what was a very pleasant connexion. But a woman could yield to a man without yielding her inner, free self. (7)

This passage, like others in *Lady Chatterley*, strikes protofeminist notes that might still resonate today: that the glorification of sex in the sordid sense was mainly the prerogative of male writers; that men are bestial in the pursuit of sexual gratification; that they try to force women to yield to them (with our twenty-first-century awareness of harassment and rape, we might also add that men may "turn nasty" but do not necessarily "flounce away"—they may sexually and physically assault a woman who does not yield to them).

Where a query might arise—and of course there could be different views on this, both within and beyond feminism—is in regard to the attribution to women of "something better" and "higher" and of a "beautiful pure freedom" that is "infinitely more wonderful than any sexual love." Perhaps flattering, in a way; but also possibly part of a more general idealization of women that raises them onto a nonsexual pedestal, repeating the idealization of women in the nineteenth century and earlier that, in the twentieth, could come to seem oppressive. One of the strands of the 1960s in particular was the assertion of a nonidealized female sexuality, of a desire equivalent in its force and insistence to that of men.

In other words, in *Lady Chatterley* and elsewhere in Lawrence's work, there is a significant element of Romantic idealization, in respect of women (as in other respects we shall consider later), which can seem like an attempt to impose stereotypes upon human beings and human behaviour. An older stereotype, going back at least to Shakespeare's *Richard III*, is evident in the novel's treatment of disability.

Disability

One of the most troubling aspects of *Lady Chatterley's Lover* in the twenty-first century is its attitude to disability. Lady Chatterley's husband, Sir Clifford Chatterley, is permanently paralysed from the waist down, and sexually impotent, as the result of a war wound. He has a wheelchair and a motorized bath chair and learns to walk on crutches. It might seem that he is coping in a brave and resourceful way with his disability and that he could be a figure of heroic stoicism, like Jake Barnes in Hemingway's *The Sun Also Rises* [aka *Fiesta*] (1926), ambulant in contrast to Clifford but likewise impotent through a war wound. Lawrence, however, repeatedly presents Clifford, even in his disability and leaving aside the many negative traits loaded upon his character (which we shall address shortly), as lacking, comic, and grotesque. He is referred to several times as "poor" Clifford in a way that is more patronizing than sympathetic. We are told that one sees in his face "the watchful look, the slight vacancy of a cripple" (6) and that he "was really extremely shy and self-conscious now he was lamed" (16). The movement of his motorized bath chair is often described by the verb "puff" (or sometimes "chuff"), which seems demeaning and belittling in the context—this "poor" fellow can only puff or chuff around, like a low-powered steam engine and of course, in the organic/mechanical binary opposition, with *mechanical* as the inferior term, which the novel deploys, the fact that Clifford relies strongly on a mechanical, motorized device to move around, is a further mark against him—whereas we might see him today, in light of Donna Haraway's idea of the cyborg as a model of human existence (see Haraway), in a more positive way, without minimizing the extent of his disability: all human beings, we could argue, are cyborgs when they use a stick or a spade or spectacles or any other prosthetic device to assist their sensory and motor capability.

In Chapter 5, when Clifford gets out of his motorized bath chair into a wheelchair, the narrative stresses his upper body strength but quickly descends into an emphasis on his weakness and dependency: "Clifford managed to swing himself over on to the low, wheeled house-chair; he was very strong and agile with his arms. Then Connie lifted the burden of his dead legs after him" (51). The adjective *dead* is pejorative here, because Clifford's paralyzed legs are not dead but part of a living body and consciousness; and *dead* is much used elsewhere in the novel to disparage attitudes and activities that Connie—and the narrator—see as inert and sterile, a perception and implied judgement that would not be universally shared.

Lawrence uses Clifford's disability as a symbol of a more general failure of male sexuality and indeed of life itself. This symbolic appropriation of disability to represent negativity is highly questionable—why should a disabled person be seen as less vital and alive?—and it is compounded by the way in which the narrative loads Clifford with negative qualities, to such an extent that it is difficult to see why Connie stays with him as long as she does.

Trolling

Although Clifford has become a successful writer, Connie and the narrator are determined to denigrate him in this as in other respects. Clifford is seen as concerned, in his literary career, with serving what the narrator calls "the bitch-goddess," success (he attributes the term to Henry James [65] but its source is a letter [11 September 1906] from Henry's brother, William James, to H. G. Wells [2, 260]). He makes money but also "seemed to care very much whether his stories were considered first-class literature or not" (66). The desire for both financial remuneration and literary esteem might seem valid and understandable in a writer in the early twentieth century, or at most other times—indeed, Lawrence might once have shared it, though it looked, by the time he wrote *Lady Chatterley*, increasingly unlikely to be fulfilled—but the narrative adduces them as further proof of Clifford's weakness.

When Connie asks herself what she is serving in sacrificing herself to Clifford, her inner reply is:

> A cold spirit of vanity, that had no warm human contacts, and that was as corrupt as any low-born Jew, in craving for prostitution to the bitch-goddess, Success. Even Clifford's cool and contactless assurance that he belonged to the ruling class didn't prevent his tongue lolling out of his mouth, as he panted after the bitch-goddess. (75-76)

The narrative here relentlessly applies negative terms to Clifford: *cold* (contrasting with *warm*); *vanity*; *cool* (in the sense of lacking in emotion or enthusiasm rather than attractive or impressive as in the 1960s phrase "Cool, man!"); *contactless* (in a novel that stresses the importance of contact and touch and that long preceded the contactless payment card of the twenty-first century); the employment of an anti-Semitic and socially snobbish simile; and the use of a reductive canine metaphor. One might say that this faithfully reproduces the way Connie, or someone like her, might well think—anti-Semitism, for instance, was routine among the upper classes in 1920s Britain. But again one has the sense here, as throughout the novel, that Connie's inner voice receives the endorsement of, and sometimes merges into, the narrator's and no contrary or countervailing voice is allowed to emerge.

Connie finds Clifford more and more disagreeable: he tends "to become vague, absent, and to fall into fits of vacant depression. It was the wound to his psyche coming out" (66). This makes Connie "want to scream. Oh God, if the mechanism of the consciousness itself was going to go wrong, then what was one to do? Hang it all, one did one's bit! Was one to be let down *absolutely*?" (66-67; italics in original). The use of the noun *mechanism* here, applied to Clifford's consciousness, is a further way of putting him down, implying his lack of organic being, his automaticity.

Connie's reaction to Clifford's psychological distress, within a loveless marriage, is understandable but she seems incapable, until near the end of the novel, of taking any appropriate action, which might involve, for example, consulting a psychoanalyst (not a course of which Lawrence would have approved) or, simply, given that their relationship seems to have irretrievably broken down, of leaving him, since each of them has an independent income and Clifford could find someone to care for him less resentfully than Connie does—indeed, Mrs Bolton starts to do so during the course of the novel (then Connie also resents her!). In Chapter 7, when Connie is in London and her sometime lover Michaelis tells her to "chuck" Clifford, "Connie's heart simply stood still at the thought of abandoning Clifford there and then. She couldn't do it. No ... no! She just couldn't" (82; ellipsis in original). But her adherence to Clifford is not convincingly motivated and seems more like a plot device to keep her entrapped so that her only way out is through an extramarital affair.

Of course, on one level it is inappropriate to suggest, for characters in a fiction, alternative courses of action to those the fiction makes them follow; they are products of, and elements in, a fictional pattern and not autonomous human beings; but the process of speculating on alternative course of actions for fictional characters occurs naturally in the process of reading or watching a fiction and indeed may mirror the psychological processes of the characters themselves when they think about or discuss alternative possibilities—as Connie does, but in a rather limited way, in that all she can propose for herself is having an affair with, and possibly marrying, a truly passionate man, embodied in the gamekeeper Mellors, and bearing a child. By the end of the novel, it seems that they are going to live together and that she will have his baby and that eventually they will marry, if their divorces from their original spouses are granted; but the reader might wonder how long it will before Mellors, and/or the baby, make her "want to scream."

Clifford is also presented as a capitalist who wants to make money by introducing modern methods in his mines, and as an aristocrat who dislikes upward mobility in the lower orders. For instance, when Connie tries to suggest to him that there might be "something special" about the gamekeeper, Mellors, Clifford rejects the idea and Connie sees in him "the peculiar tight rebuff against anyone of the lower classes who might be really climbing up, which she knew was characteristic of his breed" (72).

One could in fact assemble from *Lady Chatterley's Lover* a compendium of insults directed at Clifford, almost amounting to what would today, in a social media context, be called *trolling*. In the encounter in Chapter 7 with Hilda, for example, he is described as "boiling with rage," as "yellow at the gills with anger," and as "rather like a huge, boiled crayfish" (81). The unremitting hostility to Clifford, and the lack of alternative perspectives, make one wonder what Clifford, if he had kept a diary or put his wife in a novel, would have thought of Connie—or of Lawrence. It is difficult to imagine

George Eliot, one of Leavis's other "great tradition" novelists, mounting such a total character assassination.

It is not that Clifford does not have faults—as an individual, an aristocrat, and a capitalist—but Lawrence's representation of him lacks that balance and roundedness that would give him his full humanity and becomes a relentless and rather unsubtle caricature, as if the novelist had done something that, in Lawrence's view, a true novel should not let one do—put "his thumb in the scale, to pull down the balance to his own predilection" ("Morality and the Novel" 528). In *Lady Chatterley*, it is more as if a whole fist has been put in the scale and is pounding spasmodically, to make Clifford, the village of Tevershall, and ultimately the whole of modern industrial civilization, representative of elements to which Lawrence's Romanticism is most strongly opposed.

Romanticism

Lawrence was a late Romantic who rejected most modernist literary innovations except his own and adapted the incendiary and incandescent imagery associated with William Blake to a concern with sexuality that coincided with post-Freudian attitudes but largely avoided psychoanalytic concepts, perspectives, and terminology. His Romanticism is most evident in his deployment of binary oppositions between the mechanical and the organic, the spontaneous and the automatic, the mental and the physical, the dead and the vital—and in his negative attitude to the results of the Industrial Revolution. There is a repeated emphasis on the ugliness of the industrialized Midlands as Connie Chatterley—and the narrator—see them. In Chapter 2, for instance, Tevershall village, which starts at the gates of the park of Wragby Hall where Sir Clifford and Connie live, is described as trailing "in utter hopeless ugliness for a long and gruesome mile: houses, rows of wretched, small, begrimed, brick houses, with black slate roofs for lids, sharp angles and wilful, blank dreariness" (14). The next paragraph speaks of "the utter, soulless ugliness of the coal-and-iron Midlands" (14), heralding a series of pejorative references—in Chapter 7, for example, we have "these filthy Midlands" (79)—to a part of England that was and remains agreeable in many respects and still retains much agricultural land. The novel does not present only the housing and industrial plant of the region in this wholly negative way: "The people were as haggard, shapeless, and dreary as the countryside, and as unfriendly" (15). The adjectives *utter, gruesome, wretched,* and *dreary* and the noun *ugliness* and its associated adjectives, recur in the descriptions of the village and of its industry in the novel.

It may be said that this is the way Connie, a woman from a privileged background who has married into the aristocracy, sees it; but usually in these descriptions her perceptions and thoughts coincide with or merge into those of the narrator, and there is no dialogic element, no countervoice(s) to offer a different perspective—to point to, or evoke, the intense life that might unfold in those small houses, the possibilities of aesthetic perception that might be open even to their materially deprived inhabitants, the way in which, in the actuality of the Midlands at the time, they would have been set in open countryside. Throughout the novel there is an insistence on the industrial villages and industrialized landscape that is utterly hostile, failing to see either their material advantages—there were some, compared to agricultural labour—or their aesthetic possibilities. Perhaps the most extensive and notable example in the novel of this hostility occurs in Chapter 11, when the Chatterley chauffeur, Field, drives Connie through Tedershall toward Uthwaite:

> The car ploughed uphill through the long squalid straggle of Tevershall, the blackened brick dwellings, the black slate roofs glistening their sharp edges, the mud black with coal-dust, the pavements wet and black. It was as if dismalness had soaked through and through everything. The utter negation of natural beauty, the utter negation of the gladness of life, the utter absence of the instinct for shapely beauty which every bird and beast has, the utter death of the human intuitive faculty was appalling. The stacks of soap in the grocers' shops, the rhubarb and lemons in the greengrocers! the awful hats in the milliners! all went by ugly, ugly, ugly, followed by the plaster-and-gilt horror of the cinema with its wet picture announcements, "A Woman's Love!," and the new big

Primitive chapel, primitive enough in its stark brick and big panes of greenish and raspberry glass in the windows. (158)

This continues for some time, but the quotation is sufficiently long to show its strategy. There is the reiteration of familiar adjectives— *ugly* thrice, *utter* four times—and the insertion of exclamation marks to try to drive home an attitude that is not wholly supported by the images evoked through, for instance, a phrase such as "the black slate roofs glistening their sharp edges." Might not an Impressionist or post-Impressionist painter, a Manet or Van Gogh, have found aesthetic qualities in that village, despite its undoubtedly displeasing elements? Why should the "stacks of soap" reinforce the idea of ugliness and utter negation, given their value in terms of personal hygiene, especially in the skin-blackening environment of a mining community, and in light of the possibility that an artist, or even an inhabitant of the village who wanted a refreshing wash, might see them as aesthetically as well as practically pleasing? Why are the "rhubarbs and lemons" singled out as exemplifying ugliness and utter negation when they might be seen as forms of "natural beauty" by a customer or passer-by or a still life artist—what might Cézanne make of them? Are all the hats in the milliners, briefly glimpsed from a passing car, truly *awful*? What sartorial standards does this rapid and generalized judgement imply? Why should the cinema, a building that makes the great popular art of the twentieth century comfortably accessible to the impoverished as well as the elite, be a horror rather than a stimulus to the imagination? It may be said that Lawrence is referring here to the plaster-and-gilt decoration of the cinema exterior but his aversion extends to its screenings as well—he had particular problems with movies (see Tredell). "[S]tark brick" and "greenish and raspberry glass" may sound a little abrasive and bilious, but why should they, in a post-Constructivist and post-Fauvist era, necessarily be aesthetically obnoxious?

The tutelary spirit of Lawrence's aesthetics in this passage, though not of his style, is John Ruskin, and Lawrence's attitude shows how much he still belongs to the anti-industrial spirit of the nineteenth century, how much he is a late Romantic astray in a world that bothers and bewilders him rather than a true modern. But the passage also exemplifies the deficiency of *Lady Chatterley* as a novel—to borrow Lawrencian rhetoric, its "utter negation" of nuance, subtlety, and perception; its "utter negation" of the capacity, to adapt a line from Matthew Arnold's poem "To a Friend," to see life steadily and see it whole; its "utter negation" of a reverence for life in all its complex variety and contradiction. This is exaggerated, of course, as late Lawrencian rhetoric itself so often is; *Lady Chatterley* is not as absolutely negative as that; and there is one element in its rejection of industrialization that could be rescued for the twenty-first century,

Ecology

This is its ecological element. Industrialization, in the mining villages or the big cities, was never as wholly negative as Lawrence and other anti-industrial writers suppose; but it did exploit and diminish human beings and it did despoil the environment. One positive aspect of *Lady Chatterley* is its evocation of the woods through which Connie walks, which are "unspoilt" (except, significantly, by Clifford's motorized bath chair, but this is a minor intrusion). In these evocations, Lawrence's botanical knowledge, acquired during his teacher training, comes into play, enabling precise identification and evocation of the flowers and shrubs Connie encounters. Take this from the start of Chapter 12, for example:

> Connie went to the wood directly after lunch. It was really a lovely day, the first dandelions making suns, the first daisies so white. The hazel thicket was a lace-work, of half-open leaves, and the last dusty perpendicular of the catkins. Yellow celandines now were in crowds, flat open, pressed back in urgency, and the yellow glitter of themselves. It was the yellow, the powerful yellow of early summer. And primroses were broad, and full of pale abandon, thick-clustered primroses no longer shy. The lush, dark green of hyacinths was a sea, with buds rising like pale corn, while in the riding the forget-me-nots were fluffing up, and columbines were unfolding their ink-

purple ruches, and there were bits of blue bird's eggshell under a bush. Everywhere the bud-knots and the leap of life! (172)

This is Lawrence at his lyrical best, where specific descriptions build up rhythmically and semantically into a final affirmation that, despite its generalizing quality and its exclamation mark, seems justified, prepared for, and substantiated by what has gone before—in contrast to the generalizations and exclamation marks of the description of Tevershall village.

The problem is that these descriptions are contained, in the formal structure and imaginary topography of the novel, in the grounds of the Chatterley country seat, Wragby Hall, within privately owned land to which the public does not have legal access (hence the penalties visited on poachers). They never spill out into the descriptions of the village—but it is surely possible, indeed quite likely, that at least some of its inhabitants would have, without formal training, a measure of botanical knowledge and expertise gained from experience, would be able, for instance, to identify and aesthetically appreciate flowers. But the novel maintains a strict binary division, modeling the social division, between the grounds of Wragby Hall and the village. There is no conception of what Ashton Nichols calls "urbanature" ("Urbanature,"*Beyond Romantic Ecocriticism*)—the interaction and interfusion of human structures such as villages, towns, and industrial plant, and the natural world (which human beings, especially in the agricultural Midlands, have usually shaped to a greater or lesser extent). An ecological reading of *Lady Chatterley* today might scrutinize the text for any signs of possible ways in which the division the novel tries to maintain between the private wood and the public village may be breached. But it would have to work against the grain of a novel whose only explicit recommendation seems to be to return to a preindustrial era; and Lawrence does not return upon himself to question this.

Conclusion: No Return

In Chapter 9 of *Lady Chatterley*, the account of Connie listening with slightly shameful fascination to Mrs Bolton talking to Clifford about the lives of the Tevershall villagers slides into general narratorial reflections on life and the novel:

> It is the way our sympathy flows and recoils that really determines our lives. And here lies the vast importance of the novel, properly handled. It can inform and lead into new places the flow of our sympathetic consciousness, and it can lead our sympathy away in recoil from things gone dead. (105)

Judged by these implied criteria, the problem with *Lady Chatterley* is that it is too hectoring and insistent in its attempt to "lead our sympathy away in recoil from things gone dead" and that it pronounces things "dead" without checking for vital signs. In *Lady Chatterley*, *dead* appears to be an adjective and a concept applied to people, emotions, attitudes, and behavior that Connie/Lawrence dislikes and there is no sign of what Matthew Arnold, in his essay "The Function of Criticism at the Present Time," called, in relation to Edmund Burke, a "return [...] upon himself": the process in which, "when one side of a question has long had your earnest support, when all your feelings are engaged, when you hear all round you no language but one," you are "still to be able to think, still to be irresistibly carried, if so it be, by the current of thought to the opposite side of the question" (Arnold 1865). He is talking here of nonfiction, but it applies even more to fiction in light of Lawrence's own 1925 definition of a novel as a medium that "won't *let* you tell didactic lies" ("The Novel" 417; italics in original). *Lady Chatterley*, however, never allows "the opposite side of the question" to emerge in its full force and complexity and never turns the diagnosis of deadness against the diagnostician.

The effect of the delayed publication of the unexpurgated edition of *Lady Chatterley*, and the publicity surrounding the 1960 trial, was to make the novel, and Lawrence's work as a whole, seem much more modern than it was, reinserting its combination of a late Romantic sensibility with an early twentieth-century sexual fixation into the tumults of the 1960s. In a sense, "the *Chatterley* ban," as Larkin called it, prolonged the shelf life of the novel, and its author's oeuvre, well beyond its best-by date. Thus the end of the ban was both the apotheosis of Lawrence's reputation and the start of his dislodgement (to use a Leavisian 1930s term); it began the process of enabling his work to be seen steadily and whole, as a distinctive and energetic contribution to modern fiction and thought that is nonetheless, in the long perspective of time, dated.

Works Cited

Arnold, Matthew. "The Function of Criticism at the Present Time." In *Essays in Criticism* (1865). www.fortnightlyreview.co.uk/the-function-of-criticism-at-the-present-time.

_____. "To a Friend" (1849). www.bartleby.com/254/7.html.

Haraway, Donna. "A Cyborg Manifesto" (1991). www.web.archive.org/web/20120214194015/http://www.stanford.edu/dept/HPS/haraway/cyborgmanifesto.html.

James, William. *The Letters of William James.* 2 vols. Edited by Henry James, Longmans, Green, 1920.

Kermode, Frank. *Lawrence.* Fontana Modern Masters. Fontana/Collins, 1973.

Larkin, Philip. *The Complete Poems.* Edited with an introduction and commentary by Archie Burnett, Faber & Faber, 2012.

Lawrence, D. H. *Lady Chatterley's Lover* (1928; unexpurgated edition, 1960). Penguin, 2011.

_____. "Morality and the Novel" (1925). In *Phoenix: The Posthumous Papers, 1936.* Penguin, 1978, pp. 527-32.

_____. "My Naughty Book" (1929). In *The Complete Poems.* 2 vols. Selected and edited with an introduction and notes by Vivian de Sola Pinto and Warren Roberts, Heinemann, 1972, vol. 1, pp. 491-92.

_____. "The Novel" (1925). In *Phoenix II: Uncollected, Unpublished and Other Prose Works.* Collected and edited with an Introduction and Notes by Warren Roberts and Harry T. Moore, Heinemann, 1968, pp. 416-26.

Leavis, F. R. *D. H. Lawrence: Novelist.* London: Chatto & Windus, 1955.

_____. *The Great Tradition: George Eliot; Henry James; Joseph Conrad.* Chatto & Windus, 1948.

_____. "The New Orthodoxy." *Spectator,* 17 Feb 1961. http://archive.spectator.co.uk/article/17th-february-1961/13/by-f-r-leavis.

_____. "The Orthodoxy of Enlightenment" (retitled version of "The New Orthodoxy"). In *Anna Karenina and Other Essays*. Chatto & Windus, 1967, pp. 235-41.

_____. *Thought, Words and Creativity: Art and Thought in Lawrence*. Chatto & Windus, 1976.

Nichols, Ashton. *Beyond Romantic Ecocriticism: Toward Urbanatural Roosting*. Palgrave Macmillan, 2011.

_____. "Urbanature." *Romantic Circles: A Refereed Scholarly Website Devoted to the Study of Romantic Period Literature and Culture*. 17 Sep 2008. www.rc.umd.edu/blog_rc/urbanature.

Rolph, C. H., editor. *The Trial of Lady Chatterley: Regina v. Penguin Books Limited: The Transcript of the Trial*. Penguin, 1961.

Tredell, Nicolas. "Panoramic Sleights: Figures of Cinema in Literature." *PN Review 146*, Jul-Aug 2002, pp. 17-21.

Williams, Raymond. "Seeing a Man Running." In *The Leavises: Recollections and Impressions*. Edited by Denys Thompson, Cambridge UP, 1984, pp. 113-22.

Interanimations: William S. Burroughs's *Naked Lunch*

Nicolas Tredell

William S. Burroughs's *Naked Lunch* (1959) remains one of the most notorious of banned books, a novel that has become canonical, in the sense that no history of American and Anglophone fiction or culture would be complete without a discussion of it, but which remains difficult to assimilate fully, stays on and beyond the edge, at and over the limit, of our current cultural norms as of the somewhat different norms of the 1950s when it first appeared. A section of the novel published in the *Chicago Review* in 1958 provoked an outrage that led to the magazine's closure for a time. The following year Maurice Girodias's Olympia Press, the original publisher of a range of otherwise banned books, such as Vladimir Nabokov's *Lolita* (1955), which would later become famous and circulate widely, brought out an edition under a title that included the definite article: *The Naked Lunch*. The changes of the 1960s— not least the lifting of the ban, at the start of the decade, on the UK publication of an unexpurgated edition of D. H. Lawrence's *Lady Chatterley's Lover*, a novel discussed earlier in this volume— created a more open cultural climate, and *Naked Lunch*—this time without the definite article—achieved its first American publication in 1962. In 1964, the British publisher John Calder, well known for his promotion of avant-garde work and opposition to censorship, brought out an edition of Burroughs's writing that included *Naked Lunch* and a collection of pieces called *Dead Fingers Talk*. This was timely; Burroughs was one of those older figures who gained a kind of guru status in the 1960s as a precursor of and example for the counterculture, even though, in terms of his background, appearance, and manner he was rather respectable—in contrast to, for example, his fellow Beat writer Allen Ginsberg. His status was confirmed by his inclusion in the pantheon of figures on the cover of the Beatles LP *Sgt. Pepper's Lonely Hearts Club Band* (1967). In his later years, he would enjoy a quasi-mythical status and become an icon of consumer culture more than counterculture, making cameo appearances in films such as Gus Van Sant's *Drugstore Cowboy* (1989) and Michael Almereyda's *Twister* (1989), and featuring in advertisements for The Gap and Nike. Without denying the cultural importance of this apotheosis, or supposing that it can simply be set aside without influencing the interpretation of his texts, it is important, in a literary context, to recall Samuel Beckett's appraisal of Burroughs, which Burroughs himself treasured: "Well, he's a writer" (qtd. in Morgan 576). This essay will focus on his writing in his best-known work, *Naked Lunch,* and aim to identify those features that make it distinctive. It will make particular use, as a term and concept, of the prefix *inter*, meaning among or between, and will apply this to the novel's geography, genres, characters, and aesthetics, all of which interanimate one another.

Interzone

Interzone is a term Burroughs himself employs in *Naked Lunch* and elsewhere in his writing to denote the peculiar geography of his fiction which exists in an imaginary space where different times, places, and states of being and consciousness intersect. The thirteenth chapter of the novel, *"the market,"* opens with a "Panorama of the City of Interzone," "The Composite City where all human potentials are spread out in a vast silent market" (89):

> Minarets, palms, mountains, jungle … A sluggish river jumping with vicious fish, vast weed-grown parks where boys lie in the grass, play cryptic games. Not a locked door in the City. Anyone comes into your room at any time. The Chief of Police is a Chinese who picks his teeth and listens to denunciations presented by a lunatic. Every now and then the Chinese takes the toothpick out of his mouth and looks at the end of it. (89; ellipsis here and in subsequent quotations in original unless otherwise indicated)

There are, clearly, Orientalist stereotypes here, palms and minarets, the Chinese police chief, metonymies for the exotic East, with its appeal and menace, as seen by Western eyes; but to recognize their stereotypical aspects is not wholly to annul their evocative power (which is, indeed, partly due to their stereotypical nature). But there is also an inversion of urban pastoral that calls to mind the negative images of the River Thames in Joseph Conrad's *Heart of Darkness* (1902) and in T. S. Eliot's *The Waste Land* (1922), the modernist poem Burroughs saw as the initiator of the so-called cut-up method that he and Brion Gysin would later use ("Interview" 153, "Last European Interview" 82, 92). The river of Interzone is not sprightly but "sluggish" and while, as in George Gershwin and DuBose Heyward's song "Summertime" (1935), the fish are "jumping," the impression of vitality this verb might give is complicated by the adjective "vicious," rhyming internally with "fish" as if to drive home an inevitable coupling that brings out piscine predatoriness. The "parks" are "vast," which might at first suggest a generous provision of urban recreational space, but this is undermined by "weed-grown," implying neglect and lack of nurture. The idea of boys lying in the grass playing games might suggest innocent enjoyment (even if, inevitably in Burroughs, with an erotic element), but the adjective "cryptic" introduces an element of puzzlement, mystery, and possible deceit and trickery. The "denunciations presented by a lunatic" is an intertextual echo of Macbeth's "tale[s] / Told by an idiot" (*Macbeth* 5.5.26-7), and the fact that the police chief listens to them suggests a city in which attention may be paid to insane accusations that may provide (given the police chief's power) the pretext for punitive action against those falsely fingered. The last sentence in which the chief of police looks at what is on the end of his toothpick recalls Burroughs's own interpretation of the title for his novel that Jack Kerouac provided: "NAKED Lunch—a frozen moment when everyone sees what is on the end of every fork" (199; capitals in original).

We can see from this analysis, which is by no means exhaustive, how much Burroughs can pack into his sentences; it is in this sense that he is, in the complimentary sense of Beckett's words, a *writer* for whom words are not merely a transparent medium through which to see a preexisting reality but a way of constructing a reality in an interzone where different times, places, and categories of being intersect and interact—and different genres.

Intergenre

Whereas many banned books—*Lady Chatterley's Lover* and *Lolita* would serve as prominent examples—load their controversial content into fairly conventional forms, *Naked Lunch* breaks up the structure of the novel, mixing fragments associated with different genres. There is an aesthetic rationale for this, insofar as these two terms can be used appropriately in relation to Burroughs, whose work challenges both the aesthetic and rationality, and it is explained in what he calls an "atrophied preface," which, defying sequence, occurs as the penultimate chapter of the novel and which we shall consider in the Interaesthetic section below. In this section we shall focus first on the experience of reading the novel in relation to generic expectations, positing, to begin with, an imaginary reader familiar with different kinds of fiction but with no prior knowledge of *Naked Lunch* (admittedly an unlikely situation in actuality today, given Burroughs's considerable cultural presence, but a useful hypothesis).

The opening has the manner of a thriller, a fast-paced first-person narration that introduces the themes of flight and pursuit, of possibly justified paranoia, with an occult tinge: "I can feel the heat closing in, feel them out there making their moves, setting up their devil doll stool pigeons" (3). It segues into sharp social observations and satire, as the narrator, vaulting the turnstile at Washington Square Station and clanging down iron steps, catches a New York subway train:

> Young, good looking, crew cut, Ivy League, advertising exec type fruit holds the door back for me. I am evidently his idea of a character. You know the type: comes on with bartenders and cab drivers, talking about right hooks and the Dodgers, calls the counterman in Nedick's by his first name. A real asshole. (3)

At this point, our hypothetical first-time reader might think the novel had established, economically and effectively, a style and situation that it would follow through and develop—but it does not, although traces of that style and situation recur at various points. In a sense, we might take this "advertising exec type" who assumes an easy familiarity, across social divisions, with those who labour in service industries and who likes "characters"—a little later the narrator calls him "a character collector" (5)—as a parody of a typical novel reader, especially of the 1950s; though homosexual, he is, it goes without saying, white, with an elite education and lucrative career who likes to feel the novel offers representations of "characters" and intimate access to those in a "lower" social sphere from himself, proving that we are all the same despite inequities of income and power. The narrator's deflation of him anticipates the way in which the novel will deflate the expectations of such a reader.

There is of course an irony here that pertains to the author's biography but is not irrelevant to an assessment of his achievement. Burroughs himself came from a comfortably off family; he was not, as one newspaper article on his lethal shooting of his wife suggested, the heir to the fortunes of the famous adding machine company that shared his name (Miles 152), but his grandfather had founded the company and invented the device that was crucial to its success ("Interview" 144, Morgan 15-19); and Burroughs's parents provided him with a regular income that helped to finance both his drug and writing habits; he had a degree from an Ivy League university, Harvard; he was a white male with a respectable manner and appearance that would have enabled him to pass in the upper echelons of professional and social society had he wished to do so; he was homosexual but married and produced a son; if he had followed a more conventional course, he might well, in early adulthood, have been an "advertising exec type," like the young Scott Fitzgerald. It was this background and its expectations against which he rebelled—and this is evident in his writing as well as his life.

Even when, at the end of the first chapter of *Naked Lunch*, the narrator (we assume it is the same one as at the start) moves out of New York, we are, in a sense, linking with what looks like a familiar story, especially in American culture—lighting out for the territory, as at the end of *Huckleberry Finn,* going west as in Kerouac's *On the Road*: "So we stock up on H, buy a secondhand Studebaker, and start west" (8). In a further echo of *On the Road*, this narrator, by Chapter 3 of the novel, "*the rube*," goes over the frontier into the USA's alluring and menacing Other:

> Something falls off you when you cross the border into Mexico, and suddenly the landscape hits you straight with nothing between you and it, desert and mountains and vultures; (14)

Our hypothetical first-timer might feel by this point that *Naked Lunch* is a modern picaresque tale and begin to anticipate the further adventures that this sharp-tongued streetwise narrator will encounter down Mexico way. And there are indeed picaresque elements playing through *Naked Lunch*. But this is an intergeneric novel that mixes picaresque narrative, horror story, absurdist narrative, and science fiction—this list is not exhaustive—and eschews sustained narrative connections. Indeed the ideas of a thriller, socially satirical or picaresque narrative have already been complicated by Chapter 2 of *Naked Lunch*.

In this chapter, we enter different generic territory and meet a different kind of character, The Vigilante: "He stood there in elongated court room shadow, his face torn like a broken film by lusts and hungers of larval organs stirring in the tentative ectoplasmic flesh of junk kick" (8-9). Here are recurrent motifs in *Naked Lunch*: bodies are unstable, punctured, unpredictable, likely to generate alien growths: larval means having "the active immature form of an insect or other animal that undergoes metamorphosis," such as a caterpillar or tadpole (*Concise Oxford Dictionary*). The sense that a body—at least one ravaged by narcotics, but, characteristically, the text implies this as a possibility for all human bodies—can produce rudimentary organs that will change into a more developed life form, conveys a sense of physical instability that goes to the core of identity. The term "metamorphosis" in the *Concise Oxford Dictionary* definition of *larval* we have just quoted is especially apposite as it calls to mind the classic example of such instability in twentieth-century literature: Franz Kafka's novella *Metamorphosis* (1915). But although Kafka's Gregor Samsa undergoes a sudden and alarming bodily change, it only happens once; he is still more stable than the metamorphosing figures in *Naked Lunch*, which are encapsulated in the description of The Vigilante that concludes the second chapter of the novel: "no organ is constant as regards either function or position [...] the entire organism changes color and consistency in split-second adjustments" (9). Moreover, this could describe not only the figures who emerge, change, and fade out in *Naked Lunch*, but also the textuality of the novel itself, with its moment-to-moment changes that require, from the reader who persists with it, constant rapid adjustments. Recasting the statement we have just quoted in generic terms, we might say that, in *Naked Lunch*, no generic marker is constant as regards function or position; the entire novel changes consistency in split-second adjustments.

This instability also applies to markers of character in the novel; the reader who is a character collector, like the young "advertising exec type" (3) on the A train, will not find in *Naked Lunch* the fully rounded characters of, say, George Eliot's fiction, or the consistent eccentric types of Dickens (though Burroughs's grotesquerie is closer to Dickens than to George Eliot). But, with a certain adjustment of expectations, this kind of reader will find that there are figures who emerge from *Naked Lunch* who, while not being characters in the rounded or typical sense, have enough characteristics to make them memorable, even to give them an imaginative life that enables them to float free of their text of origin, becoming cultural points of reference in their own right. They exist, as it were, between different kinds of characterization so that we might call them intercharacters. We shall now consider three examples of these.

Intercharacters

The first is Doctor Benway, "a manipulator and coordinator of symbol systems, an expert on all phases of interrogation, brainwashing and control" (19). When he works in the Freeland Republic (another country in Burroughs's interzonal geography), Benway largely eschews physical repression, favouring guilt-inducing "prolonged mistreatment": the subject "must be made to feel that he deserves *any* treatment he receives because there is something (never specified) horribly wrong with him" (19). Benway's manipulative skills make him especially useful to "the control addicts" who cloak and assuage their craving in bureaucracy: "The naked need of the control addicts must be decently covered by an arbitrary and intricate bureaucracy so that the subject cannot contact his enemy direct" (19).

We can again see Kafkaesque resonances here, the idea of "an arbitrary and intricate bureaucracy" that constantly baffles and defeats the individual, as in Kafka's novels *The Trial* and *The Castle*. But Burroughs adds the concept, crucial to *Naked Lunch* and to his whole oeuvre, of the desire for control as itself an addiction to a narcotic as draining as any chemical drug; in this perspective, the urge to control chemical narcotics, any kind of "War on Drugs," is itself a form of addiction. The same is true of the censorship that *Naked Lunch* encountered. As it says in Chapter 15 of *Naked Lunch* *"You see control can never be a means to any practical end ... It can never be a means to anything but more control ... Like junk ...* " (137). Today's notion of the "control freak" partly originates in Burroughs, for whom addiction is not confined to the junkie but is the driver of any bureaucracy or big business that works to enmesh its subjects in its intricacies.

Doctor Benway recurs in the seventh chapter of the novel, called *"hospital,"* where, among other things, he gives a demonstration to medical students of his operating skills with this commentary:

> "Now, boys, you won't see this operation performed very often and there's a reason for that ... You see it has absolutely no medical value. No one knows what the purpose of it originally was or if it had a purpose at all. Personally I think it was a pure artistic creation from the beginning. Just as a bull fighter with his skill and knowledge extricates himself from danger he has himself invoked, so in this operation the surgeon deliberately endangers his patient, and then, with incredible speed and celerity, rescues him from death at the last possible split second ... " (52)

This routine—*routine* in the sense of "a set sequence in a theatrical or comic performance" (*Concise Oxford Dictionary*)—is characteristically Burrovian (an adjective derived from Burroughs's surname on the model of "Shavian" from Shaw). *Naked Lunch* is rich in routines and their crucial performative element is language. But though they are performed for the reader in print, in a novel, they constantly suggest oral routines, with appropriate accompanying body language, in another kind of performance space—the carnival tent, a place of subversion, of scabrous and scatological exuberance, of turning the world, at least temporarily, upside down. In this context, it is notable that one of the novel's most memorable intercharacters, and one of Benway's most memorable routines, is a story *about* a routine in a carnival that gets out of hand—though a metaphor drawn from a lower part of the anatomy might seem more appropriate here. The intercharacter here is the loquacious anus, or, to put it in a more robust Burrovian register, the "talking asshole."

As we have seen, the term *asshole* occurs in the first paragraph of the text (3), in the dismissive summation of the young man who holds the subway train door open for the narrator, and who figures both as an image of the conventional 1950s reader and of the conventional man the narrator—and Burroughs himself—might have become. When, in Chapter 14 of *Naked Lunch*, "*ordinary men and women*," the Burrovian-Benway routine takes up this term again, it is to present a literal embodiment of the idea of a person who, in the colloquial phrase, is "talking through his ass." It is, in a sense, an adaptation of the tale of the ventriloquist whose dummy takes him over (as in the film *Dead of Night* [1945]), but in this case the dummy is a part of the ventriloquist's own anatomy that, in a characteristic Burrovian way, turns against its supposed controller, develops a life of its own (111).

A carnival entertainer develops an act in which he teaches his anus to talk and banters with it; for example, he asks "are you still down there, old thing?" and the anus replies: 'Nah! I had to go relieve myself'" (111). At first this is, according to Benway, really funny but then starts to assume a more sinister, though still darkly comic aspect as the anus starts talking on its own, ad-libbing, which at first makes it easier for the entertainer, who does not have to work out his routine in advance, but becomes more disturbing as the orifice develops "sort of teeth-like little raspy incurving hooks" (111) and starts eating. Increasingly it gets out of control, "talking on the street, shouting out it wanted equal rights," getting drunk and having "crying jags" (111).

The anecdote, exemplifying the intergeneric quality of *Naked Lunch* as a (fragmented) whole, starts to turn into a mixture of horror story and science fiction; the anus decides it no longer needs the man because, in addition to its original function, it can also talk and eat. The man starts to awaken each morning "with a transparent jelly like a tadpole's tail all over his mouth" (111). This jelly is "Undifferentiated Tissue, which can grow into any kind of flesh on the human body" (111). The man tears it off his mouth but the pieces "stick to his hands like burning gasoline jelly and grow there, grow anywhere on him a glob of it fell" (111). Finally it seals his mouth over so that his whole head "would have amputated spontaneous" (111) except for the fact that the anus needs the man's eyes since "the one thing [it] *couldn't* do was see" (112). But "nerve connections were blocked and infiltrated and atrophied so the brain couldn't give orders any more. It was trapped in the skull, sealed off" (112). Finally, it seems that "the brain must have died, because the eyes *went out*, and there was no more feeling in them than a crab's eye on the end of a stalk" (112).

This routine, which encompasses humour, horror, and science fiction, finally, in a last metamorphosis, becomes an image of self-reproducing bureaucracy that creates inner division, takes over bodies, blindly proliferates, severs brain and eyes from voice, and ultimately proves lethal: and it seems to be Doctor Benway who acts as interpreter of this image here, glossing it thus:

> A bureau takes root anywhere in the state, turns malignant like the Narcotic Bureau, and grows and grows, always reproducing more of its own kind, until it chokes the host if not controlled or excised. Bureaus cannot live without a host, being true parasitic organisms [...] Bureaucracy is wrong as a cancer, a turning away from the human evolutionary direction of infinite potentials and differentiation

and independent spontaneous action to the complete parasitism of a virus. (112)

If Benway has earlier been a sinister figure, using his manipulative skills in Freeland to help the control addicts, and performing unnecessary and potentially lethal operations for kicks and to demonstrate his own skills, here (and we should not expect consistency in Burroughs's intercharacters), he is a sharp diagnostician of an endemic disease and advocates control and surgery for benign purposes, to contain and cut out the malignant bureaucracy the craving of the control addicts has generated—though there is perhaps also an implication that this desire to control control addicts may, as with the Narcotic Bureau, itself become a form of control craving.

There are also figures in *Naked Lunch* that belong more to science fiction and fantasy, though the novel refuses to contain them safely within those genres; such generic containment might itself be seen as a form of control. Perhaps the most striking science-fictional figures are the Mugwumps, whom the reader first encounters in the sixth chapter of the novel, "*the black meat*," in the Meet Café in the City of Interzone:

> On stools covered in white satin sit naked Mugwumps sucking translucent, colored syrups through alabaster straws. Mugwumps have no liver and nourish themselves exclusively on sweets. Thin, purple-blue lips cover a razor-sharp beak of black bone with which they frequently tear each other to shreds in fights over clients. (46)

Though their name makes them sound like amiable characters in a children's story, and their sucking of syrups and sweets may sound harmless, the last sentence sharply conveys their aggression and destructive capacity, linking up with the "vicious fish" (89) in the Interzone river and with many other violent incidents in *Naked Lunch*. Moreover, the Mugwumps, as pushers, necessarily prey on their clients, who crave the addictive fluid the Mugwumps produce, which lengthens life by slowing down metabolism. Its addicts are called Reptiles, who "flow over chairs with their flexible bones and black-pink flesh" in the Meet Café, and absorb the addictive fluid by means of a "fan of green cartilage covered with hollow, erectile hairs" that "sprouts from behind each ear" (46). The figures of Mugwump and Reptile bring together the Burrovian motifs of addiction and the desire to stave off death, a desire which, as the passage indicates, can itself become addictive, especially if it finds a means that does actually seem to extend existence: "all longevity agents have proved addicting in exact ratio to their effectiveness in prolonging life" (46).

There are many other intercharacters in *Naked Lunch*: a paragraph in the penultimate chapter of the novel, the "*Atrophied Preface*" that bears the title "WOULDN'T YOU?" offers a list (not exhaustive) where the names and nicknames run from normalcy to anomaly: "The Vigilante, The Rube, Lee The Agent, A. J., Clem and Jody The Ergot Twins, Hassan O'Leary the After Birth Tycoon, The Sailor, The Exterminator, Andrew Keif, 'Fats' Terminal, Doc Benway, 'Fingers' Schafer" (186). Among these, Salvador Hassan O'Leary is especially protean, even in Burroughs's shapeshifting pages: "He has held 23 passports and been deported 49 times—deportation proceedings pending in Cuba, Pakistan, Hong Kong and Yokohama" (131). His aliases include The Shoe Store Kid, Wrong Way Marv, After Birth Leary, Slunky Pete, Placenta Juan, K. Y. Ahmed, El Chinche, El Culito and more, "for fifteen solid pages of dossier" (131). But there is a unity to his activity that shows that it is not only bureaucracy but also big business that creates labyrinthine confusion that can enmesh individuals: "A squad of accountant investigators have made a life work of Sal's international dossier … His operations extend through the world in an inextricable, shifting web of subsidiaries, front companies, and aliases" (131).

After listing the names of a range of the novel's intercharacters, the "*Atrophied Preface*" makes a further point: that, differentiated though they are by name and activities, they "are subject to say the same thing in the same words, to occupy, at that intersection point, the same position in space-time. Using a common vocal apparatus complete with all metabolic appliances—that is, to be the same person—a most inaccurate way of expressing *Recognition*" (186).

In other words, the intercharacters are not consistently confined within one identity but may overlap and interchange qualities, without becoming "the same person." The idea that they do not, ultimately, become "the same person" works against one possible way of interpreting *Naked Lunch*, which would be to read it as an Expressionist text, in which all the intercharacters, intergeneric elements, and interzonal locations were supposedly unified by being interpreted as the product of one mind, as the sustained fantasy of an author deeply influenced by drugs (which would account for its dreamlike qualities and drastic shifts). Such an interpretation would return the novel, if rather uneasily, to a traditional aesthetic realm in which it was the expression of its implied or actual author. It would leave aside, however, the interaesthetic aspect of the novel, the way it exists among and between, and disrupts, traditional aesthetic positions (which by 1958 would include Modernist ones). It is to this aspect that we shall now turn.

Interaesthetics

The most sustained statement of this aspect of the novel is in the "*Atrophied Preface*" from which we have just quoted, but before addressing this, we shall examine some references earlier in the novel, in Chapter 13, "*the market*." A section of this (94-98) mocks the idea of a prophet, particularly one who presents himself as a white-haired elderly man:

> Are we never to be free of this grey-beard loon lurking on every mountain top in Tibet, subject to drag himself out of a hut in the Amazon, waylay one in the Bowery? 'I've been expecting you my son,' and he make with a silo full of corn. 'Life is a school where every pupil must learn a different lesson. And now I will unlock my Word Hoard ... ' (97)

This seems to satirize the turn to supposed prophetic wisdom in 1950s Beat culture itself and, anticipatorily, in 1960s counterculture—though it has been preceded by a similar satire on the major religious figures of the past, so it does not make a distinction between authentic and phony prophets, implying that all of them are false. But the significance of the satire is complicated by the phrase "unlock my Word Hoard," an intertextual reference to the phrase "wordhord onleac," meaning "word hoard unlocked," which occurs five times in Old English verse: twice in the poem *Andreas* and once each in the poems *Beowulf, The Metres of Boethius*, and *Widsith;* this last, for instance, has "Widsið maðolade, *wordhord onleac*" / ["Widsith spoke, *unlocked his word-hoard*"] (*Widsith*, 1.1, italics added; see Videen, "Old English Wordhord: About"). This ancient provenance gives the phrase a certain cultural authority that complicates any simple dismissal of it as corny.

Moreover, the phrase recurs later in *Naked Lunch*, and it does so in a first-person sentence in the "*Atrophied Preface*" that is attributed to a speaker who identifies himself by Burroughs's own two forenames: "Now I, William Seward, will unlock my word hoard" (192). It should be said that the Corgi paperback edition of the novel, based on the John Calder edition, has "horde" (*The Naked Lunch* 256) and one may question its emendation to "hoard" in the "restored text," since "horde" stays closer to the original Old English spelling, makes a good pun, and creates an intertextual link with the "hooded hordes swarming / Over endless plains" in Eliot's *Waste Land* (73; 5, 368-69). But whether one opts for "horde" or "hoard," or keeps both in mind, its attribution to "William Seward" gives it added authority, almost as if it came directly from the author himself, and again suggests that the "grey-beard loon" (97) evoked in the earlier chapter of the novel may not be altogether mad or silly. It is as if Burroughs, the Burroughs we can infer from the text, both assumes the prophetic mantle, anticipating his own guru status in the 1960s, but also tears it off, so that he himself is a kind of intercharacter in his own novel, inhabiting a space between prophet and fool.

In that earlier chapter, shortly after the use of the term "word hoard," there is a paragraph whose source is unclear but that seems partly to relate to the aesthetics enunciated in the penultimate chapter, though not in a fully concordant way:

So I got an exclusive why don't I make with the live word? The word cannot be expressed direct ... It can perhaps be indicated by mosaic of juxtaposition like articles abandoned in a hotel drawer, defined by negatives and absence ... (97)

This offers an aesthetic of indirection, which both recalls that of Henry James's observation that "romantic," as opposed to the "real," "stands ... for the things that ... we never *can* directly know" (15; ellipses added), and anticipates the post-structuralist view that the gap between signified and signifier can never be wholly closed. By contrast, however, a passage in the "*Atrophied Preface*" seems to acknowledge the possibility of direct verbal recording:

There is only one thing a writer can write about: *what is in front of his senses at the moment of writing* ... I am a recording instrument ... I do not presume to impose "story," "plot," "continuity" ... Insofar as I succeed in *Direct* recording of certain areas of psychic process I may have limited function ... I am not an entertainer ... (184)

The emphasis on sensory presentations and the claim to the status of a recording instrument may initially seem to suggest a stance like that summed up in the second paragraph of Christopher Isherwood's novel *Goodbye to Berlin* (1939): "I am a camera with its shutter open, quite passive, recording, not thinking" (9). In that passage, the mind is conceived of as a lens turned outward to the physical world, registering without active thought and not turning inward to take a mental selfie (as it were); but the mention of "psychic process" indicates that the instrument here is not conceived as simply a mechanical instrument that registers external phenomena but as the node of psychological processes that may present imaginary as well as actual objects to the senses, the stuff of dreams and hallucinations as well as empirical perception. The passage suggests that it may be possible to record this in language to some degree, but only if the writer aims to seize the moment in words without too much inhibiting attention to the wider and more abstract demands of story, plot, or continuity, which may drain the moment of its intensity. This is much closer to the Beat aesthetic than the Jamesian or post-structuralist one, and both Ginsberg in his poetry and Kerouac in his prose also tried to practice it.

The rejection of story, plot, and continuity also has implications for the reader and, as it were, user of *Naked Lunch* that the "*Atrophied Preface*" draws out: "You can cut into *Naked Lunch* at any intersection point ... *Naked Lunch* is a blueprint, a How-To Book ... How-To extend levels of experience by opening the door at the end of a long hall .... Doors that only open in *Silence* ... *Naked Lunch* demands Silence from The Reader. Otherwise he is taking his own pulse ... " (187). This gives the reader a measure of freedom: it is not necessary to read the novel in a linear way; dipping into it is possible and permissible. It also presents *Naked Lunch* as a vade mecum, a self-help book to assist experiential expansion; and it finally requests the reader to stay silent, as if the book were a hushed library, to eschew imposing their own frameworks upon it, to turn off the mind and be fully open to what its words have to offer.

Conclusion: Censorship, Aesthetics, Erotics

To be fully open to what the words of *Naked Lunch* have to offer implies an eschewal of what is, in a Burrovian perspective, another kind of addictive control: censorship. This may come from outside the reader, in its many forms from punitive bans to discreet omissions from reading lists, or inside the reader, in its many forms from dropping the book in disgust to inwardly playing down its more disturbing passages. In its challenge to censorship, however, *Naked Lunch* may only be exemplifying, at an extreme, what words, in literature and life, always have the power to do anyway: topple our towers of preconceived notions and perceptions and tip us into new interzones of experience.

As the "*Atrophied Preface*" of Burroughs's novel proceeds it does indeed suggest that the nature of *Naked Lunch* is the nature of language, the Word, itself:

> The Word is divided into units which be all in one piece and should be so taken, but the pieces can be had in any order being tied up back and forth in and out fore and aft like and aft like an innaresting

sex arrangement. This book spill off the page in all directions, kaleidoscope of vistas, medley of tunes and street noises ... (191)

Here the idea that the book we are reading can be approached in any order, that it is multidirectional and offers constantly changing visions and aural mixings, combines with an implied erotics of reading in the simile of the interesting sex arrangement, which might, indeed, be a capsule description of the whole novel. It is thus hardly surprising that it has attracted the strictures of censors, whose driving obsession is often to obscure interesting sex arrangements.

Naked Lunch provides no complete and coherent aesthetics but, characteristically, inhabits an interzone between aesthetic positions, and offers, both in its explicit statements such as the one just quoted, and in its overall textual activity, fascinating aesthetic, erotic, imaginative, and visionary interanimations.

Works Cited

Burroughs, William. "Interview by Conrad Knickerbocker." In *Writers at Work: The* Paris Review *Interviews*. Secker and Warburg, 1968, pp. 141-74.

_____. "The Last European Interview." 1974. In Hibbard, pp. 80-89.

_____. *The Naked Lunch*. 1959. Corgi, 1968.

_____. *Naked Lunch*. The restored text. Edited by James Grauerholz and Barry Miles, Harper Perennial, 2005.

_____. "Talking with William S. Burroughs." 1974. Interview by William Bates et al. in *Conversations with William S. Burroughs*. Edited by Allen Hibbard, Mississippi UP, 1999, pp. 90-94.

Eliot, T. S. *The Waste Land*. In *The Complete Poems and Plays*. Book Club Associates by arrangement with Faber and Faber, 1977, pp. 59-80.

Isherwood, Christopher. *Goodbye to Berlin*. 1939. Vintage, 1998.

James, Henry. "Preface". *The American*. 1877. The Chiltern Library. John Lehmann, 1949, pp. 7-21.

Miles, Barry. *William Burroughs: El Hombre Invisible*. 1992. Virgin, 1993.

Morgan, Ted. *Literary Outlaw: The Life and Times of William S. Burroughs*. 1991. Pimlico, 1996.

Shakespeare, William. *Macbeth*. Edited by George Hunter. Penguin, 2005.

Videen, Hana. "Old English Wordhord: About." www.oldenglishwordhord. com/about.

Widsith. www.sacred-texts.com/neu/ascp/a03_11.htm.

Efforts to Ban Harper Lee's *To Kill a Mockingbird*___

Phill Johnson

Harper Lee's *To Kill a Mockingbird* has long been hailed as a classic of modern American literature. Published in 1960, *Mockingbird* was immediately and immensely popular and garnered Lee the Pulitzer Prize just one year later. Characterized as both a Southern Gothic novel and a bildungsroman, it has been a staple in school reading programs for most of its existence. But despite its stature as one of the most beloved books in the world, challenges to it being taught in schools have come regularly, sometimes as often as several times a year. In fact, just six years after publication the novel was pulled from the shelves of Virginia schools because it was deemed to be immoral and therefore unsuitable for young readers. Because of the great number of challenges to *Mockingbird*, it would be beyond the scope of this chapter to cover them all. Instead, the focus will be on challenges that took place after 2000.

Muskogee, Oklahoma, 2001

One of the earliest twenty-first century challenges to Lee's novel came during the summer of 2001 in the northeastern Oklahoma community of Muskogee. The community of nearly 40,000 residents is home to four institutions of higher education and two public school districts. *Mockingbird* came under scrutiny in one of the public school districts during its annual high school curriculum revision. During that process, a committee determined that the novel was unsuitable for the required reading list for freshman high school students. According to members of the committee, the book was not actually being banned per se, but was instead being delisted from the curriculum.

According to Muskogee High School principal Terry Saul, a panel of "teachers and administrators made the decision because the book contained derogatory and racist language that could offend African-Americans" ("High School Yanks" n.p.). Saul reported that the high school had a "59 percent African-American population" and when a school has a population that diverse it has "to be sensitive" to issues of race. ("High School Yanks" n.p.). Saul went on to say that the school wished "to develop a climate of mutual respect among all kids" and that the administrators "didn't want a book that would make students feel uncomfortable" ("High School Yanks" n.p.).

Reaction to the novel being removed from the required reading list was swift. Michael Camfield, an attorney for the American Civil Liberties Union chapter in Oklahoma, argued that "'To Kill a Mockingbird' is about as overtly anti-racist as you can get in a novel." He went on to say that he thought "the anti-racist message would be apparent to any reasonable reader" ("High School Yanks" n.p.). Joann Bell, director of the Oklahoma chapter of the American Civil Liberties Union, called the ban "ludicrous" and said "If you want to look for racism, you can find it anywhere" ("Novel Removed" n.p.). The American Library Association also chimed in when the director of their office for intellectual freedom, Judith Krug, said the book "is material that I believe can well be read in high school and what better place to talk about these kinds of issues" ("Novel Removed").

Unlike most instances when a book is challenged, in Muskogee the novel was not actually banned or even removed from the high school library. Principal Saul noted that the decision was not based upon student or parental complaints but had instead been made solely by the committee that sets curriculum for Muskogee High School students. Saul made it clear that the book was freely available to those students wanting to read it ("High School Yanks"). Despite that fact, by October of 2001 the school board voted to reverse its decision to remove *Mockingbird* from the required reading list. Commenting on the reversal, assistant principal Dan Hattaway said, "If you threw out everything that was objectionable to people, we'd be using a watered-down version or we'd all be reading Dr. Seuss" ("School Board Reinstates" 2A)

Glynn County, Georgia, 2001
The second challenge in 2001 came later in the year from the coastal area surrounding Jekyll Island in Georgia. This time the challenge

did not begin with *Mockingbird* but instead originated from parental complaints about J. D. Salinger's novel *The Catcher in the Rye*. After hearing complaints from parents, the Glynn County School Board decided to expand the ban beyond *Catcher* and began "considering a comprehensive anti-profanity policy that would ban any books, programs and activities that contain bad words" ("Glynn Board Upset" F6). That move immediately brought *Mockingbird* into the fold.

According to an Associated Press report in the *Atlanta Journal-Constitution*, board member Pat Ulmer was the first to consider removing Salinger's acclaimed novel from Glynn County schools. The article also noted that the novel was to be excluded from the high school curriculum because it "contains multiple uses of profanity and references to homosexuality and drinking alcohol" ("Glynn Board Upset" F6). Still others found the 1951 novel "offensive because of the narrator's use of profanity and his cynical, rebellious attitude" ("Barnes Dislikes" C5).

As a result of the comprehensive antiprofanity policy, *Mockingbird* soon became a part of the discussion. The blanket policy quickly drew sharp opposition. Associated Press reports from the time indicated that "150 parents, teachers and students crowded into a school board meeting" to complain about the plan ("Glynn Board Upset" F6). Many local high school teachers chimed in, asking questions such as "Who can judge what is profanity?" and "Who will decide and how will they decide?" Ingrid Metz, a Brunswick High School teacher, noted that "The Bible, Shakespeare and the dictionary all have profanity. Are we going to ban them?" Ulmer, the board member who initiated the challenge, said "such material conflicts with the state's mandated character education program, which states that '... profanity will not be used in any instructional program or activity'" ("Glynn Board Upset" F6). According to one report, however, eventually "no action was taken, and the book was retained" (Sova 277). Incidentally, this was not the first time the Glynn County Board of Education had dealt with a request to remove materials from the required reading list. In 1997, a student complained that *Catcher in the Rye* contained "690 cuss words" and said she believed she was "as qualified as anyone to judge the quality" of high school reading materials (qtd. in Cragin 7).

Normal, Illinois, 2003

Mockingbird landed on another list of so-called undesirable novels in 2003, this time in the Unit 5 school district of Normal, Illinois. Besides *Mockingbird*, the list of novels considered for removal from sophomore literature classes included John Steinbeck's *Of Mice and Men*, Mark Twain's *Adventures of Huckleberry Finn*, and Lorraine Hansberry's *Raisin in the Sun*. The objections to the novels arose based upon the number of racial slurs they contained. One complainant, Normal resident Jerry James, said, "There needs to be a lot more discussion and there needs to be different opinions discussed." James went on to say, "Nobody is willing to deal with the deep psychological issues" the books might arouse. Rozalind Hopgood, the parent of a Normal student, noted that the concerned parents had "never asked that these books be banned" but instead "asked that they be removed from the required reading list" (Loda, "Turning" A8).

The initial board meeting to discuss removal of the novels focused mostly on Steinbeck's *Of Mice and Men*, with the majority of speakers indicating they wanted the novel removed from the sophomore literature class. One parent initially complained that "it contains racial slurs, profanity and violence" and that it "does not represent traditional values, is culturally insensitive and conflicts with a board policy regarding educational materials." (Loda, "Book Battle" A1). The daughter of that parent told reporter Rebecca Loda of the *Pantagraph* that "she felt degraded by the novel and spent several weeks in the library while it was being studied in class" (Loda, "Book Battle" A1). While the majority of speakers at the board meeting opposed the novels, three Normal Community High School students spoke up in support, with one student saying "the language made her angry and is meant to be analyzed," and that "the language promotes change" (Loda, "Book Battle" A14).

In response to the parental complaints, the district formed the Unit 5 Diversity Advisory Committee. Made up of parents and community members, the committee provided alternative reading titles for students who were offended by novels such as *Mockingbird* or *Of Mice and Men*. At the same time, the committee also recommended removing certain titles from the required reading list for sophomore-level literature classes taught in the district. Of the initial list of titles, the advisory committee voted to retain *Mockingbird*, *A Raisin in the Sun*, and *Adventures of Huckleberry Finn*. For the books not recommended for retention, the group suggested alternative books be selected instead.

The district's executive director of secondary education, Bruce Boswell, said the district planned to purchase all of the recommended alternative books but that they intended to discuss the other committee recommendations. One thing everyone agreed upon was the diversity committee's recommendation that "teachers learn about diversity and sensitivity in the classroom" and that "read-along guides should be sent home while a book is being studied" (Loda, "Turning" A8).

Columbus, Indiana, 2003

A different type of challenge to *Mockingbird* came in late 2003 when a high school stage production of the novel was canceled on account of complaints. At issue was Lee's use of a racial slur, which led Columbus East High School to cancel a scheduled three-day run of the play. Oddly, the novel had been part of the school's curriculum for many years prior to the play's cancellation, as it was part of the ninth-grade required reading list. However, the Columbus-Bartholomew Chapter of the National Association for the Advancement of Colored People (NAACP) opposed it on the ground that it contained offensive racial slurs.

According to reporting by Peter Szatmary in the *Indianapolis Star*, the play director at Columbus East consulted with Gwen Higgins, president of the local chapter of the NAACP, who was "at first warily supportive" but "ultimately opposed it because of the racial slur against blacks" (Szatmary, "Reading" E1). Szatmary reported that it was unclear whether Higgins "spoke on the chapter's behalf or gave her private opinion." The NAACP had at one point "recommended modifying or eliminating the word" as administrators at Columbus East worked with them and the parents of students who would be offended by the racial epithet (Szatmary, "Reading" E1).

In an attempt to avoid canceling the play, the director of the Columbus East production initially held rehearsals without using the slur (Szatmary, "School Theater" A1). In fact, the director planned to have "onstage disclaimers, post-show discussions and classroom follow-ups," but upon requesting the change from Dramatic Publishing, the company that owned the rights to the play, their request was denied. The play's publishers, according to the *Star*, cited censorship and violation of copyright laws as reasons for their denial (Szatmary, "Reading" E5). Assistant principal Gary Goshorn, who asked the publisher for the change, said, "It would have been easy to just" put on the play as planned, "and we've found [that] some communities have" done so, but he questioned "what message that would send to the kids" (Szatmary, "Reading" E5).

After weeks of work preparing for the play, especially in building the stage, the unexpected cancellation left the Columbus East theater department scrambling to find an alternative work to perform. However, members of the local community banded together to hold a stage reading of *Mockingbird* at the Crump Theater. The group, calling themselves The Show Must Go On Productions, created the stage reading to "ensure that the individual patron of the arts has the choice to decide whether or not a play is offensive," arguing that *Mockingbird* "tackles themes of racial tolerance, gender identity, gun control and racial profiling" (Szatmary, "Reading" E5). The reading, which included black cast members, was staged on multiple nights.

Brentwood, Tennessee, 2006
In Brentwood, Tennessee, a communications glitch in early 2006 would result in an anonymous effort to remove *Mockingbird* from Williamson County Schools. The glitch in question prevented Brentwood Middle School principal Kay Kendrick from receiving

an e-mail from the parent of an eighth-grade student. According to Kendrick, neither she nor the student's teacher received the e-mail expressing the parent's desire that the student not read *Mockingbird*. The principal later stated that had either of them received the e-mail they "would have instantly pulled that student from the classroom" (Booth, "Brentwood" 7). However, because neither responded to the initial e-mail, the parent anonymously mailed a paper petition to parents asking for their support to ban the book from all Williamson County Schools.

The petition, which went out to the parents of nearly 900 students, claimed *Mockingbird* "'promotes racial hatred, racial division, racial separation and promotes white supremacy,' due to its use of racial slurs" (Booth, "Brentwood" 7). The writer of the petition also contacted the *Tennessean* with yet another anonymous statement, this time to ask why a school board would let black children read a book that the writer claimed would harm them. According to reporter Charles Booth, the statement's writer asked, "What is the motive for having an African American child read this book? Is the Board or is America trying to secretly destroy the self image, self confidence and self worth of African American children?" Furthermore, the writer alleged that "To Kill a Mockingbird can be seen as an instruction manual on racism—all in the name of 'classical literature' and it has no place in the public schools of America" (Booth, "'Mockingbird' Debate" 7).

Reaction to the petition, and especially to the anonymity of the writer, was mixed. Most disagreed with the attempt to ban the novel, and many took offense at the unsigned petition. Booth reported that "Brentwood Middle parent Jeri Daniels said what struck her about the petition was that it was unsigned," and that she thought that was "kind of chicken" (Booth, "Petition" B1). Brentwood resident Edythe Nash noted the book "could be interpreted" as racist, but she argued that its purpose was to depict a father who "is trying to teach his children that racism and discrimination and hatred is not a way that he wants them to act" (Booth, "Brentwood" 7).

This was not the first instance of a challenge to an award-winning novel dealt with by the Williamson County School Board.

Just five years earlier, there had been a challenge to Kurt Vonnegut Jr.'s National Book Award winner, *Slaughterhouse-Five* (Booth, "Brentwood" 7). In that case, the board voted to retain the novel with a 5-to-3 vote, just as it would later vote to retain *Mockingbird* in 2006. Thanks to the board's decision to retain *Mockingbird*, the Williamson County Board of Education would go on to win the SLATE Intellectual Freedom Award, which was presented by the National Council of Teachers of English, for taking a "stand in favor of classic American literature" (Giordano U3).

Cherry Hill, New Jersey, 2007

A little-reported incident that resulted in a unanimous resolution to keep *Mockingbird* in the Cherry Hill High School English curriculum occurred in the 2007 academic year when an attempt to ban *Mockingbird* came before the local board of education. According to reporter Barbara S. Rothschild of the Camden, New Jersey, *Courier-Post*, a local resident "objected to the novel's depiction of how blacks are treated by members of a racist white community" and "feared the book would upset black children reading it" (Rothschild, "Cherry Hill" 18B).

In response to the resident's complaint, the school board formed a committee that included two board members, a teacher, an assistant principal, the director of curriculum at Cherry Hill, the assistant superintendent, and the superintendent. The committee found that *Mockingbird* should remain in the curriculum and as a result the board voted 8 to 0 to retain the novel. However, the board took additional steps to ensure it was being taught in a sensitive manner. According to Rothschild, "all high school English teachers will undergo in-service training focused on the book, emphasizing sensitivity when addressing racism of any kind and better awareness of student reactions to such material" (Rothschild, "Cherry Hill" 18B).

This was not the first instance of objections to literature taught at Cherry Hill. In 1996, local residents objected to the content in *Huckleberry Finn* and the "way it was being taught in the high schools." Danny Elmore, a member of the Cherry Hill African

American Civic Association, was quoted by Rothschild as saying, "we dealt with the *Huck Finn* issue and thought it was over. It wasn't. Students are still suffering" (Rothschild, "Cherry Hill" 18B).

Brampton, Ontario, 2009

Students attending St. Edmund Campion School in Brampton, Ontario, found themselves at the center of another attempt to ban *Mockingbird*, as principal Kevin McGuire pulled the novel from their reading list in 2009 because one parent had personally complained to him. As is often the case with Lee's novel, this attempt to ban it was based upon Lee's use of a particular racial slur. The book, which was part of the Grade 10 reading list, was removed as a result of a single complaint. Ironically, Ontario education minister Kathleen Wynne saw the removal as "a great opportunity to find a Canadian novel to put on that course's reading list" ("Open Books").

Response to the Brampton ban was not much different from most attempts. One editorial writer noted "the ludicrous scenario of protecting 15-year-old Grade 10 students from a naughty word in a book when, long before they reached high school, they were well-versed in all the naughty words English has to offer" ("Open Books" n.p.). Still others reacted to the ban in a positive manner, with one person calling principal McGuire "enlightened." That person went on to say that *Mockingbird* and similar books "are outdated, racist and do not belong in school" (Keith, "Racist Reading" n.p.). Journalist Natalie Alcoba reported that "proponents [of the novel] agree it is sensitive material that requires thoughtful discussion and analysis, but not censorship, while critics say the solution is not to ban, but rather to widen the lens through which a seminal moment in civil rights history is understood" ("To Ban" n.p.).

Interestingly enough, principal McGuire banned *Mockingbird* without having the parent file a written complaint. Instead, he banned the novel based upon a single verbal objection from the parent, although the parent did indicate an intention to file a written complaint in the fall. Such a complaint would have triggered a review by the Challenged Materials Review Committee. According to the *Brampton Guardian*, that review would typically involve additional "input from board librarians, religious coordinators, trustees, and local superintendent and parents" (Belgrave, "Wrong" n.p.).

Plaquemines Parish, Louisiana, 2013

Unlike other bans and challenges mentioned in this chapter, the events that took place in Plaquemines Parish warrant discussion because a ban of *Mockingbird* was reversed after twelve years. Interestingly, members of the Plaquemines Parish School Board did not know that a ban was in place and only became aware of it when it was brought to their attention that local teachers were reading the novel to their students in violation of the 2001 edict.

Upon learning of the ban, copies of *Mockingbird* were quickly removed by the district while administrators sorted matters out. Learning of this action, the American Civil Liberties Union of Louisiana demanded the novel be returned to the classroom. According to reporting by news station WAFB, Marjorie Esman, the executive director of the ACLU of Louisiana, said the ban had "been there for quite some time" and "never should have been implemented in the first place" ("12-Year Ban" n.p.). District officials noted they "took the initial action after they received complaints from some parents who believed the material, which deals with rape and racial prejudice, was inappropriate." After looking into the matter, they said that while the book was "deemed unsuitable" in 2001, the "ban had largely gone unenforced in recent years" ("School Board Lifts Ban" n.p.). They then held a special meeting that resulted in the immediate reinstatement of *Mockingbird*. Superintendent Denis Rousselle also recommended that the board remove "any limitations on instructional materials" and implement reviews of policies and procedures for school texts and literature ("School Board Lifts Ban" n.p.)

Whether or not local teachers knew of the ban remains unclear. Some reports stated they did not know, while other reporting indicated that they were surreptitiously sidestepping the ban by quietly teaching the novel (Rawley n.p.). Esman, speaking for the ACLU, said, "obviously the teachers didn't agree with [the ban] and they've been teaching the book anyway" ("12-year Ban" n.p.).

Accomack County, Virginia, 2016

In Accomack County, Virginia, an attempt to ban both *Mockingbird* and *Adventures of Huckleberry Finn* came after a parental complaint that a racial slur appears 48 times in *Mockingbird* and 219 times in *Huck Finn*. As a result, and in accordance with the Accomack Public Schools policy manual, both titles were temporarily suspended from use in classrooms and libraries throughout the county school district. According to superintendent Chris Holland, a committee was formed to look into the complaint prior to any action being taken. That committee consisted of "the principal, the library media specialist, the classroom teacher (if involved), a parent and/or student, and the complainant" (Chesson, "Parent" A3).

Marie Rothstein-Williams, the white parent of a biracial child, initiated the complaint, saying, "there is so much racial slurs in there and offensive wording that you can't get past that." She also stated that she understood the books are literary classics, but that "at some point I feel the children will not or do not truly get the classic part" (Chesson, "Accomack" A5). A number of students and parents disagreed with her assessment of the novels and protested outside the local courthouse during a rally in support of both books. The students also gathered signatures for two separate petitions—one to reinstate both books and the other seeking a referendum to have school board officials elected rather than appointed.

The Accomack County School Board ultimately voted to return both titles to classrooms and libraries. While agreeing "that some of the language is offensive and hurtful," chairman Ronnie E. Holden went on to say that the county's "excellent teachers and media center specialists have a wonderful talent for conveying the bigger meanings and messages of literature." As a result of the challenge, Holden initiated a new process where the superintendent would have discretion to keep challenged materials in the schools until the review process was completed (Chesson, "Accomack" A5).

Biloxi, Mississippi, 2017

Without so much as a vote by the local school board, *Mockingbird* was pulled from eighth-grade English language arts classes after complaints about its language. Kenny Holloway, vice president of the Biloxi School Board, noted the decision to pull the book was the result of an "administrative and departmental decision" and "not something that the school board voted on." However, the board would soon become heavily involved as the school district became the focus of a national outcry over the decision to ban the award-winning novel.

According to Holloway, there were multiple complaints about the language used by Lee in *Mockingbird*. Noting there is "some language in the book that makes people uncomfortable," Holloway said the school district can "teach the same lesson with other books." While assuring people the book would remain in the library, he indicated that the school would indeed use another book for the course. While not mentioning *Mockingbird* by name, and seemingly sidestepping the controversial decision, superintendent Arthur McMillan also indicated that there "are many resources and materials that are available to teach state academic standards to our students." Many were not happy with the decision to pull the novel, with readers telling the Biloxi *Sun Herald* that the decision was made "mid-lesson plan, the students will not be allowed to finish the reading of 'To Kill a Mockingbird' … due to the use of the 'N' word" (Nelson, "Biloxi School District" n.p.)

It took only a matter of weeks for school officials to reverse course and reinstate the book, though with added oversight and curricular changes. Students were still able to read the novel but only after first asking to participate and with a permission slip signed by a parent. Parents were also informed that *Mockingbird* would not be on the required reading list for students but would instead be part of "an in-depth book study of the novel during regularly scheduled classes as well as the optional after school sessions." Moreover, while the intensive book study would not take place every day, principal Scott Powell indicated it would be completed in less than two months ("Mississippi School District" n.p.).

Duluth, Minnesota, 2018

Another attempt to ban both *Mockingbird* and *Adventures of Huckleberry Finn* came after years of complaints about racial slurs, this time in Minnesota. According to reporting in the Appleton, Wisconsin, *Post-Crescent*, the concerns about language in both books had been raised by parents, students, and community groups. Duluth's district director of curriculum and instruction Michael Cary reported that the "feedback that we've received is that it makes many students feel uncomfortable." The move was also said to be "part of an effort to be considerate to all students, particularly students of color." Cary also asserted that "Conversations about race are an important topic" and that the district wanted to make sure they "address those conversations in a way that works well for all of our students" ("Minnesota District" A9).

The attempt to ban *Mockingbird* at Duluth's Denfeld High School was supported by at least one English teacher. Brian Jungman, who had used the novel in his classes for years, said that he understood "that other books might resonate more with today's students." Noting that Lee wrote *Mockingbird* to "explain racism to primarily a white audience," Jungman went on to say that his school's "African-American population doesn't need to have racism explained to them." Duluth's NAACP chapter agreed with Jungman and said the curriculum change was "long overdue." Others rose to the defense of *Mockingbird*, including the National Coalition Against Censorship, which called that book and other challenged titles "literary masterpieces" and suggested "We're potentially treating students too delicately." Former student Crystal Wirtz said that she didn't "remember feeling uncomfortable while discussing the book as one of only a few African-American students in her classroom." Wirtz went on to say that her teachers "were straightforward about the language" and "made clear that it's not appropriate to use today" (Louwagie, "In Book Debate" A1).

Monona Grove, Wisconsin, 2018

Yet another challenge to *Mockingbird* would take place in 2018 as the Monona Grove School Board rejected a complaint brought by the parents of a ninth-grade student. Tujama and Jeanine Kameeta, parents of a Monona Grove High School freshman, said that Lee's novel "provides no educational value" and is itself racist "due to how themes are presented and because of its use of racial slurs." Though the Kameetas found the book suitable for library use, they deemed it inappropriate for the ninth-grade English curriculum (Rivedal, "Harper Lee" B2).

After the Kameetas filed their complaint in December of 2017, the Monona Grove School Board formed a committee to review the matter. Two months later, that committee voted 4 to 1 "to retain the novel with further examination by the English Department" (Wroge, "Board Votes" A12). After learning of the committee's vote, the Kameetas appealed the decision to the full board. In April, six of the seven members of the board met and deadlocked in a 3 to 3 vote to uphold the committee's decision. In a follow-up meeting in May, the board voted 6 to 1 to uphold the committee's decision to retain *Mockingbird*. As part of that vote, the board also allowed "the English Department to further examine the novel, the context [in which] it is taught, other equivalent readings and other ways the book could be used in class" (Wroge, "Monona Board" A4).

As is often the case, supporters for and against retaining the novel provided input during the multiple board meetings. Jeremy Duss, a Monona Grove teacher, considered it "critical that the School Board and district administrators continue to trust the English Department," arguing that their department should not be one "that bans books and avoids difficult topics." Others argued that the "School Board represents minority students along with its teachers" and that they should "empathize with the experience of students of color" (Wroge, "Board Votes" A12). Board member and associate principal James Kamoku said that although *Mockingbird* is an "awesome read," he would like to "see the number of books in the ninth grade English class that deal with issues of racism expanded" (Wroge, "Parents Appeal" B2.)

Conclusion

Challenges to *Mockingbird* have occurred regularly since shortly after its publication in 1960. Despite being hailed as one of the greatest works of twentieth-century literature, it has repeatedly been challenged, and sometimes banned, when it has been part of public school curricula. As the foregoing reports suggest, the novel has been the target of numerous challenges, mostly on account of its use of the N-word. However, its discussions of sexuality and rape have also resulted in challenges. Moreover, while many people see *Mockingbird* as an inherent indictment of racism, others argue it is racist itself, or even that it promotes racism. This argument is not all that surprising as the novel honestly and accurately portrays the ways racists typically speak. The problems *Mockingbird* raises exemplify the problems raised by many other classics of American literature.

Works Cited

"12-Year Ban on 'To Kill a Mockingbird' Lifted." WAFB-TV, 23 Oct. 2013. www.wafb.com/story/23768565/12-year-ban-on-to-kill-a-mockingbird-lifted.

Alcoba, Natalie. "To Ban a Book, To 'Erase History.'" *National Post* [Toronto, ON], 6 Oct. 2009. www.pressreader.com/canada/national-post-latest-edition/.../282746287820575.

"Barnes Dislikes Banning Books." *Atlanta Journal-Constitution*, 30. Aug. 2001, p. C5. www.newspapers.com/clip/28041456/the_atlanta_constitution.

Belgrave, Roger. "Wrong to Kill Mockingbird with Just a Single Shot." *Brampton Guardian* [Ontario], 22 Aug. 2009. www.bramptonguardian.com/opinion-story/3072185-wrong-to-kill-mockingbird-with-just-a-single-shot.

Booth, Charles. "Brentwood Buzzes Over Petition to Ban 'Mockingbird.'" *Tennesseean* [Nashville, TN], 31 Jan. 2006, pp. 1, 7. www.newspapers.com/image/277511838.

_____. "'Mockingbird' Debate Continues." *Tennessean* [Nashville, TN[, 2 Feb. 2006, pp. 1, 7, www.newspapers.com/image/276299155.

_____. "Petition: Kill 'Mockingbird' in County Schools." *Tennessean*, 28 Jan 2006, p. B1. www.newspapers.com/image/?spot=27076333.

Chesson, Hillary T. "Accomack School Board Reinstates Suspended Novels." *Daily Times* [Salisbury, MD], 8 Dec. 2016, p. A5. www. newspapers.com/image/250049489.

_____. "Parent: Books Validate Racist Words." *Daily Times* [Salisbury, MD], 2 Dec 2016, p. A3. https://www.newspapers.com/clip/25191724/the_daily_times.

Cragin, Edward J. "Down for the Count." *Atlanta Journal-Constitution*, 23 Feb. 1997, p. 7. www.newspapers.com/image/?spot=27127283.

Giordano, Maria. "'Mockingbird' Decision Wins Schoolboard an Award." *The Tennessean* [Nashville, TN], 29 Aug. 2007, p. U3, www. newspapers.com/image/278400114.

"Glynn Board Upset by 'Catcher' Words." *Atlanta Journal-Constitution*, 15 Aug. 2001, p. F6. www.newspapers.com/clip/28041310/the_ atlanta_constitution.

"High School Yanks 'Mockingbird' from Reading List." *Chicago Tribune*, 4 Aug. 2001. www.chicagotribune.com/news/ct-xpm-2001-08-04-0108040184-story.html.

Keith, Jocelyn. "Racist Reading." *The Calgary Herald* [Calgary, ON], 18 Aug, 2009. www.pressreader.com/canada/calgary-hera ld/20090818/281844344653600.

Loda, Rebecca. "Book Battle Draws Crowd." *Pantagraph* [Bloomington, IL], 9 Oct. 2003, pp. A1, A14. www.newspapers.com/image/75726683.

_____. "Turning the Page: Unit 5 Ends Book Controversy with Alternate Pick." *Pentagraph* [Bloomington, IL], 26 July 2004, pp. A1, A8. www.newspapers.com/image/75655254.

Louwagie, Pam. "In Book Debate, A Painful Turning of the Page." *Minneapolis Star Tribune*, 11 Feb. 2018, p. A1. www.newspapers. com/image/?spot=27154939.

"Minnesota District Drops 2 Classic Novels, Cite Racial Slurs." *Post-Crescent* [Appleton, WI], 9 Feb, 2018, p. A9. www.newspapers.com/clip/27155603/the_postcrescent.

"Mississippi School District to Resume Teaching 'To Kill A Mockingbird.'" *Clarion Ledger* [Jackson MS], 25 Oct. 2017. www.clarionledger. com/story/news/local/2017/10/25/mississippi-resume-teaching-to-kill-mockingbird/801212001.

Nelson, Karen. "Biloxi School District Pulls 'To Kill A Mockingbird' from Eighth-Grade Lesson Plan." *Clarion Ledger* [Jackson, MS], 13 Oct. 2017. www.clarionledger.com/story/news/local/2017/10/13/biloxi-school-district-pulls-to-kill-mockingbird-8th-grade-lesson-plan/762213001.

"Novel Removed from Reading List." *NewsOK.com*, 3 Aug. 2001. newsok.com/article/2750367/novel-removed-from-reading-list.

"Open Books, Open Minds." *Calgary Herald* [Calgary, ON], 16 Aug. 2009. www.pressreader.com/canada/calgary-herald/20090816/281736970470018.

Rawley, Joe. "'To Kill a Mockingbird' Banned in Plaquemines Parish." WGNO-TV, 16 Oct. 2013. www.wgno.com/2013/10/16/to-kill-a-mockingbird-banned-in-plaquemines-parish.

Rivedal, Karen. "Complaint: Harper Lee Classic 'Provides No Educational Value.'" *La Crosse Tribune* [La Crosse, WI], 26 Jan. 2018, p. B2. www.newspapers.com/image/516789572.

Rothschild, Barbara S. "Cherry Hill to Keep Book in Curriculum." *Courier Post* [Camden, NJ], 24 Jan. 2008, p. 18B. www.newspapers.com/clip/27133143/courierpost.

"School Board Lifts Book Ban, Reinstates 'To Kill a Mockingbird.'" WDSU-TV, 22 Oct. 2013. www.wdsu.com/article/school-board-lifts-book-ban-reinstates-to-kill-a-mockingbird/3366543.

"School Board Reinstates 'To Kill a Mockingbird." *Baltimore Sun*, 11 Oct. 2001, p. 2A. www.newspapers.com/image/377858480.

Sova, Dawn B. *Literature Suppressed on Social Grounds*. Rev. ed., Facts on File, 2006.

Szatmary, Peter. "Reading Addresses Controversy." *Indianapolis Star*, 30 Jan. 2004, pp. E1, E7. www.newspapers.com/image/127325765.

_____. "School Theater Walking Fine Line." *Indianapolis Star*, 17 Oct. 2003, pp. A1-A11. www.newspapers.com/image/127285441.

Wroge, Logan. "Board Votes to Retain 'Mockingbird.'" *Wisconsin State Journal* [Madison, WI], 11 May 2018, p. A12. www.newspapers.com/image/431274342.

_____. "Monona Board Votes to Retain 'To Kill a Mockingbird.'" *Wisconsin State Journal* [Madison WI], 10 May 2018, p. A4. www.newspapers.com/clip/27869339/wisconsin_state_journal.

_____. "Parents Appeal Decision That Would Keep 'Mockingbird' in Curriculum." *La Crosse Tribune* [La Crosse, WI], 16 Mar. 2018, p. B2. www.newspapers.com/clip/27868697/the_la_crosse_tribune.

To Kill a Mockingbird in Columbus, Indiana: A Community Divided_____

Robert C. Evans

It began innocently enough: a high school in Columbus, Indiana announced, in the fall of 2003, a planned production of Christopher Sergel's play based on *To Kill a Mockingbird*, the famous novel by Harper Lee first published in 1960 that became a popular movie in 1962. By 2003, both the novel and the film were considered American classics, and the dramatic adaptation had been performed countless times. Columbus East High School's theater department, intent on raising funds for a prestigious forthcoming trip to Scotland, decided that Sergel's play would be a surefire moneymaker. The English department announced plans to have students read the novel that fall. "After the students read the book," said an article published on September 29 in Columbus's excellent local newspaper, the *Republic*, "they will have the chance to see the play. The community should feel proud of East's Theatre Troupe's immense achievement. To be accepted to attend the Fringe Festival [in Edinburgh, Scotland] so many months in advance is a very extraordinary occurrence" ("Theatre Department" 10).

Everything seemed propitious. The students were excited; the set was nearly finished; rehearsals had begun. But then, the following week, the *Republic* published this brief, cryptic notice: "Columbus East High School's fall drama production, 'To Kill a Mockingbird,' has been canceled. ... 'We regret any inconvenience to our patrons,' said East drama director Janelle Runge" ("East's Play" A8). Three sentences: that was it. What had happened? A lengthy article published the next day (October 8) bore this headline: "School Cancels Play Due to Slur / NAACP Unhappy with Language in 'To Kill a Mockingbird'" (Werner, "School Cancels" A1). According to reporter Nick Werner, Gwen Wiggins, an official of the local chapter of the National Association for the Advancement of Colored People (NAACP), said Janelle Runge, an East drama teacher, called her late last month for advice on how to handle the word "nigger" in the script. "I told her I could not give her permission to call any of the students using that word," Wiggins said. Parents of black actors had told Wiggins their children were uncomfortable when white students used the slur to refer to them, she said. "I know for sure they would've had a hard time finding a black person to play the role of Tom Robinson [a black character unjustly accused of raping a white woman]," Wiggins said. "There are too many incidents in school every day where students say nigger."

The drama department called Dramatic Publishing, which owns rights to the play, asking the company for permission to change the word to a less offensive one. Dramatic Publishing refused, Wiggins said, and East canceled the play. Columbus East Assistant Principal Gary Goshorn said the school ... did not want students to become part of a racial or political controversy. ("School Cancels" A9)

Thus began (ironically enough) a racial and political controversy that deeply divided the community and drew national attention. It would quickly grow and deepen, leaving the community shaken and somewhat embarrassed. Paradoxically, the school's desire to forestall conflict had inadvertently created one.

The *Republic* was the sort of publication that seems rarer and rarer these days in small-town America. It printed numerous articles, letters to the editor, and editorials on the *Mockingbird* dispute, thus providing probably one of the fullest records ever amassed, in one place, of how diversely communities can react when issues of race, censorship, and alleged book bannings arise. Over ensuing months, many citizens would be heard from. Many articulate arguments would be offered. The play, as it happens, *would* eventually be performed—but not at the high school—and community forums would allow people to talk to one another face to face, not merely in letters to the editor. My purpose in this essay is to survey at least part of the published record. Practically every imaginable point of view was expressed, and often the personal experiences recounted were forceful and moving. The debates in Columbus in 2003 epitomize similar debates before then and later.

Many Opinions

Nick Werner's article continued to quote assistant principal Goshorn, who said "I'm just not sure this is the right time to put the play on." But Werner also quoted sophomore Mark Presto, who had been working on the set, and who thought "the language would have been suitable for the audience. 'Maybe younger kids won't understand, but teenagers like us should,'" Presto commented. Gwen Wiggins, of the NAACP, said that she herself had "enjoyed reading the play but worried it would set a bad example for the school. 'They are going to think, "If you can do it in the play, then you can do it outside the play,"' she said. Wiggins said "she appreciated East speaking with the NAACP but wished the school corporation would alter its high school required literature, which includes 'To Kill a Mockingbird' and 'Huckleberry Finn.' 'There are better books about African-American history and literature,' she said" (Werner, "School Cancels" A9).

It did not take long for other local people to respond. *The Republic* itself, on October 9, editorialized that the play's cancellation amounted to "a failure of leadership" by both the school board and the NAACP and accused school officials of having chosen "the path of least resistance." The editors thought audiences could have been prepared for the play's "impact." The newspaper conceded that the N-word "is especially troubling and even traumatic to many black people" and that to "some degree, school officials" must "be sensitive to the feelings of students and parents. But they are also," the editors continued, "responsible for exposing [students] to a diverse education." The school, the paper suggested, could have held

> a panel discussion before each performance to talk about the play and its content, emphasizing the time frame in which the original material was written and how it came to play a critical role in the civil rights movement. It is not just the hundreds of hours spent in preparing for this production that were lost. Far more important was the knowledge that this play could have imparted to people of all colors. ("Killing Play" A4)

Here and in other responses to the controversy, the newspaper tried to suggest compromise.

An article by Werner ("Cancellation" A1, A9), also published on October 9, quoted the playwright's grandson, Chris Sergel III, vice president of the company that had denied permission to alter the play's dialogue. Sergel (surely reluctant to set any such precedent) said, "'I wish they would produce the show as it is. ... It's a very strong show" and its message "'needs to be heard.'" According to Werner, Sergel felt "that removing the word would soften the script's portrayal of racism. 'The fact that this word is uncomfortable doesn't make it go away,'" Sergei said.

School administrators, however, seemed eager to move on. According to Werner, "East officials have said the community is unfairly turning the cancellation into an issue of racism and censorship" ("Cancellation" A1):

> The dispute between play supporters and opponents, ... Goshorn said, is an example of why the school canceled "To Kill A Mockingbird" in the first place. "It was never the intent to try to make the theater department the focus of a controversy," he said. "We were caught in the middle between two extremes." Continuing the play without NAACP support, Goshorn said, would cause an even bigger uproar, an uproar the [school's theater] troupe could not afford, because it is in the middle of efforts to raise about $100,000 for a trip to perform in Scotland this summer. "If we erred, we erred on the side of trying to be collaborative with a group we were working with," he said. ("Cancellation" A9)

Werner noted that according to Sergel, "260 amateur theaters, including Decatur Central High School in Indianapolis, have produced 'To Kill a Mockingbird' in the past three years." Werner added that

> Will Wilson, a black Decatur Central senior, played Tom Robinson, a black man wrongly accused of raping a white woman in the play. He said the story, despite its language, is a lesson about acceptance. "It's a play, and it's telling a story," he said. "You have to understand that it's a production and what's coming out is not the feeling of

the actors." One local black activist agrees. Paul Jones, co-founder of Addressing Columbus Cultural Education and Promoting Trust, said communities must acknowledge racism and slurs to defeat them. "I'm kind of angry about it being shut down," he said. "It's part of the play, and you got to hear that stuff for people to feel the pain and start healing." ("Cancellation" A9)

Jones eventually played a major role (in several senses of that term) in attempting to help the community deal with the controversy. His status as a respected black leader was significant. In the meantime, Werner added further details, noting that the school board,

> which was not involved in the decision to cancel the play, has struggled to take a stance. Member Billie Whitted said she was disappointed and Russell Barnard said the cancellation seemed like an overreaction. Mindy Lewis, however, said she supported East's decision. The decision has been made in "the best interest of what's important for the school population and community as a whole," she said. "So let's respect that decision and move on." ("Cancellation" A9)

Werner closed by reporting that "Fabulous Fifties Affair," a murder mystery set in the 1950s, would be the substitute production but was expected to bring in only half of the profits the school had expected from *Mockingbird* ("Cancellation" A9).

An article by Jerry Battiste, published in the same issue as Werner's, reported that local libraries carried "multiple copies" of Lee's novel and that librarians said "no one has ever complained." The book had been the focus of recent community readings, and librarians reported no "fallout from the decision." Yet although Vicki Butz, one librarian, reported receiving no complaints, she admitted that "the library tried to avoid controversy. 'We really didn't try to emphasize the racial aspect ... because there are so many other positive aspects to focus on, like friendship, family and community,' she said" (Battiste A9). The librarians noted that the novel, popular among patrons, was borrowed frequently and without complaint.

Harry McCawley, an editor at *The Republic*, raised an interesting concern in an October 9 column. He reported that a prominent local businessman had recently warned that Columbus risked economic decline if businesses considered the local school system weak. McCawley used this concern to attack what he perceived as censorship of *Mockingbird*. He called the play's cancellation "a defeat for everybody," especially "bitter foes of racism. The play should not only be staged, but ... should be required reading" for all students in Columbus." However, it "should not be offered in English literature but in American history," he said, because he thought Lee had exposed the ugly realities of racial prejudice. Expressing an opinion that would soon be frequently echoed, he wrote that the "book was set in the South in the early 20th century," when "'nigger' was commonly used to describe black people. To have replaced it with any other word would have been to tell a lie. It is awful," McCawley continued, "but people need to know that there were awful times and awful people in this country. That we have come so far from the time in which that word was so common," he thought, "is something to be celebrated. Most importantly, it is something to never forget" (McCawley, "Cruel Word" A4).

Letters, Letters, and More Letters
Now that local leaders had started to have their say, letters to the editor began arriving. In fact, the letters provide some of the most interesting of all responses, partly because of their sheer diversity in viewpoints, attitudes, evidence, and tones. On October 11, for example, Roma Downen said it "would be a gracious gesture" if the NAACP, along with Wiggins, Goshorn, and a few others "responsible for stopping the presentation of the play ... would make a generous contribution to the Scotland trip fund." She wondered why no objections had been raised until so recently, especially since the play had been "selected and approved in May." And then she expressed an opinion that others would later challenge: "Columbus has a reputation as a warm, welcoming ethnic community," adding that "something like this can change the climate very quickly. We must realize we cannot change history by banning plays, books or

cultural arts in general. The students read this book in school, so I believe they are aware of the offensive word already. And it is," she conceded (as did practically everyone else) "an offensive word," although she thought that "in the context of the play it has a place" (Downen B5). As will soon be seen, some letter writers argued that black students were indeed familiar with the offensive word, not simply from reading it in books but from hearing it spoken derisively in classrooms, hallways, and locker rooms and while playing sports.

But Downen's letter was just one of *many* published on October 11. A letter written by Nioka Wiggins claimed that Columbus had long had real problems with race relations, saying the city was "stuck in a time zone" in that respect. The cancellation, she said, "was made by the Columbus East Theater department, not by the NAACP." She advised the school to "find another play to do and get over it. The form of non-support by the NAACP was based on the fact of racial tensions that has [sic] been in the Columbus high schools here recently, and if you want to get down to it, the racial tensions has [sic] been going on forever and a day" (B5).

A letter from Page Gifford, also published on October 11, asserted that the "NAACP is correct. The work does contain racial slurs. That's the point! But that's not what it's about." Gifford argued that the play's purpose is to *attack* prejudice, not endorse it—a common argument in ensuing weeks. Gifford, like many later letter writers, accused the NAACP of censorship (B5). Sally Van Dyk also regretted the play's cancellation. She argued that although some people may have learned bigotry from some American classics, they would probably have become bigots no matter what they read. Van Dyk felt that many more readers had probably learned from such books "how not to think, speak and treat people of colors different than their own." She thought the "play should be performed ... to show what once was and, hopefully, will never be again." And then, in an especially interesting passage, she wrote that her "grandfather lived in the deep South for many years, and I heard many things from him that I wish I had not heard. I had negative pictures of black people imprinted on my mind at a very young age. Books such as 'To Kill a Mockingbird' later helped to alter my thinking about racial differences" ("No" B5) his was one of the first—and also one of the briefest—examples of letter writers describing how their own lives had affected their attitudes. Most writers rooted their arguments in abstract principles (such as opposition to censorship or concern about students' feelings). But a few writers spoke movingly and intriguingly from very personal points of view. In contrast, a few others, such as Larry E. Arnolt of Yelm in Washington state, were less reflective and thoughtful. Arnolt merely urged local opponents of the production to "get your head out of the sand" (B5). Not the most helpful contribution, but at least evidence that news about the controversy had now spread to the West Coast and throughout the rest of the nation.

Some letters reiterated points already made by others. Thus Kelly J. Branum recounted being required to read *Mockingbird* in school and how she "learned a lot from its message." Branum thought the NAACP should be proud that such a story "was still taught because the book could teach tolerance": "The NAACP" should support the play and "anyone trying to spread its message." It should not oppose the play over "a few words that are just what they are, words." Why, she wondered, didn't "the NAACP boycott MTV or BET cause [sic] I guarantee you will hear ... 'nigger' or 'nigga' a hundred times in one day" (B5). This point would also be made and addressed by other writers.

In the meantime, Georgeanna Dent added a few new details about local conditions, explaining that as "the dance teacher at Columbus East," she knew about recent

> racially motivated incidents ... at both [local] high schools. And while the administration and the NAACP acted with the best of intentions, I believe they are misguided. The messages that I remember from "To Kill A Mockingbird" are that only ignorant people use ... "nigger" and that one should do what is right, even when it is not popular. These are messages that I would have thought that the administration and the NAACP would not only endorse, but embrace. Other schools outside of [Columbus] were scheduled to attend performances .... Clearly, they realized an important learning opportunity was being presented. These messages cannot be learned if they are not allowed

to be taught. *We will continue to experience unrest in our community* if we do not address racial issues directly and stop trying to be so politically correct. (B5; italics mine)

The fact that other local schools saw no problem with the play was a fact that later letter writers—and even the African American head of such a school—would mention when defending the now-cancelled production.

Two more letters published on October 11 added to the discussion. Thus Joetta Fee echoed Harry McCawley's warning that if Columbus schools were considered inferior, the local economy might suffer. But she also wondered how many students wanted to abandon the production and how many local black residents had been "consulted prior to the leader of the NAACP speaking on their behalf." Fee said she did not "assume that the entire African American community" agreed with the cancellation, especially since individuals have individual opinions (B5). Finally, Denise Goodin wrote that she would "never forget the impact" *Mockingbird* had had on her "when I was a student at Columbus High School. The use of racially derogatory language made me wince, but sparked some lively discussion in the classroom about real issues that should matter to all of us—morality, compassion, injustice, alienation, courage, and of course, prejudice. ... The lessons still ring in my ears" (B5). But for every seemingly persuasive point made by any single letter writer, there would be an opposite plausible point made by another. If nothing else, the debate showed (and still shows) how difficult making rational, principled decisions can be when rational principles sometimes conflict.

Yet More Letters (and Articles, Editorials, and Columns)
When one reads the many letters citizens wrote, one often feels genuine respect for these people. Despite often disagreeing strongly and often talking past one another (few minds were probably changed), they were frequently intelligent, well-spoken, and *thoughtful* (which is something different from mere intelligence). For example, Tom Lane, on October 14, eloquently argued for more

dialogue and less debate. Debaters, he said, feel (and want to feel) right, but dialogue means being genuinely open to considering others' opinions. Debate is combat; dialogue is conversation (A4).

In fact, desire for dialogue encouraged several local theater people to announce a stage reading of the suppressed play. On October 15, Nick Werner reported that Sharon Blackerby, Suzette Holmes, and Andrew Ranck had formed an ad hoc production company called "The Show Must Go On" and were planning a full-scale reading of the drama (featuring numerous actors), "with proceeds going to the East drama department": "Ranck said [that] by staging a reading," the group would make it possible for "Columbus residents ... to decide for themselves about whether the script is offensive. The reading" would "not include a set or costumes," but the producers hoped "to include student actors from East in roles they would [originally] have played" ("Troupe" A1). But the producers weren't entirely optimistic, saying they would "cancel the reading if they" could not "find black actors to play black roles" (10). Apparently, however, finding African American actors was not a problem: the stage reading *did* eventually take place and ran for many nights. Not all local African Americans, apparently, agreed with the NAACP.

Before the show "went on," however, the debate continued. Nancy Warren on October 15 expressed "sadness and distress" that the controversy had apparently "opened old wounds of racism and, perhaps, fueled ... new ones." But then she remembered "that, throughout history, meaningful and lasting changes have begun in the midst of controversy and conflict." She had, she said, always considered herself unprejudiced,

> but I could not pass [a simple] test. Ask yourself the question: "In this culture, would I want to be anything other than white?" The answer will give you the truth about yourself. That level of honesty can begin the process toward healing, respect and acceptance among people of all skin colors. The work of changing and healing is ours, light skin and dark skin alike. Only when we are willing to see past the color to the soul ... will we recognize the oneness which we share. (A4)

Warren's striking letter was soon followed by a new opinion piece by Harry McCawley, the *Republic*'s associate editor. He hoped there would be a full cast for the planned public reading. Especially interesting, however, was his assessment that the play had

> become a lightning rod. Some might say it has divided the community, and there are those who say that it has divided the black community. If it has, think of the courage it would take for a black person to step forward and agree to a part in which another actor would call them a nigger. It would not just be the sting that word would have (even if used in a performing format) but the act of stepping outside a group which feels very deeply about the word. Some might choose to call it an act of betrayal. Let us hope we are not that divided. I don't think we are. I don't think all blacks in this community march in lockstep with one another just as I don't believe all whites are cloned from the same source. I think there are blacks and whites who are intelligent enough to see that this particular work of art now must be performed before a Columbus audience. ("Now" A4)

McCawley also confirmed an impression many will probably share:

> I have never seen more candid thoughts expressed as have appeared in letters to the editor this past week. They're not just the thoughts of ignorant rednecks or angry brothers and sisters, but they are the honest and repressed opinions of people with good intentions .... ("Now" A4)

McCawley thought the "school corporation should embrace this production. For that matter, so should the NAACP. And no one should be concerned about what others might think if they take part in the production" ("Now" A4). Apparently (since the show *did* go on over many nights), the producers were able to fill all the slots available for black characters with black actors. That fact alone says much about the sheer diversity of opinion about the play, even within the African American community.

Unfortunately, Andrew Ranck, a producer of the show, published a letter containing some possibly regrettable language. After celebrating literature's power to transport people to new imaginative places, he called it a "shame" that "because of *a few misguided souls*, 46 students and a city of 40,000" would miss "an instructive journey to the not-so-distant past of the Deep South circa 1932" (my italics). Ranck was "shocked that a school system which tried to teach me right from wrong through similar examples is now burying this vital message" (A4). Presumably the "few misguided souls" were either the NAACP, the school administrators, or both. Calling them "misguided souls," however, might not have done real justice to their genuine concerns and good faith. In this controversy, few if any villains (or misguided souls) can be found. If villains *had* been easily visible, the whole controversy would have been much simpler. Instead, *both* sides made valuable points.

Ironically (in light of Ranck's letter) the *Republic* soon called it "critical that [the] Community get past any us-against-them attitudes" (4). The paper also said that the planned stage reading had "already generated significant [community] support." The paper said Ranck and the other "organizers wisely" stressed that their play was not "a slap at the NAACP, the school corporation or any individuals … personally offended" by "racial language in a public setting." The producers had also offered students from the original cast "first preference on the roles they had in the school play." According to the *Republic*'s editorial, the producers had also

> gone to lengths in reaching out to the local black community to support and participate in the production. The community reaction to the original cancellation has, for the most part, facilitated that effort. The vast majority of the critics have stayed away from personal attacks on any one individual and also have emphasized the positive message in the play rather than slip into racial stereotyping. Yet much remains to be done in staging this production in a way that it could be presented to a universal audience rather than wind up with a whites-only crowd. Some have suggested that a panel discussion be included as part of the production, and that would certainly add to the educational element. But the dialogue that has already begun should be ongoing up to and even after the restaging. ("Restaging" A4)

Apparently the staged reading *did* receive community support. A theater was quickly found; auditions were announced; local feedback was called "positive"; "about a dozen phone calls" offered the producers thanks and support; and several "businesses and individuals ... offered to help pay for production costs" (see Werner, "Crump to Host" 10).

Letters and columns continued to express varied opinions. Sharon Drach Mangas, a community columnist and one-time teacher, recounted how she had once tried to share *To Kill a Mockingbird* with a "recalcitrant student" (who promptly dropped Mangas's class). Mangas said that although she had "read many controversial books," she "never thought 'To Kill a Mockingbird' would be tossed on the bonfire," especially in view of its "prevailing message" "of tolerance, standing up for what you believe in and, oh, a little bit of redemption and forgiveness, too" (B5). A long, intriguing letter by Brenda Pitts and Dennis Roberts, published on October 22, stated that although both writers were African Americans "and members of the local ... NAACP," both were also "independent thinkers who evaluate all information presented to us and then form an opinion" (A4). Even in the already relatively civilized discussion that had been going on in the pages of the *Republic*, this letter was exceptionally rational in attitudes and tone. Pitts and Roberts counseled everyone to try to truly understand each other's opinions, not simply insist on being "right." Then they offered their own insights:

> We believe that one side of the situation, censorship, has been explored very well. However, the other side, trying to understand the feelings of some of the African Americans in our community and the reasons for those feelings, has not been explored very well. In fact, we see very little interest expressed in trying to understand the strong feelings within the African American community regarding this issue. Citizens who have never walked in our shoes have been so busy trying to tell us how we are to think that they have not thought to ask us. Quite frankly, we resent being told how we are to think and then being degraded for daring to be different and not going along with the majority. We thought this whole censorship issue was about the freedom to express ourselves.

A few sentences later, they continued:

> It is difficult for many African Americans to worry about censorship when their basic need for being treated with dignity and respect goes unmet. Many feel that they live, work and go to school in an environment that is hostile and unreceptive to listening to their needs. In fact, many of our children have had to face not only being called derogatory names such as the n-word in school but having to sit through discussions of books and plays that focused on that word and where their classmates used this as an opportunity to degrade them further. Before we argue about our right to do a play, why not first try to understand why some people are so opposed to this play? Some of the questions we should explore are: What were the purpose and criteria for selecting this particular play? If we are attempting to create understanding of racism, what other alternatives were explored? Given the school system has a tolerance policy that forbids the use of derogatory language, particularly the n-word, what is their policy on teaching literature that includes derogatory language? What has been the experience of teenage African Americans in the community and school and how do they feel about their school producing a play that contains derogatory language and how do they feel about appearing in such a play? In our opinion, rushing to produce this play in our community only affirms the right of the majority to do what they want to do. (A4)

This was an exceptionally long letter. No paraphrase or series of lengthy quotations can do it justice. It ended not only with some concrete suggestions for improving local race relations but also with a tone of genuine civility:

> Again, thanks for the opportunity to present another perspective on this controversy and thanks to those who have taken the time to try to understand both sides of this issue and are interested in healing the wound that is festering currently in our community. (4)

Other letters added few new insights, although an intriguing column by John Clark did raise some interesting questions:

Sure, "To Kill a Mockingbird" has a powerful, positive message and carries a vital insight into the minds of certain people at a certain time. But it also carries that word, and it is a word that would be said by our public schoolchildren on a public-owned stage. No one said so, but the worry of a slippery slope has to play into this discussion. If you approve of the artistic kids using the word in a play, how do you stop the pranksters from using it as a joke? And then how do you keep the locker room bullies from using it "all in fun" and the bigots from spray-painting it on a locker? (A4)

Clark felt middle-class whites should not "get to decide for everyone else what is offensive or what is not. ... Only a black person," he continued,

gets to decide when and if he is offended by the "N" word; and a Gentile can't decide that Jews shouldn't be offended by a caricature. If you are in doubt about whether a broad-brush comment on another race, religion or ethnicity is out of bounds, then it probably is. And if you are still in doubt, go try it out on a few of your closest black or Jewish friends to test the waters. If you don't have a close black or Jewish friend, I think you already know the answer to your question. (A4)

More and more opinions similar to Clark's now began to appear. One especially moving piece came from Pat McClendon and was published on October 23. It argued that "there are many citizens of Columbus who do not understand the pain ... associated with using or hearing the 'N' word" (A5). McClendon offered a list of points to consider:

1. As a parent, I had to prepare my children from the age of 5 on how to handle a situation when called a "N." As a parent did you have to destroy the innocence of one of your babies in order to protect them? To give them an action plan for their safety when confronted?

2. As a parent, have you had to wipe away the tears and soothe the soul of a young child the first time they are called a "N"? I have. In 1989 not 1968, my oldest daughter was sent home from

a neighborhood birthday party. (The invitations had been handed out at school.) The mother said, "I don't allow "n....." to play with my children or be in my home. You have to leave." So my beautiful and loving child walked home crying and heartbroken while her friends remained at the birthday party. The mother wouldn't even let her call me. The word "N" excludes, hurts and starts the division in children that becomes the huge wall of racism that becomes too wide to cross.

3. Have you had to explain to your high school senior why some students in her American History class when given specific instructions NOT to read the "N" word out loud (*Huckleberry Finn, To Kill a Mockingbird*) but to change it to Negro, can't seem to do it? Who blurt out the "N" word during their reading and then look over at her to see her reaction, the only black student in the class, all the while laughing under their breath. (2003)

4. What about during athletic competition? Ask some of the past Central football players who had to play Martinsville about the "N" word on the football field. Ask any Black athlete in Columbus their experience in athletics and the use of the "N" word.

5. Every time the word is used, said or discussed, I can recall the first time I was called a "n....B." As a result, you work and pray not to hate. You teach your children not to hate. You teach your children not to make distinctions based on skin color or ethnic background but on the content of a person's character because it is the right thing to do even when it doesn't feel fair to them or you.

These are just a few insights. Don't be fooled into thinking that they are isolated incidents. Don't think the use of the word stopped with the end of slavery or the Civil Rights era. Every parent who has a Black child knows even today they must prepare their children for this ugly attack on their character and self-esteem but still prays it never happens. So when given a choice as Ms. Wiggins was to voice her opinion about the use of the word in a play, she chose not to condone its use. Not because "To Kill a Mockingbird" is not a great play or book but because we as a society can not yet handle the issues the novel and play confront. Because as demonstrated by the example above, some high school students are not mature enough to handle the subject in a classroom let alone in a play for the public. Because some American citizens are still practicing passive racism by not speaking out against the use of the "N" word just because they don't use the word themselves. The "N" word and all it represents is like the Berlin wall, until it is totally torn down, eradicated and no longer used, it will always be a barrier to the true brother and sister relationship God intended for us. (A5)

Of all the letters the controversy generated, this one may be the most heartfelt and moving.

Further Responses and a Stunning Revelation

On October 23, Sharon Blackerby, one producer of the planned show, thanked locals for their "enthusiastic response." But she warned about the dangers of the N-word, whether used by whites about blacks or by blacks about each other. She also noted that a week earlier "Eastern Oklahoma State College performed 'To Kill A Mockingbird.' The Friday night performance," she said, "was sponsored by the NAACP." From this, Blackerby concluded that "[a]pparently, theirs is an optimistic community"—as Columbus could also be (A5). David A. Moore, on the same day, recognized the N-word's dangers if commonly used but cautioned against censoring it from an antiracist play. He regretted that a "handful of people" had succeeded in getting the play cancelled (A5). Kate Craig, also on October 23, opined that only the illiterate or biased could object to the play (A5), while Roberta J. Irwin compared the cancellation to Nazi book-burning (A5). On October 24, Joseph Nuby observed that despite claims for *Mockingbird*'s beneficial effects, it had "been out for many years" and had "not done any good yet." Nuby suggested, instead, that residents should "do something about the [biased] legal system here." He recalled that as a student he "did not want to read" books like *Mockingbird*, "and my kids do not either" and suggested that if locals "really want something done about the racism maybe they should read a book from the black point of view." Instead, "people who have never and aren't currently living through being black in this town or country [are] telling us how we feel" (5). Alternatively, Tom Lane counseled readers not to lose touch "with the beauty of simply being an aware and alive human" (A5).

But a letter from a white woman, Sally Van Dyk of Columbus, responded directly to the moving letter from Pat McClendon (already quoted), which Van Dyk found "painful to read." Van Dyk, who had written a previous letter opposing the cancellation, now added some new, shocking, and quite personal information:

> My mother and grandparents lived in the deep South and were fully indoctrinated by southern whites in the use of the "n" word and anything else that displayed hatred for black people. My grandfather, I learned a few years ago, took part in the angry mob hanging of a black man. I spent my young life adoring my grandfather, who never used language or displayed hatred of blacks where his grandchildren could see or hear it. To me, he was just my wonderful grandpa. Learning of that part of his life served two purposes. One was to destroy many of the images I had of my grandfather. The other was to strengthen my resolve to not be like him. The hatred my grandfather had for blacks was born of hatred shared by hundreds of thousands of angry, bigoted, prejudiced white people who had been taught hatred by their parents, who had, in turn, been taught by their parents. Prejudice and bigotry can stop only when the teaching of it stops. That teaching in my family stopped with me. I know my children are only a tiny part of the populace, but they will teach their children and their grandchildren will teach their children. Maybe, someday, no one will ever know what bigotry was. In the meantime, my thinking about "To Kill a Mockingbird" remains the same. While I will never understand the hatred white people have for black people, or blacks for whites, only education will, I believe, some day put an end to racial injustice. Education works both ways, too. Blacks need to teach their children that many whites harbor no ill feelings toward them and that whites today should not be held responsible for the actions of their ancestors. One means of educating is to show how things once were and how they still are too many. Burying our heads in the sand or sweeping racism under the rug will not make it go away. Instead, I would hope those attending the play would watch and truly see, listen and truly hear what hatred is about and choose not to be part of it. ("Eradicating" B6)

Inevitable limitations of space prevent much further quotation from letters, but anyone interested in the controversy should certainly read Carl Moore's passionate account of his own experience with racial discrimination. He noted that in 1968 he "was drafted, fought in Vietnam but couldn't eat in restaurants back home." He observed that in *Mockingbird*, the falsely accused black man winds up dead even though his innocence was proved. No matter how hard Atticus Finch's life was (Moore noted), Robinson's was worse. Moore also commented that he had been hearing "that the kids today don't even care that much and the [N] word is dead. My youngest son plays football at Northside Middle School; every day he tells me just how much that word is alive and well in their locker room. So don't worry about the freedom of speech for our kids; their parents are passing it on so very well." But then Moore ended with a striking story of his own:

> When I was a little boy I was laughing at another child who had gotten hurt and was crying, and I called him a sissy and told him to "get over it." My grandfather who was standing by came over and kicked me in the shin. When I started to cry he said "never tell a hurt man how to holler." It is easy to say get over it if you have never felt the pain. For all of those who only saw the glory of the book, the magnificence of the writing: you have never felt the pain. (B6)

Conclusion
Let me end with just one more letter from among many more. This one, published on October 25, was from Buddy King, an African American who wrote as follows:

> The story I would like to write someday is about what happened to me, growing up in Columbus, as a colored boy. When I write that story it must contain the so-called "offensive language" of my experiences. How else would my story be correct or inclusive? So [Harper Lee] was simply "telling it like it was." The story would have no purpose otherwise. (B5)

"Following generations," he thought, "would have no accurate accounting of what it was like to be colored in that time and culture" if Lee had *not* used the N-word (B5). King advised everyone, black and white, to focus on the present and future rather than the past: "let the story stand. Our youths will learn something about our history they need to know. In the learning they will likely not repeat the problem. If we allow them to be informed and show them that our own prejudices are more of a problem than stories like Ms. Lee's, we can get on with living and loving" (B5).

The debate continued for many more weeks. There is no way, here, to include all the evidence. In letting Buddy King have the last word, so to speak, I don't mean to imply that I necessarily agree with his position. In fact, my experience of reading *all* the letters, articles, and columns has left me feeling much less certain of my own opinions than I was when I began this project. And perhaps that is a good thing. Perhaps that is one of the real values of hearing as many sides as possible of any issue. Perhaps, when we do so, we realize that there are more ideas worth considering than simply our own.

Works Cited or Consulted

Arnolt, Larry E. "Depiction of Bigotry." *Republic* [Columbus, IN], 11 Oct. 2003, p. B5.

Battiste, Jerry. "'To Kill a Mockingbird' Favored at Nearby Libraries." *Republic* [Columbus, IN], 9 Oct. 2003, p. A9.

Blackerby, Sharon. "Be Optimistic about Community, It's People." *Republic* [Columbus, IN], 23 Oct. 2003, p. A5.

Branum, Kelly J. "Harmful Approach." *Republic* [Columbus, IN], 11 Oct. 2003, p. B5.

Clark, John. "It's Not for Us to Decide." *Republic* [Columbus, IN], 22 Oct. 2003, p. A4.

Craig, Kate. "Wake Up, People." *Republic* [Columbus, IN], 23 Oct. 2003, p. A5.

Dent, Georgeanna. "Misguided Action." *Republic* [Columbus, IN], 11 Oct. 2003, p. B5.

Downen, Roma. "Students Need Support." *Republic* [Columbus, IN], 11 Oct. 2003, p. B5.

"East's Play Canceled." *Republic* [Columbus, IN], 7 Oct. 2003, p. A8.

Fee, Joetta. "Freedom Denied." *Republic* [Columbus, IN], 11 Oct. 2003, p. B5.

Gifford, Page. "Missing the Point." *Republic* [Columbus, IN], 11 Oct. 2003, p. B5.

Goodin, Denise. "Enduring Lessons." *Republic* [Columbus, IN], 11 Oct. 2003, p. B5.

Irwin, Roberta J. "Great Lesson." *Republic* [Columbus, IN], 23 Oct. 2003, p. A5.

"Killing Play Wrong Way to Educate." *Republic* [Columbus, IN], 9 Oct. 2003, p. A4.

King, Buddy. "Get On with Living." *Republic* [Columbus, IN], 25 Oct. 2003, p. B5.

Lane, Tom. "Debate vs. Dialogue." *Republic* [Columbus, IN], 14 Oct. 2003, p. A4.

_____. "Words Have Power." *Republic* [Columbus, IN], 24 Oct. 2003, p. A5.

McCawley, Harry. "Cruel Word, Unjust Times Need to be Remembered." *Republic* [Columbus, IN], 9 Oct. 2003, p. A4.

_____. "Now Is Time for Community to Show What It Believes In." *Republic* [Columbus, IN], 16 Oct. 2003, p. A4.

McClendon, Pat. "'N' Word a Barrier." *Republic* [Columbus, IN], 23 Oct. 2003, p. A5.

Mangas, Sharon Drach. "You Can Read My Life Like a Book." *Republic* [Columbus, IN], 19 Oct. 2003, p. B5.

Moore, Carl. "Pain Lives On." *Republic* [Columbus, IN], 25 Oct. 2003, p. B6.

Moore, David M. "Handful Decides." *Republic* [Columbus, IN], 23 Oct. 2003, p. A5.

Nuby, Joseph. "I Can Speak for Myself." *Republic* [Columbus, IN], 24 Oct. 2003, p. A5.

Pitts, Brenda, and Dennis Roberts. "A Different Perspective." *Republic* [Columbus, IN], 22 Oct. 2003, p. A4.

Ranck, Andrew. "Show Must Go On." *Republic* [Columbus, IN], 16 Oct. 2003, p. A4.

"Restaging Needs Broad Support." *Republic* [Columbus, IN], 17 Oct. 2003, p. A4.

Van Dyk, Sally. "Eradicating Bigotry." *Republic* [Columbus, IN], 25 Oct. 2003, p. B6.

_____. "No Censorship." *Republic* [Columbus, IN], 11 Oct. 2003, p. B5.

Warren, Nancy. "Time for Healing." *Republic* [Columbus, IN], 15 Oct. 2003, p. A4.

Werner, Nick. "Cancellation Ignites Racial Controversy." *Republic* [Columbus, IN], 9 Oct. 2003, pp. A1, A9.

_____. "Crump to Host Disputed Play." *Republic* [Columbus, IN], 16 Oct. 2003, pp. A1, A10.

_____. "School Cancels Play Due to Slur." *Republic* [Columbus, IN], 8 Oct. 2003, pp. A1, A9.

_____. "Troupe to Stage 'Mockingbird.'" *Republic* [Columbus, IN], 15 Oct. 2003, pp. A1, A10.

Wiggins, Nioka. "Get Over It." *Republic* [Columbus, IN], 11 Oct. 2003, p. B5.

Informal Censorship: The Literary Feud between Frank Chin and Maxine Hong Kingston

Liyang Dong

Very few American writers are actually banned or censored these days. The First Amendment to the Constitution is still strong enough to prevent that from happening often. Certain books, of course, *are* kept out of various classrooms, sometimes because they are seen as too sexually explicit but increasingly because they are seen as offensive by members of particular races, ethnic groups, or gender categories. But *informal* censorship or banning does occur, or is at least still attempted. Some works, for example, which do not toe a particular political line, are simply never reviewed by major newspapers, magazines, or other media outlets. Even when they become best sellers they are often ignored by the so-called prestige press, such as the *New York Times* or the *Washington Post*.

However, yet another kind of attempted censorship sometimes occurs within the literary community itself. Writers, after all, are the persons most likely to have especially passionate feelings about other writers and other kinds of writing. Sometimes authors offer ringing endorsements of other writers who resemble themselves and of other writings that resemble their own. And sometimes they publish savage attacks on writers who differ from themselves and condemn works that contrast with their own. Such attacks—*by* well-known and respected writers on other authors trying to seek recognition or maintain prominence—are often the most damaging of all. Typically, the writer being attacked feels the need to respond to, and try to refute, the original accusations. And then the original writer responds to the response. And thus a literary feud is born.

One especially interesting feud is the one that arose in the 1970s between Frank Chin and Maxine Hong Kingston, two of the most important Asian American writers of the past half century. Chin rose to prominence first: he was the first Asian American playwright to see his works performed on New York stages. By the mid-1970s,

Chin was probably the most visible and respected of all Asian American writers. Soon, however, Chin would have to contend with the rise of other Asian American authors whose fame and financial success quickly began to eclipse his own. One of these authors was Maxine Hong Kingston, whose 1976 autobiographical novel *The Woman Warrior* has now become a classic of recent American literature. One of the few people who did *not* admire Kingston's book, however, was Frank Chin. The story of his long-running dispute with Kingston is an intriguing example of literary politics that can seem either highly principled or extremely petty, or perhaps a mixture of both. And it is also an example of how the tables can turn—how the writer who starts out as an alleged censor can come to feel that he himself has become a victim of censorship.

Background

Edward Iwata, writing for the *Los Angeles Times* in June 1990, has provided one of the fullest accounts of the origins and development of the dispute. Iwata's article was preceded by an editorial summary—a kind of extended headline—asking and answering a couple of pertinent questions:

> Is it a clash over writing philosophies, myths and culture? Or is it just an anti-feminist vendetta? No matter. The long feud between two of the brightest lights in Asian-American letters has reached a boil. What's the dispute between best-selling author Maxine Hong Kingston and the man sometimes called the Chinese-American Norman Mailer, playwright Frank Chin? Why are they . . . Word Warriors? (n.p.)

Iwata himself, after establishing some background, reported that since "the debut of 'Woman Warrior' in 1976, Chin has attacked Kingston in forum after forum, in essay after essay. He charges her writing is 'white, racist art' that distorts beloved Asian myths and folk tales to fit her feminist views" (n.p.) Iwata noted that although Kingston had remained "silent on the issue for years," she had "spoken out in recent months. In an interview at her home in Oakland last fall, she compared Chin's views to censorship in

China: 'I'm afraid Frank is staging his own Cultural Revolution in this country'—a stinging allusion to the famous and very violent purge that took place in China during the 1960s and '70s. Kingston, according to Iwata, was now seeking peace, whereas Chin, in contrast, continued to mock "Kingston in his new book of short stories, 'The Chinaman Pacific & Frisco R. R. Co.' (Coffee House Press). In one tale," Iwata noted, "Chin parodies 'Woman Warrior' by writing of a woman author who changes the Joan of Arc myth by turning [Joan] into a man who is castrated and burned at the stake" (n.p.). Iwata noted that many academics had hoped for a formal confrontation or actual, open debate between Chin and Kingston. But he also reported that Chin chose to stay away from all events where Kingston would be present. According to Iwata, in 1989 Chin turned down an opportunity to lecture at UCLA alongside dozens of other Chinese American authors. Iwata argued that the feud between Chin and Kingston amounted to more than mere literary bickering and in fact carried a deeper cultural meaning. This was especially true, Iwata suggested, since Americans of all sorts were now taking a deeper interest in Asian American literature.

The Feud

Iwata reported that Chin and Kingston were both descendants of first-generation Chinese immigrants and were both born in the 1940s. Both majored in literature at the University of California at Berkeley, and each admired the other's literary talent early in their careers. Iwata noted that Chin rose to fame first, at the dawn of the 1970s. His two significant plays, *Chickencoop Chinaman* and *Year of the Dragon*, made it to New York, where they were staged Off Broadway. Iwata observed that Chin's plays were lauded for their intensity, originality, and humor. According to Iwata, Chin in these works exposed and ridiculed the vulnerable psyche of Asian American males, sneered at negative stereotypes such as Charlie Chan and Fu Manchu, and fumed about common images of Asian American men as eunuchs or symbols of a "yellow peril" (n.p.). According to Iwata, Chin was compared to Malcom X by the African American writer Ishmael Reed because of his straightforward style and his exposure and criticism of weaknesses of people belonging to his own ethnic group. But Iwata observed that by the time his own article was composed, Chin had "written little fiction since his glory days. He teaches sporadically. Many speak of him today as if he's a relic of a more militant era" (n.p.).

In contrast, Iwata observed that Kingston, unlike Chin, had risen to great literary prominence by the late 1970s—prominence that continued undiminished in the decades since then. Her books *Woman Warrior* and *China Men* (focusing on female and male characters, respectively) won her great fame and admiration. Her works had soon become must-reads in many disciplines, especially literature, women's studies, history, and sociology. She had earned the esteem of numerous readers, especially in the Asian American community. Chin, however, was not one of her admirers, either at first or later on. Iwata reported that the dispute between them started with a letter in 1976. Kingston had sent Chin a galley of *The Woman Warrior* before its official publication to ask for his feedback and, perhaps, endorsement. The book's publisher, Knopf, had added a subtitle to the book, "Memoirs of a Girlhood Among Ghosts," to sell it as an autobiography. Chin's response was harsh: "you've used all your craft and skill with words ... and you are good, no doubt about it ... to hide yourself. I see what you're trying to do in your work ... the making of mythical connections with all sorts of pasts and cultures out of the stuff of everyday Chinese American girlhood ... I wish you'd pushed harder, let go and done it instead of being so prissy and sissy" (qtd. in Mackin 513). When Kingston suggested that Chin had been too bitter, he responded with even greater anger:

> You call me a screamer? You mouthe [sic] off your assumption that lit is white and I'm writing from whiteness when you blow Norm Podhoretz and the New Critics at me. I'm all over the place coming on as a yellow writer talking to a yellow writer and you lay down and suck white fanatasay [sic] bout [sic] being just plain universal and raceless. You're the screamer, child. (qtd. in Mackin 513)[1]

Iwata reported that although Chin admired some aspects of Kingston's writing, he felt that he could not endorse her first novel because he considered it mainly an attempt to win approval from whites. He had hoped that Kingston's book would be a work of Asian art by an Asian artist, not something to be exploited by mainstream publishers trying to create "another Pocahontas" (n.p.).

According to Iwata, the initial dispute between Chin and Kingston quickly escalated into a full-scale battle. Chin even "refused to fly to Hawaii to speak on a panel on Chinese-American literature" because Kingston would also be there.

> His friends, though, dominated the panel. Chin's pals lionized the absent playwright, calling him "a literary giant." Echoing Chin, they raked Kingston's new book, "Woman Warrior." An angry Kingston rose from the audience to defend herself. In a quavering voice, she told her critics that her work [spoke] for itself. They had "misread" her book, she argued. (n.p.)

Iwata noted that the conflict between Chin and Kingston soon became a major topic at academic conferences. He reported that Chin's aggressiveness often repelled many Asian American women educators in particular, who quickly began to shun him at meetings. According to Iwata, many outside observers asserted that the squabble resembled the strife between Ishmael Reed and Alice Walker when Reed accused Walker of reinforcing negative stereotypes of African American males in her novel *The Color Purple*. But Iwata reported that some commentators considered Chin "guilty of censorship. 'I admire Frank's work very much,' said playwright [David] Hwang. 'I also admire Yeats, but I don't admire that he embraced fascism once in his life'" (qtd. in Iwata, n.p.).

Chin's Charges

Because these accusations—that Chin was a censor who resembled a famous fascist sympathizer —may sound extreme, perhaps it is best at this point to review some of Chin's own accusations against Kingston. They may help explain the nature of the dispute and why Chin expressed himself as passionately as he often did. Many of Chin's accusations can be found in a long essay titled "Come All Ye Asian American Writers of the Real and the Fake," which was the lead piece in an important (reissued and revised) collection of Asian American creative writing. This book, *The Big Aiiieeeee! An Anthology of Chinese American and Japanese American Literature*, published in 1991, was the sequel to an even earlier, similarly titled collection.

Chin's essay returned repeatedly to Kingston, whom he regarded as a main creator of "Fake" (as opposed to "Real") Asian American literature. In fact, very early in the essay, Chin asserted that what

> seems to hold Asian American literature together is the popularity among whites of Maxine Hong Kingston's *Woman Warrior* (450,000 copies sold since 1976); David Henry Hwang's *F.O.B.* (Obie, best off-Broadway play) and *M. Butterfly* (Tony, best Broadway play); and Amy Tan's *The Joy Luck Club*. These works are held up before us as icons of our pride, symbols of our freedom from the icky-gooey evil of a Chinese culture where the written word for "woman" and "slave" are the same word (Kingston) and Chinese brutally tattoo messages on the backs of women (Kingston and Hwang). (2)

Chin considered all three writers to be authors of inauthentic Asian American literature—literature designed to appeal to whites and literature that distorted the true heritage of Asian culture. But of all the "fake" writers he attacked, Chin criticized Kingston most often and at greatest length.

According to Chin, in *"The Woman Warrior*, Kingston takes a childhood chant, 'The Ballad of Mulan,' which is as popular today as 'London Bridge Is Falling Down,' and rewrites the heroine, Fa Mulan, to the specs of the stereotype of the Chinese woman as a pathological white supremacist victimized and trapped in a hideous Chinese civilization" (3). He argued that the engravings of Chinese characters on Fa Mulan's back, which he said were actually carved into the back of an entirely different figure (Yue Fei) in Chinese legend, reinforced the negative stereotype that Chinese men tortured and abused Chinese women. Chin maintained that David Henry Hwang and Amy Tan had followed Kingston's lead in this regard. He claimed, in fact, that

Kingston, Hwang, and Tan are the first writers of any race, and certainly the first writers of Asian ancestry, to so boldly fake the best-known works from the most universally known body of Asian literature and lore in history. And, to legitimize their faking, they have to fake all of Asian American history and literature, and argue that the immigrants who settled and established Chinese America lost touch with Chinese culture, and that a faulty memory combined with new experience produced new versions of these traditional stories. This version of history is their contribution to the stereotype. (Chin 3)

Chin argued that the works of Kingston, Hwang, and Tan are "not consistent with Chinese fairy tales and childhood literature" (8). He then wondered how one could explain their similarities with one another and with previous publications by Asian Americans, including "the first book ever published in English, in America, by a Chinese American—*My Life in China and America* by Yung Wing, 1909" as well as "Jade Snow Wong's *Fifth Chinese Daughter*"— which Kingston claimed had positively and substantially influenced her own works (8). Chin provided three answers to his own question. First, he stated that "all the authors are Christians" (8). His second explanation was that autobiography, as "an exclusively Christian form," was the only genre of works by Chinese American writers that acclaimed American publishers would produce (except for cookbooks). Additionally, he contended that all these "Christians" unanimously

write to the specifications of the Christian stereotype of Asia being as opposite morally from the West as it is geographically. The social Darwinists of the turn of the century regowned this stereotype in social scientific jargon, and white writers—from Jack London to Robert Heinlein—made art of the stereotype. The stereotype, and its corroboration in science and art, sharpened the racist laws against Chinese and Japanese, from Congress to city hall. The stereotype—as moral, scientific, artistic, entertaining, and legal fact—taught, inspired, and haunted the first American-born, English-speaking generations of Chinese Americans and Japanese Americans who would become the first authors of Asian American works in English. (8)

Chin asserted that all autobiographies and autobiographical fictions by Chinese Americans, from as early as Yung Wing, Leong Gor Yun, and Jade Snow Wong to Kingston and Amy Tan, have been "written by Christian Chinese perpetuating and advancing the stereotype of a Chinese culture so foul, so cruel to women, so perverse, that good Chinese are driven by the moral imperative to kill it. Christian salvation demands the destruction of all Chinese history," which he compared to "the Second Commandment" (11).

In Chin's view, Christians (including Chinese Christians) see only misogyny in Chinese civilization and think all Chinese females are victimized. He claimed that these "Christianized writers" look up to "America and Christianity" as the only hope for "freedom from Chinese civilization. In the Christian yin/yang of the dual personality/identity crisis," Chin wrote, "Chinese evil and perversity is male. And the Americanized honorary white Chinese American is female" (26). Chin blamed Kingston for perpetuating and strengthening the tradition of writing "fake" works. He concluded that *Woman Warrior* marked a turning point where "we have given up even the pretense of reporting from the real world," and he attacked the idea that Kingston was helpless in front of a cruel Chinese culture. He believed this sense of being persecuted was "informed only by the stereotype communicated to her" through the tradition of "Christian Chinese American autobiography," noting that Kingston even openly and repeatedly gave credit to the Christian writer Jade Snow Wong for "'giving [her] strength'" (26). Chin asserted that Kingston had inherited a legacy from "missionary novels, autobiographies and biographies" and "social Darwinist works of science and fiction" which are "forgotten" by most readers today (26). All that is left from these works, he said, is "the sensibility they produced, the racist mind" which, he thought, is still evident in "the voice of Maxine Hong Kingston" (26). He attributed this stereotypical, racist influence on Kingston not only to certain Asian American writers who had preceded her but also to "Chinese and Japanese sociology and Hollywood" (26). According to Chin, by the 1970s, the racist stereotype—of despicable Chinese men propelling a sadistically misogynistic culture that had no moral right to survive, and of victimized Chinese women seeking rescue and moral superiority in American and Western values—had so completely displaced history that it didn't need to be argued; it didn't even need to be asserted. (26)

Chin asserted that whereas Jade Snow Wong and Betty Lee Sung sought to legitimize their Chinese identity by publishing Chinese food recipes, "Kingston, with a stroke of white racist genius, attacks Chinese civilization, Confucianism itself, and where its life begins: the fairy tale" (27). He said Kingston presented herself as a "victim of Chinese misogyny," and he blamed her for designating "The Ballad of Mulan" as the "source of the misogynistic emphasis of Chinese ethics" (27). He criticized her for transforming Mulan into a "champion of Chinese feminism and an inspiration to Chinese American girls," who, according to Chin, were being encouraged by Kingston "to dump the Chinese race and make for white universality" (27). According to Chin, Kingston had defended her revisionist approach to Chinese history, civilization, and children's literature and tales by reiterating white supremacist stereotypes about Chinese people and their culture. Chin charged that Kingston, in an interview with Frank Abe in 1989, had implied that the first Chinese Americans were (in Chin's words) "incredibly stupid and forgetful" (29). Chin argued that the "fake" tradition started with Jade Snow Wong and Kingston, whose works he considered devoid of reality and set in a "pure white dreamland, where the real has no existence, no presence" and where the only truth left is the "destruction of Chinese history, culture, and literature in a single stroke" (29). He attacked Kingston for telling Frank Abe that "'I think to write true biography means you have to tell people's dreams. You have to tell what they imagine. You have to tell their vision. And, in that sense, I think I have developed a new way of telling a life story'" (29). Chin disparaged Kingston's abilities as a writer, saying her work was rooted in a "biased Christian autobiographer's intelligence informed only by autobiography." He considered her guilty of "dreaming up the imaginings and visions of the immigrants" and of trying, unconvincingly, to duplicate "immigrants' mental processes" (33). Chin sarcastically quoted Kingston as claiming "I'm not even saying that those are Chinese myths anymore. I'm saying I've written down American myths. Fa Mulan and the writing on her back is an American myth. And I made it that way" (50).

Chin agreed with her (or at least with his characterization of her views) and charged that Kingston had invented a fake Mulan. He mocked all the alleged achievements of Chinese American literature up to his time, belittling them as "seven decades of nothing but one Christian autobiography after another" and arguing that they have caused "self-contempt" among Chinese Americans so that the community is not even aware of the fake writing done by Kingston and "her literary spawn, David Henry Hwang and Amy Tan" (50). According to Chin, the Chinese American community took

> no offense . . . at [Kingston's] characterizing Chinese fairy tales and children's literature of the heroic tradition as teaching both contempt for women and wife beating. Without batting an eye, the average Chinese American born here in the 1970s, or before, will applaud the notion that Chinese history and literature are irrelevant to the understanding of Chinese American history and writing. Clearly, Chinese American writing by Christian autobiographers has had the effect of displacing history with the stereotype. An attitude of racist prejudice about illiterate Chinese with bad memories and no self-respect, and that no good drives their belief and their dreams zapped all fact, all the real. (50)

Kingston's and Others' Responses to Chin's Charges

Iwata, once again, is a fine source of information about the entire conflict, including how, exactly, Kingston responded to Chin's charges. Iwata wrote that in

> recent interviews, Kingston has insisted that Asian Americans must create their own unique mythology. She believes the tales will die if they do not change for a modern audience.
> "I don't claim I'm an archivist preserving myths, writing the exact, original version," she said. "I'm writing a living myth that's changing all the time." (qtd. in Iwata, n.p.)

According to Iwata, Kingston believed that she had stayed true to the spirit of the original myths even if she had sometimes changed certain details. For example, in Kingston's version of the Mulan tale (Iwata reported), Mulan was inspired by vows engraved onto her back by her mother. However, in actual Chinese myth, those vows were featured in a different tale altogether and were engraved onto the back of a male hero, Yue Fei. Kingston responded to criticism of this change by saying that although she had altered some details in the Mulan myth, she had not altered its spirit or deeper meanings. But Chin felt that Kingston had not only distorted important Chinese myths but had also rejected the whole tradition of male heroism in Chinese culture. According to Iwata, Chin drew on ancient Chinese works as his own sources for Chinese American mythology. He especially valued the tradition of male heroism found in works about outlaws and martial art strategists—such as the "Romance of the Three Kingdoms" and "The Art of War." Chin valued those works because he thought they extolled such virtues as "courage, loyalty and integrity," virtues that had been abandoned by the Chinese when they immigrated to the New World (Iwata, n.p.). But according to Iwata, some recent scholars of Asian American literature have dismissed the heroic tradition because they believed it celebrated violence and warfare while neglecting or even demeaning women. Chin, however, argued that traditional Chinese folklore actually endorsed, or at least displayed, gender equality. He denied that Chinese literature featured women with bound feet, claiming instead, Iwata reported, that the Christian Bible and Greek literature featured more misogyny than traditional Chinese tales (n.p.).

Iwata recounted one public appearance by Kingston in which she read a graphic scene from her novel *Tripmaster Monkey*, in which the protagonist—Wittman Ah Sing—makes love to a white woman and kisses her toes, which looked human and attractive, unlike the toes of some stereotypical Chinese female ancestors who had bound feet. She wrote this scene, Iwata reported, to celebrate a new emphasis, in the United States, on Chinese American physical beauty and to liberate her ancestors, at least imaginatively, from generations of bound feet and sexual repression. Ironically, many readers have interpreted Wittman Ah Sing, Kingston's protagonist, as her version of Frank Chin. Such readers have seen *Tripmaster Monkey* as, in part, a satirical response, by Kingston, to all of Chin's charges against *her*. Kingston herself has sometimes denied this interpretation, although people who think she is mocking Chin in this novel have found plenty of evidence to support their suspicions.

In fact, in one interview from 1989, Kingston herself admitted some similarities between Wittman and Chin:

> [Interviewer]: Wittman seems to bear a striking resemblance to Frank Chin. A lot of people think it is him. There's some references I can see. How much of that is true?
>
> MHK: I suppose he resembles Frank—and a lot of people. You know, when I try to write about myself, I think I may end up writing about Frank because his background and mine are very similar.
>
> We were born exactly the same year, we identify with being dragons and come from northern California. I guess he comes from Oakland, and I live in Oakland. We went to school [at U.C. Berkeley] exactly the same time, too, and had the same teachers.
>
> I think he may have been the only Chinese American male English major of that period. I may have been the only Chinese American girl English major. I know the same teacher appreciated both our work and encouraged us. I think we come from such similar backgrounds with so many similar concerns and values. If I write about myself I probably end up resembling him because I do resemble him in real life, although he's tall and I'm short (she laughs). (Blauvelt)

Then the interviewer asked some questions especially pertinent to the present essay:

> [Interviewer]: Everyone knows that Frank Chin is your most vocal critic and sort of bothers you....
>
> MHK: Oh yeah. He threatens me. It's not just bother—he threatens me.
>
> [Interviewer]: Is *Tripmaster Monkey* or Wittman a way of getting even, so to speak, or a way of answering Frank Chin?
>
> MHK: Oh I don't know. I actually don't believe in revenge. I see this book as a kind of big love letter. If it is answering—if it is—then it's

like him sending me hate mail, and I send him love letters, it's like that. I sure hope his soul is big enough to understand that.

Oh. That reminds me: I just saw the *Seattle Weekly*, and Sam Solberg wrote a review in which he says my book is a roman a clef, saying it's really all about Frank and other people, and you just have to match up things. He says it's a very bad portrait of Frank. He's saying I'm trying to imitate Frank's language and doing it badly. I think it's just a mistake, because it is not a roman a clef and I'm not trying to capture Frank or his language. I just think Solberg never read my book for itself. (Blauvelt)

According to Iwata, in 1989 Kingston praised Chin's early successes as a dramatist: "It was a very daring breakthrough," she said. "The music of his language was beautiful." But she said that she now thought he might be caught in the past. Iwata himself argued that Chin's criticism of Kingston had had a strong impact not only on her psyche but on her writing itself. He reported that some observers believed that Kingston had come to regard Chin as her "male alter ego." She even wrote to Chin, in 1976, that "If I am to grow at all as a writer and a person, . . . I have to wrestle with an understanding about men and write about them/you." Moreover, she even—according to some of their mutual friends—grew worried that Chin might be right about some of the praise *The Woman Warrior* had received from some white commentators. Some of that praise could be interpreted as condescending and even subtly racist, as if Kingston were depicting an alien, mysterious ethnic group rather than credible, complicated human beings. According to one friend of the two writers, "Maxine was afraid a lot of the praise she was getting was racist praise . . . . You can imagine how terrible this was when she wanted to promote understanding, not confirm stereotypes. In a way, Frank Chin was right" (qtd. in Iwata, n.p.).

Chin's Further Charges

Chin's outrage at Kingston, which had begun in the 1970s, was still going strong in the first decade of the twenty-first century. In a series of blog posts uploaded in 2007, Chin continued to attack Kingston not only personally but also as a symbol of everything he felt was wrong with most Asian American writers as well as with the academic study of Asian American literature. He accused Kingston and the Asian American academics who admired and promoted her work of being "white racists," reiterating his original charges that Kingston had grossly distorted ancient Chinese folktales, especially the one about Mulan ("Chin to China, part 1," n.p.). But, in a very interesting turn of events, it was Chin himself who now began to speak as if he were being either censored or ignored. He wrote, for instance, that "Amy Tan accuses the nameless critics of her work of jealousy and refuses to talk about criticism of her and Kingston" ("Chin to China, part 1," n.p.) Throughout this post, in fact, Chin expressed frustration that his ideas were either being suppressed or were being politely (or not so politely) disregarded. In other words, the man who had once seemed—at least to Kingston—a kind of censor now felt increasingly censored himself.

Several passages in the 2007 blog post indicate Chin's sense that he had increasingly become a marginalized figure, an embarrassment to many other Asian American intellectuals. For example, Chin asserted that in the summer of 1999, at the Naropa Institute's Jack Kerouac's School of Disembodied Poetics in Boulder, Colorado, he

> presented the Arthur Waley translation of [the] real BALLAD OF MULAN . . . and my own translation to demonstrate that the translation process doesn't create new facts . . . . I was greeted with nonplussed silence. One student asked a question that he confessed was asked because he was embarrassed for me not getting any questions. [The possibility that] Kingston's Mulan might be phony had never occurred to them. ("Chin to China, part 1," n.p.)

Why did this Colorado audience have no questions for Chin? Several possibilities suggest themselves. Perhaps the audience felt that Chin's criticism of Kingston's alleged "fakery" was pointless. Perhaps they felt that Kingston had a perfect right to make any creative changes she wished in the source materials she used. Perhaps they were embarrassed by Chin's attacks on Kingston and preferred to avoid discussing them. Maybe they thought that, rather than encouraging the feud and provoking more charges from Chin, they should just remain quiet. Chin probably felt embarrassed and annoyed by the lack of questions, as if he were being insulted and as if he had failed to generate any real interest, let alone any converts.

Many of the same questions can be asked about another incident Chin relates:

> Later I was approached by a yin yang team of white faculty who glowered at me and said I should be ashamed to be a man instructing whites on Chinese culture.
>
> "Huh?"
>
> "You had no right to say those terrible things about Maxine Hong Kingston's heroic book." ("Chin to China, part 1," n.p.)

The fact that Chin was now being openly criticized by two whites—who were also defending and extolling Kingston—must have angered him even more than if he were being criticized by fellow Asian Americans. Perhaps he interpreted the whites' criticism of him (and their defense of Kingston) as a sign of disrespect both for his literary talents and his critical intelligence. Such charges from whites perhaps smacked of racism, not to mention arrogance and condescension. The whites' claim that Chin "had no right" to criticize Kingston must have struck him as an attempt at censorship—as if he were being told to sit down and shut up. Chin would have considered such words, especially from two whites, as evidence that Kingston had won the support of white racists, which is exactly the prediction and charge he had been making for almost thirty years. In the early 1970s, Chin himself had been perhaps the leading figure in Asian American literature, but now Kingston was being treated, by whites and by other Asians, almost as a goddess, and Chin was essentially being told to stop talking. This was worse than the silence of unasked questions; this was, he must have felt, an effort to silence *him*. Kingston had once worried about possibly being censored by Chin; now Chin was worried about being literally silenced by fans of Kingston.

Frank Chin: Victim of Censorship?

Even worse than being challenged by a couple of white academics was another incident Chin reported later in his blog: "I presented the real Mulan at the Thurber House in Columbus, Ohio. They refused to print what I had said, but paid me, and invited me to spend the night in the Thurber bed. Kingston had slept in the James Thurber bed of the Thurber House. I chose not [to] sleep in the Thurber bed that had held Kingston's body overnight" ("Chin to China, part 1," n.p.). The fact that the Thurber house "refused" to print Chin's charges against Kingston must have struck him as a true effort to censor him. Being ignored by an audience of potential questioners was one thing; being challenged by a pair of white academics was another; but seeing a respected institution refuse to publish one's words comes close to actual censorship. Of course, we have only Chin's account of what happened with the people at the Thurber House, but there seems little doubt that Chin himself would have regarded their behavior as a real decision to censor him.

Why would the Thurber House refuse—if it did refuse—to print Chin's comments? Many answers seem possible. By 2007, Kingston was perhaps the most popular and respected of all Asian American writers. Perhaps the Thurber House staff did not want to offend her, her publisher, or her many admirers, especially since Kingston herself had once been a guest at the House. Perhaps the staff of the House felt (as many people felt) that Chin had a personal vendetta against Kingston and even that his attacks were misogynistic. Better simply to pay Chin for his visit and not seem to give his attacks on Kingston any more notoriety than they had already received over many years. Why risk alienating all the people (especially Asian Americans, and particularly Asian American women and other women) who admired Kingston? Whatever the reasons for the alleged behavior by the staff at the Thurber House, it seems reasonable to assume that Chin himself probably suspected some element of anti-Asian racism.

What could be worse than a refusal to publish Chin's ideas? One possibility would be a decision to *cut, delete,* or *omit* ideas. And this, according to Chin, is precisely what happened next: "POETS &

WRITERS Magazine cut my remarks about Kingston and Tan, from an interview about Kingston and Tan and asked me for subscription to their white racist magazine" ("Chin to China, part 1," n.p.). Again, we have only Chin's testimony about this charge, but one can see why Chin, by 2007, must have felt that he was increasingly the victim of censorship. *Poets and Writers* might have worried about offending Kingston, offending her publishers, offending her many admirers, offending many of their own subscribers, and thus, in all these ways, damaging the magazine's public image as well as its future sales. In fact, Chin claimed that "The Oakland Tribune, and the San Francisco Chronicle, good old hometown papers have treated me likewise" ("Chin to China, part 1," n.p.).

From his own perspective, therefore, Chin seems to have felt as if he had become not the censor but the victim of censorship. He describes what must have seemed to him a growing conspiracy to silence him—a conspiracy that would not only prevent him from airing his views about Kingston but would also ultimately damage his own literary career. In his 2007 blog post, Chin further claimed that "[o]nly the L.A. Times, thanks to Carolyn See, mention that I call Kingston a fake, but she was careful not [to] say why" ("Chin to China, part 1," n.p.). Here again, Chin implies that other people and publications—the Thurber House, *Poets and Writers*, the *Oakland Tribune*, the *San Francisco Chronicle*, and now even the *Los Angeles Times*—were afraid to take the risk of offending Kingston and her supporters—especially female supporters. In fact, later in the same blog post, Chin himself suggests that See regarded his charges against Kingston as misogynistic. This allegation—of misogyny— is one that Chin always hotly denies, but there seems no doubt that many women readers, both within and without the Asian American community, do feel that he is guilty of this accusation.

Perhaps this reason, as well as the others already mentioned, helps explain one more anecdote Chin reports in his 2007 blog post:

"Don't get on me for Maxine Hong Kingston," a writer I used to be close to shouted, "I have a kid to support." He supports that kid by his writing and teaching AALit. So he's afraid of the Chinese children's story for the sake of his kid. He admits the program he started, is racist. He blames his being a coward on his kid. ("Chin to China, part 1," n.p.)

Who knows whether or how much of this story may be true? The important point is that Chin considers it true, and it fits into his strong sense that by 2007 it had become too dangerous for others to risk offending Kingston and her supporters. This anecdote implies that at least one very prominent academic felt he might *lose his job* or at least *damage his career* if he was seen as too closely allied with Chin. Chin, who always presents himself as fearless, expresses nothing but contempt for his former friend. But if Chin's story *is* true, the story is indeed alarming. Academics, after all, are supposed to have the right to think and say almost anything. Tenure exists so that, ideally, they can think and say what they think, honestly, without fear of losing their jobs. Chin suggests that at least one major academic felt intimidated anyway. Again: we have only Chin's word to go on, but his anecdote is one that many may consider cause for concern. In Chin's opinion, Asian American writers and academics were still, in 2007, functioning as they had always functioned—as "servants of white culture. They serve, they entertain and do what they are told" ("Chin to China, part 1," n.p.). Kingston, he believed, bore much responsibility for this alleged servitude, since he considered her guilty of it herself.

Conclusion: Other Asian American Writers as Victims of Censorship?

However, Chin in 2007 not only felt that he and a few other Asian Americans were being censored, intimidated, or subjected to fear campaigns. He additionally argued that the writings of *previous* Asian American authors had also been ignored or suppressed because they challenged white racism. He wrote, for instance, of a postwar journalist named "Ken Wong of the San Francisco Examiner. Not a page, not a word of his novel will ever be read. His name will not exist. He'll only be a memory . . . ." ("Chin to China, part 2," n.p.). Chin saw Wong as a precursor—an Asian American writer who was unafraid to tell the truth. And, because he *did* tell the truth, his works (according to Chin) had never become fashionable and were now mostly forgotten. Chin considered Wong's writing an example of what Chin called "Chinaman lit," proclaiming

> Chinaman lit isn't Christian, isn't autobiographical. And it doesn't lie. The Chinaman writers are Wong Sam & Associates (1882) and Chiang Yee of [the] thirties, stranded in Britain by WWII. He told stories in two cultures and painted in the manners of two cultures with humor and charm, in his own signature style.
> . . . If there had been a Chinese American public that read about him in a Chinese American critic's criticism in a CA magazine he wouldn't be unknown and untaught in AALit as he is today. ("Chin to China, part 2," n.p.)

Chin felt that both Wong and Yee had been, if not censored, at least neglected and forgotten. In fact, it is possible to argue that to neglect and forget a writer is even *worse* than censorship, because censorship at least implies that the writer is the subject of real attention.

Clearly, by 2007, Chin had come to feel that he himself might face a fate similar to that of Wong and Yee. His bitter blog posts can be seen as ways not only to escape censorship but to avoid being forgotten.

Note

1. As this quotation and practically all the others from Chin in this essay suggest, Chin has his own idiosyncratic style of writing, punctuation, and formatting. Anything that looks unusual in a quotation from Chin in this essay is quoted exactly as Chin wrote it.

Works Cited

Blauvelt, William Satake. "Talking with the Woman Warrior." *Conversations with Maxine Hong Kingston.* Edited by Paul Skenazy and Tera Martin, U of Mississippi P, 1998, pp. 77-85.

Chin, Frank. "Chin to China, Part 1." 6 Mar. 2007. www.chintalks. blogspot.com/2007/03/chin-to-china-part-1.html.

_____. "Chin to China, Part 2." 12 Mar. 2007. www.chintalks. blogspot.com/2007/03/chin-to-china-part-2.html.

_____. "Come All Ye Asian American Writers of the Real and the Fake." In *The Big Aiiieeeee!* Edited by Jeffery Paul Chin et al., Meridian, 1991, pp. 1-110.

Iwata, Edward. "Is It a Clash over Writing Philosophies, Myths and Culture?" *Los Angeles Times*, 24 June 1990, n.p. www.articles. latimes.com/1990-06-24/news/vw-1117_1_woman-warrior.

Mackin, Jonna. "Split Infinitives: The Comedy of Performative Identity in Maxine Hong Kingston's *Tripmaster Monkey*." *Contemporary Literature*, vol. 46, no. 3, 2005, pp. 511-34.

Alison Bechdel's *Fun Home*: The Gay Graphic Memoir as a Magnet for Censorship

Darren Harris-Fain

Like *comic book*—which is a magazine rather than a book and often is not comic—the term *graphic novel* is misleading, often used to refer to any book in comics format, whether it is novelistic or even fictional. This is especially problematic for graphic memoirs, in which authors (who are often the artists as well) present compelling narratives about key parts of their lives through the medium of comics. Important examples include Art Spiegelman's *Maus* (1986, 1991), in which the author-artist describes his relationship with his father and his father's experiences before and during the Holocaust; Marjane Satrapi's *Persepolis* (2000-2003), about the author-artist's experiences growing up in a liberal Westernized family in Iran during the Islamic Revolution; and Alison Bechdel's *Fun Home: A Family Tragicomic* (2006), about the her gradual recognition of her lesbianism and her coming out juxtaposed with the revelation of her father's closeted homosexuality and the strains placed on his marriage by his relationships with underage teen boys. All three works have been acclaimed as paragons of what graphic narrative, with its combination of text and image, can accomplish, as well as remarkable examples of life writing.

Before 2006, Bechdel was already known to some readers for her comic strip *Dykes to Watch Out For*, published in independent and LGBTQ newspapers between 1983 and 2008. The strip also brought her to public attention through a conversation between two characters that provided the basis for what is now known as the Bechdel test, widely applied to determine gender bias in entertainment. A movie, television show, or other form of narrative entertainment passes the test if it meets the following criteria: (1) Does it have at least two women in it? (2) Do they talk to each other? (3) Do they talk about something other than a man? By these criteria, Bechdel's *Fun Home* unsurprisingly passes the Bechdel test. Ironically, however, the memoir focuses on her relationship with her father, and besides her girlfriend Joan, the woman she most interacts with is her mother, and they mostly talk about a man: Helen's husband and Alison's father.[1]

Fun Home recounts Alison's childhood in Beech Creek, a small town in north central Pennsylvania, where she was raised with her two brothers in a Victorian house renovated by her detail-obsessed father, Bruce. Like the speaker of Robert Hayden's poem "Those Winter Sundays," she grew up "fearing the chronic angers of that house," caused by frequent tensions between her parents and her father's volatile furies. Thus the title is sadly ironic: home was often not a fun place. The title also derives from Bruce's part-time job as a small-town funeral home director and mortician; often enlisted to help there as well as at home, the children refer to it as the *fun home*. The graphic memoir also covers her adolescence, when she was a student of her father's, who like her mother, Helen, was a high school English teacher; her years at Oberlin College in Ohio, where she pursued her longtime interest in art, came to terms with her lesbianism, and came out to her parents; and her postcollege life in New York City. Soon after Alison comes out, Helen tells her that Bruce was essentially a closeted homosexual and had even been in trouble with the law because of his interest in underage adolescent boys. Along with her and her father's shared love of literature, their sexuality creates a bond in Alison's mind between them, but that bond is shattered by his abrupt death when he steps into the path of a truck, which she believes was a suicide.

Bechdel relates these events and relationships in carefully observed detail made more concrete by the fact that the story is not simply narrated, it is illustrated. Period details are painstakingly reproduced, and she literally inhabited the characters not simply by drawing them, but by photographing herself as a model for many of the panels—including those in which her father is depicted. Moreover, *Fun Home* is noteworthy for its layered construction: the memoir is organized into chapters thematically rather than chronologically, with some key moments revisited from a different perspective. Repeated motifs and allusions occur throughout the book, and readers learn more about Alison, Bruce, and their complicated relationship with each successive chapter.

Given the book's raw honesty, unusual family dynamics, visual and verbal artistry, and (as promised in the subtitle) its adroit combination of the comic and the tragic, it is unsurprising that it was quickly acknowledged as a masterpiece within the relatively new form of the graphic novel. Sean Wilsey called it "a pioneering work" in the *New York Times Sunday Book Review*, adding that it "quietly succeeds in telling a story, not only through well-crafted images but through words that are equally revealing and well chosen" (9). It spent two weeks on the *New York Times* bestseller list ("Hardcover Nonfiction"), and it was one of five finalists for the 2006 National Book Critics Circle Award in the autobiography/memoir category ("2006 Awards"). In 2007 it received the Eisner Award, considered the comics industry's equivalent of the Oscars, for best reality-based work ("2007 Eisner Awards"). *Fun Home* has been the subject of dozens of conference papers and scholarly articles and essays, as well as Genevieve Hudson's short autobiographical book inspired by the graphic memoir called *A Little in Love with Everyone: Alison Bechdel's* Fun Home (2018). Bechdel's graphic memoir was even adapted as a musical by Lisa Kron and Jeanine Tesori, opening Off Broadway in 2013 and at Broadway's Circle in the Square Theatre in 2015, making it the first Broadway musical with a lesbian protagonist and winning five Tony awards in the process.

Challenges and Bans

Such widespread acclaim for *Fun Home* makes it understandable why many libraries would purchase the book and why many teachers and professors would consider it for the classroom. Yet almost as soon as the book was offered in public libraries, it was challenged by some patrons. Among the first was the Marshall Public Library in Marshall, Missouri, where both *Fun Home* and Craig Thompson's semiautobiographical graphic novel *Blankets* (2003) were challenged in the fall of 2006 by a patron named Louise Mills, who first saw them, she said, in the new arrivals section of the library. In a public hearing on October 4, 2006, she said she worried the books' comics format would attract the attention of children who could see adult imagery in them (Sims), and she said, "My concern does not lie with the content of the novels [sic]," but rather with "the illustrations and their availability to children and the community" ("Graphic Novels Draw Controversy" 13). Yet in the same hearing Mills asked, "Does this community want our public library to continue to use tax dollars to purchase pornography? ... We may as well purchase the porn shop down at the junction and move it to Eastwood," adding, "Someday this library will be drawing the same clientele" (Sims). The library removed both books from the shelves while they reviewed the complaints, and in the same hearing where Mills spoke, more than three-fourths of the community speakers expressed concerns about the books while the remainder supported the library's purchases and questioned the claim that these books were pornographic.

Asked in February 2007 about the challenge and the library's response, Bechdel said, "The issue is not, as I understand it, the content of my book, but the fact that there are pictures of people having sex—not just pictures, but comic pictures, which everyone interprets as somehow geared toward or particularly appealing to children. And that's true, kids love funny drawings. So do grown-ups" ("Newsmaker" 22). However, Bechdel did not think this sufficient reason to ban books from libraries and said that, if given the opportunity to address that community in Missouri, she would ask them what they were afraid of: "What exactly is it in these images that you're concerned about? What's going to be the result of a child looking at these images?" ("Newsmaker" 22). Although Bechdel herself did not investigate homosexuality through the library until she was in college, she imagines that it would not have harmed her to do so as a child and argues that "libraries are these points at which people learn about the world"—that access to information, including information about homosexuality, is "hugely important" ("Newsmaker" 22). At any rate, the plan at the Marshall library was to keep *Fun Home* away from the children's section, shelving it in adult biographies instead (Oder 20).

On October 11, 2006, a week after the public hearing, the Marshall library board voted 7 to 1 to remove *Fun Home* and Thompson's *Blankets* from the shelves until the library's trustees developed a policy regarding the selection of materials, which it had previously lacked, at which point their status could be revisited. Five months later, at its meeting on March 14, 2007, the library's board of trustees unveiled their new selection policy. Under this policy, well-reviewed books such as *Fun Home* could be acquired by the library and offered to patrons, provided they were appropriately shelved. Thus *Fun Home* was returned to the adult section, which it had been intended for all along, and Thompson's *Blankets* was moved to adult fiction, in contrast with its earlier placement in the young adult section because of its adolescent protagonist ("Marshall Keeps Graphic Novels" 29).

However, this would not be the only challenge to the availability of Bechdel's *Fun Home* in a public library, nor did such challenges cease soon after the graphic memoir's publication. In 2016 the American Library Association released its list of the ten most-challenged books in the previous year, and *Fun Home* was among them for its "graphic images" (Waxman 1). It was the seventh-most-challenged book of 2015, coming behind John Green's *Looking for Alaska*, a young adult novel challenged for its language and sexual content; E. L. James's S&M bestseller *Fifty Shades of Gray*; two books about transgender teens; Mark Haddon's novel *The Curious Incident of the Dog in the Night-Time*; and the Bible.

Librarians routinely make the case that they exert every effort to select high-quality books that provide patrons with a wide range of reading options, even if some patrons find some books objectionable. It could be added that, when it comes to libraries, no one is forced to check out a book whose contents they might find offensive. A different issue emerges when books become required reading, and *Fun Home* has also been challenged when it has been assigned as part of the curriculum.

An early example came in 2008, when a graduate teaching assistant assigned *Fun Home* for a sophomore-level course on literary genres at the University of Utah ("Anti-Porn Group"). A student was offended by the images of sexual acts in the book and contacted a Salt Lake City–based group called No More Pornography, which started an online petition to protest the assigned book. Despite this protest, the chair of the English department, Vincent Pecora, defended the book and the professor, saying that if professors chose only "novels that have a moral point of view that we agree with, we might not have a whole lot of literature to teach." The instructor, Jennilyn Merton, said that while the graphic memoir does contain depictions of sexuality, its purpose was not to "create porn addicts with state tax dollars instead of educating its' [sic] students" as claimed by No More Pornography, but rather, she said, that sexuality has been part of literary coming-of-age stories by such authors as Kate Chopin and James Joyce. In addition to not avoiding sexuality as part of the human experience, she said, "[i]t also helps us understand the ongoing violence that happens around people's sexuality. If we can't talk about that, then I don't think we can be responsible citizens" ("Anti-Porn Group"). Her chair, Pecora, pointed out that the University of Utah allows students to request an alternate assignment for religious reasons or to leave the course without penalty and take another that fulfills the requirement. According to reporter Sarah Dallof, "The student in question accepted an alternative assignment but would like to see further changes. The university has no plans [to] make any. It says while a student has the right not to read the book, other students in the class have the right to judge for themselves."

Similar institutional support for an instructor assigning *Fun Home* and other challenged works in a graphic novels course occurred in 2015, when a student enrolled in an elective course on graphic novels and objected to four of the ten assigned books, including *Fun Home*. Saying "I expected Batman and Robin, not pornography," student Tara Schultz at Crafton Hills College, a community college in Yucaipa, California, requested that four of the assigned texts—including Satrapi's *Persepolis*, volume 1 of Brian Vaughn's *Y: The Last Man*, and volume 2 of Neil Gaiman's *Sandman* in addition to Bechdel's memoir—be removed from the reading list. Her professor, Ryan Bartlett, refused, saying, "I chose several highly acclaimed, award-winning graphic novels in my English 250 course

... because each speaks to the struggles of the human condition ..." He added that the course had been reviewed and approved by his college's administration and board, and after reviewing the student's complaint they supported his inclusion of texts with mature content for a college audience and denied her request (Murphy 15). Schultz and her parents had asked the administration not only to have the books removed from the course reading list but also from the college bookstore, or at a minimum to label them so that students would be aware of potentially offensive content—a practice at odds with the American Library Association's Office of Intellectual Freedom, which believes that such labeling could prejudice readers against particular books (Murphy 15). Initially the college proposed that a disclaimer regarding the books' mature content be added to the syllabus, but this move was vigorously opposed by the National Coalition against Censorship and the Comic Book Legal Defense Fund (a nonprofit organization designed to support the First Amendment rights of comics creators, publishers, and retailers), and the college backed away from requiring a disclaimer on the syllabi (Maren Williams, "Case Study").

Another significant challenge to a college involving *Fun Home* came when the College of Charleston in South Carolina gave copies of the book to two thousand incoming first-year students in 2013 for its summer reading program, College Reads. The university did not require students to read the memoir—indeed, many an English professor has lamented that some students don't read even when it *is* required—but it nonetheless encouraged students to read Bechdel's book before matriculating so they could participate in campus events connected to it. In response—prompted by South Carolina Republican representative Garry Smith, who said parents had expressed concerns about the book's content—the budget committee at the statehouse in Columbia voted to cut $52,000 for the following academic year from the College of Charleston—precisely the amount allocated for their summer reading program (Lauren Williams 12).[2] While the college cited academic freedom and the importance of exposing students to a variety of ideas, and though even Smith's fellow Republican representative Jim Merrill said the bill "might make us feel better, but it's kind of stupid" (Maren Williams, "South Carolina"), the proposed budget cut was ultimately approved by South Carolina's House of Representatives. The state's Senate failed to pass the measure but instead required colleges to allow for alternative assignments when students have a "religious, moral or cultural belief" that would lead them to object to an assignment, and also required the two schools to use $70,000 (the amount the house voted to cut) to teach American documents such as the Declaration of Independence, the Federalist Papers, and the Constitution, mandating not only the study of but also "devotion to American institutions and ideals" (McLeod).

In response to the furor over the state's actions, the cast of the Broadway adaptation of *Fun Home* traveled from New York City to Charleston to perform selected songs from the musical free of charge, supported in part by Bechdel, with ticket sales from the two back-to-back shows going to the university (Margolin). Todd McNerney, chair of the college's theater and dance department, noted that no taxpayer dollars were used to bring the show to Charleston but still worried that South Carolina legislators might punish them "for presenting a piece of artistic work" contrary to their values (Knich). Indeed, Representative Grooms did just that, saying in response to the shows, "If lessons weren't learned over there, the Senate may speak a little louder than the House. There would be a number of members in the Senate that would have a great interest in fixing the deficiencies at the College of Charleston" (Knich). This was not the first time state legislators in South Carolina had threatened to cut funding to universities over the content of their courses, but the dozens of students who rallied in support of LGBTQ students agreed with Bechdel, who said that Grooms was "severely out of touch" (Knich).

In 2015, Duke University also encouraged incoming freshmen to read *Fun Home*, and this time the furor arose not from state legislators (the North Carolina university is private, not public) but from students who objected to the book's content and images. Discussion among the incoming first-year students was facilitated by a Facebook group and initiated by Brian Grasso, who posted that he would not read the book "because of the graphic visual depictions of sexuality," adding, "I feel as if I would have to compromise my personal Christian moral beliefs to read it" (Ballentine). Many of Grasso's future classmates agreed, some citing similar religious convictions, others giving moral objections. One student, Jeffrey Wubbenhorst, said that the fact that the book's content was visual as well as verbal led him to decide against reading Bechdel's book: "The nature of 'Fun Home' means that content that I might have consented to read in print now violates my conscience due to its pornographic nature" (Ballentine). Other new Duke students, however, defended the summer reading book selection committee's choice. Such students pointed to its literary qualities and argued that the book would open them up to new perspectives and introduce them to topics with which they might be unfamiliar. This had been the hope of Sherry Zhang, a senior who served on the selection committee, but she acknowledged that new students were free to choose not to read the book, adding that she hoped they would at least talk about their choice (Ballentine).

Graphic Novels and Libraries

Thus we see three primary situations in which Alison Bechdel's *Fun Home* was challenged: its purchase by public libraries, its promotion as recommended reading for first-year college students, and its inclusion in a course on the graphic novel. In each case, it was challenged because of Bechdel's account of her recognition of her lesbianism and her first sexual experiences, coupled with the fact that this is a graphic memoir and these experiences are visually depicted in a realistic manner, which some considered pornographic.

Libraries in the United States other than the Library of Congress have always had to be selective in their purchase of materials for the practical reason that they lack the funds and the space to buy everything. In addition, public libraries have increasingly become de facto community centers in recent decades, and thus not only have collections aimed at children and young adults but also try to maintain a family-friendly environment for their patrons. As a result, most public libraries do not subscribe to magazines with nudity, nor do they carry pornographic films in the DVD section. Indeed, many public librarians will tell you that one of the challenges of their jobs today is policing patrons who use library computers to access images and videos that parents would not want their children to see.

Sexually explicit descriptions in printed matter have their own history of bans and challenges, but the emergence of the graphic novel in the second half of the twentieth century introduced a new element into librarians' considerations. Most libraries did not purchase comic books for a variety of reasons, but even before the comics industry began limiting their content in response to parents' and government criticism about the content of crime and horror comics in the middle of the twentieth century (Hajdu), American comic books were not sexually explicit until the arrival of alternative comix in the 1960s and '70s, and thus were objectionable in librarians' eyes for other reasons. But graphic novels were another matter. Unlike comic books, which are actually magazines rather than books, graphic novels *are* books, even if they employ the format of comics instead of poetry, prose, or drama. The history of the graphic novel is multilayered and complex (Baetens et al.), but to offer a simplified version, American comics began to mature at roughly the same time that early practitioners like Will Eisner (*A Contract with God*, 1978) began experimenting not only with the notion of a book in comics format but of a book with more mature content than readers who had not been following new developments in comics would expect of the form. The years 1986 and 1987 especially brought graphic novels to the public's attention with the acclaim that greeted the first volume of Spiegelman's *Maus* on one end of the realism spectrum and the gritty superhero works *Batman: The Dark Knight Returns* (Frank Miller, 1986) and *Watchmen* (Alan Moore and Dave Gibbons, 1986-1987) on the other. As the public became increasingly aware that there was such a thing as the graphic novel, so too public libraries sought to meet their patrons' interest in this new kind of book—a book they could actually shelve with other books, even if their pages resembled or even reprinted the comic books they tended to eschew.

But the dual verbal-visual nature of the graphic novel, along with how new publications such as *Fun Home* presented content one could never have found on a drugstore wire rack, presented librarians with a new dilemma: how to make materials with mature content available to readers without stirring up the sentiments of those who feel that visual depictions of sexuality have no place in libraries receiving their funding from the public. Returning to the controversy in Marshall, Missouri, some members of the community attacked *Fun Home* and Thompson's *Blankets* as pornographic, saying they shouldn't have been purchased at all, while others proposed keeping such books in an adults-only section or behind librarians' desks away from children. One speaker drew a parallel with R-rated movies and pornographic magazines, thus unintentionally highlighting how the visual nature of the graphic novel makes such books different from text-only publications. As Bechdel said in an interview with *American Libraries* following the 2006 Missouri challenge, "As graphic novels become considered more a legitimate literary form, libraries are going to have to grapple with this.... But I don't think you can use [graphic content] as a reason to ban books from libraries" ("Newsmaker").

One way libraries have responded to such challenges, as happened in Missouri, was to argue that they are attempting to apply the same evaluative criteria to graphic novels as they do for other purchased materials. The awards and recognition *Fun Home* received and the fact that it continues to be taught and studied in college and universities have helped, no doubt, to make a case that the memoir is a highly literary work as well as visually well crafted, and that its inclusion of the author's early sexual experiences is as much a part of her development as her voluminous reading. Such arguments may not mollify critics who see any depiction of sex (especially same-sex relationships) as morally unacceptable, but at least they can be presented in support of the view that libraries, in striving to offer a variety of materials for a variety of patrons, are guided by the effort to select items that possess, to quote from the classical legal defense against obscenity, serious literary or artistic value.

It also helps when librarians are aware of the fact that comics are not just for kids. Given the history of comic strips and comic books in America, it is understandable that many people have assumed that comics are a children's medium. One can imagine scenarios in which librarians unaware of developments within comics or the possibilities inherent within the graphic novel would wrongly assume that a graphic novel, because its pages have panels and speech bubbles instead of sentences and paragraphs, could be shelved in the children's or young adult section. But of course, as readers in Europe and Japan knew well before most Americans, neither comics nor its cinematic cousin animation is inherently juvenile in nature, even if a great amount of material in these formats has been directed toward children. Rather, librarians have learned if they did not know already that just as one can't judge a book by its cover, neither can its contents be determined by a cursory glance at its use of comics.

Graphic Novels and Higher Education

It is one thing to offer a book like *Fun Home* in a library, where patrons are free to select the books that interest them and to disregard those that do not (although as the Missouri case shows, there are patrons who believe they should have a say in what other people may choose). It is different when a book is either recommended for incoming college freshmen, as happened at the College of Charleston and Duke University, or on the reading list for a class. Even if the recommended reading for matriculating students is merely recommended, there is still some pressure to participate, given that activities around the book were planned for their first year; and if a book is assigned, certainly the instructor expects students to read it.

A few months before her high school graduation, I took my daughter for her first trip to New York City. I let her determine much of our agenda, but I insisted that we see the musical adaptation of *Fun Home* on Broadway. I did so knowing that, while the story would not gloss over Alison's lesbianism or Bruce's pedophilia, it would not be presented as graphically as in the book (which is not nearly as graphic as the sex scenes in, for instance, Alan Moore and Melinda Gebbie's *Lost Girls*). Had I learned, a few months later, that her new university was asking students to read it before the fall term began, I might have wondered about the wisdom of the selection, even though I've taught *Fun Home* on three different occasions.

My misgivings stem not from the quality of the book, which I believe is a masterpiece of graphic literature that deserves to be in libraries and the classroom, nor from its depictions of sexuality, which I consider limited, subtle, and appropriate to their context. Instead, my concerns about its appropriateness as recommended reading for first-year students come not just from my experience as a parent but as an educator myself. Most of my career has been spent at small, regional state universities in Appalachia and the South, but I have also taught at a large state university and at small private institutions. Among the many things I've learned is that students, regardless of the institution, come to college from a variety of backgrounds and worldviews—some of which may be more socially traditional or conservative, for either secular or religious reasons. Thus I've always been more cautious about selecting materials for my first-year students and even my sophomore classes, realizing that even if I don't find certain subjects shocking, many students would.

For this reason, I think that the decision to promote *Fun Home* as a book for incoming freshmen was misguided, despite my admiration for the book. Just as some conservatives seek to impose their moral standards on others through censorship, so some liberals, thinking themselves more intelligent than those they deem to possess a false consciousness and perhaps seeking to *épater la bourgeoisie,* are either oblivious to the sensibilities of those who are more conservative or believe such sensibilities need to be shaken up. *Fun Home* is a great graphic novel, but that doesn't necessarily mean that it's great for students who may already be entering college with some trepidation that the liberal professors their parents have warned them about are trying to lead them away from the values with which they were raised. It is not surprising, then, that some students objected to the recommended reading, even if it's a dangerous incursion into academic freedom for state legislators to threaten funding cuts over material they find offensive.

On the other hand, I think *Fun Home* is perfectly acceptable for a class on the graphic novel or other literature classes. By the time students take such courses, they have typically taken first-year writing classes or otherwise have some experiences under their belts as college students—experiences that should have gradually introduced them to more-mature subjects than they may have been exposed to in high school. Moreover, in a literature class, students can expect to read works dealing with a wide range of experiences that are part of the human condition, and part of that condition includes sexuality. Given the visual format of the graphic novel and the still-common assumption by some people that comics are for kids, I do tell students at the beginning of the semester that books like *Fun Home* and *Watchmen* contain nudity and sexual situations (as well as graphic violence in the latter) and thus shouldn't be kept around their homes where children might encounter them, but this is more like a word of caution than a disclaimer like the one the protesting student at the community college in California requested.

I would also strongly argue against her petition to have such books removed from the curriculum and the college bookstore. Instead, I would side with her college's president, Cheryl Marshall, who disagreed in a formal statement in support of academic freedom and an open learning environment, which may include exposure to controversial material. Banning such exposure, she argued, might reaffirm students' values, but students cannot learn and grow if they are presented only with materials that validate their existing beliefs.

Contrary to popular belief, most university instructors are not trying to destroy their students' faith or alter their political views to match their own. We don't expect students to conform to our worldview or even to like everything we ask them to read. We do expect them to learn that the world includes people who are not like them who have ideas and beliefs different from theirs, but there are ways to teach this that ease students into these differences without alienating them. But of course for this to happen, academic freedom is of paramount importance, as is access to all kinds of materials in libraries—including Alison Bechdel's finely wrought memoir *Fun Home*.

Notes

1. Bechdel's relationship with her mother is the focus of her sequel to *Fun Home*, the 2012 graphic memoir *Are You My Mother? A Comic Drama*.

2. The committee also voted to cut around $17,000 from the University of South Carolina's Upstate campus in Spartanburg, where Ed Madden and Candace Chellew-Hodge's gay-themed *Out Loud: The Best of Rainbow Radio* had been assigned.

Works Cited

"2006 Awards." National Book Critics Circle. www.bookcritics.org/awards/past_awards#2006.

"2007 Eisner Awards." Comic-Con International: San Diego. www.comic-con.org/awards/2000s.

"Anti-Porn Group Challenges Gay Graphic Novel." *Q Salt Lake,* 7 April 2008. www.gaysaltlake.com/news/2008/04/07/anti-porn-group-challenges-gay-graphic-novel.

Baetens, Jan, et al., editors. *The Cambridge History of the Graphic Novel.* Cambridge UP, 2018.

Ballentine, Claire. "Freshmen Skipping 'Fun Home' for Moral Reasons." *Chronicle* [Duke University], 21 August 2015. www.dukechronicle.com/article/2015/08/freshmen-skipping-fun-home-for-moral-reasons.

Dallof, Sarah. "Students Protesting Book Used in English Class." *KSL.com*, 27 March 2008. www.ksl.com/?nid=148&sid=2952660.

"Graphic Novels Draw Controversy." *American Libraries,* November 2006, p. 13.

Hajdu, David. *The Ten-Cent Plague: The Great Comic-Book Scare and How It Changed America.* Picador, 2009.

"Hardcover Nonfiction." *New York Times*, 9 July and 16 July 2006.

Knich, Diane. "C of C Drama Continues: Crowds Pack Memminger for Controversial 'Fun Home.'" *The Post and Courier* [Charleston, SC], 20 April 2014. www.postandcourier.com/archives/c-of-c-drama-continues-crowds-pack-memminger-for-controversial/article_db40526e-7ef5-53f2-9b99-759e2a60360d.html.

Margolin, Emma. "College of Charleston Protests with Gay-Themed Play 'Fun Home.'" *MSNBC*, 22 April 2014. www.msnbc.com/msnbc/college-of-charleston-stages-fun-home-gay-themed-play-protest.

"Marshall Keeps Graphic Novels." *American Libraries,* May 2007, p. 29.

McLeod, Harriet. "South Carolina Senate Won't Cut College Budgets over Gay-Themed Books." *Business Insider,* 13 May 2014. www.businessinsider.com/r-south-carolina-senate-wont-cut-college-budgets-over-gay-themed-books-2014-13.

Murphy, Anna. "CA Graphic Novel Complaint." *Library Journal,* 1 August 2015, p. 15.

"Newsmaker: Alison Bechdel." *American Libraries,* February 2007, p. 22.

Oder, Norman. "Graphic Novels Called Porn." *Library Journal,* 15 November, p. 20.

Sims, Zach. "Library Board Hears Complaints about Books," *Marshall Democrat-News* [Marshall, MO], 5 October 2006. www.marshallnews.com/story/1171432.html.

Waxman, Olivia B. "The 10 Most Controversial Books of 2015." *Time,* 10 May 2016, p. 1.

Williams, Lauren. "LGBT-Themed Books Controversy Threatens Funding." *University Business,* April 2014, p. 12.

Williams, Maren. "Case Study: *Fun Home.*" *The Comic Book Legal Defense Fund.* www.cbldf.org/banned-challenged-comics/case-study-fun-home.

_____. "South Carolina Legislator Tries to Punish College for *Fun Home* Selection." *Comic Book Legal Defense Fund*, 21 Feb. 2014. www.cbldf.org/2014/02/south-carolina-legislator-tries-to-punish-college-for-fun-home-selection.

Wilsey, Sean. "The Things They Buried." *New York Times Sunday Book Review*, 18 June 2006, p. 9.

A Recent Attempt at Book "Censorship": The Conejo Valley Dispute

Robert C. Evans

Anyone who thinks that the issue of alleged book "censorship" is passé in the United States today may want to consider a recent case. It occurred in California in 2017 and involved the Conejo Valley Unified School District. It began as a dispute over whether Sherman Alexie's novel *The Absolutely True Diary of a Part-Time Indian* should be required reading in high school English classes. Alexie's book, in fact, has been the subject of similar controversies throughout the nation in the years since its initial publication in 2007. But the controversy about Alexie's novel in the Conejo Valley soon generated claims that other books might be similarly "censored." Among the titles often mentioned as possible targets of such "censorship" were *I Know Why the Caged Bird Sings*, by Maya Angelou; *The Bluest Eye*, by Toni Morrison; *The Catcher in the Rye*, by J. D. Salinger; *Snow Falling on Cedars*, by David Guterson; *The Things They Carried*, by Tim O'Brien; *The Kite Runner*, by Khaled Hosseini; *The Handmaid's Tale*, by Margaret Atwood; *The Tortilla Curtain*, by T. C. Boyle; *Bless Me, Ultima*, by Rudolfo Anaya; *Bless the Beasts and the Children*, by Glendon Swarthout; and *Thousand Pieces of Gold*, by Ruthanne Lum McCunn, among roughly two hundred other possible titles.

I have placed the word "censorship" inside quotation marks because I want to indicate that this was (and *often* is) very much a disputed term. People accused of trying to "censor" texts or films rarely think of themselves as doing so; people making the accusation typically claim that "censorship" is indeed the real purpose and result of the efforts they oppose. As will be seen in the Conejo Valley case, almost no one (if anyone) admitted to wanting to censor anything, but "censorship" was the charge most often leveled by their opponents. The Conejo Valley case is typical of many other such cases that have occurred recently and that undoubtedly will continue to occur. The arguments made by both sides seem worth serious consideration. In fact, the arguments made were detailed and numerous, and some of them are ones I have not read before in examining other, similar cases.

The Conejo Valley Controversy

The Conejo Valley controversy began in the spring of 2017. According to an article by Wendy Leung published on June 22 in one of the three local newspapers that heavily covered the dispute, "fears of a book ban ... were stoked" when "Trustee Mike Dunn, the Conejo district board president, said he would spend a couple of weeks reading a 'controversial' book"—Alexie's novel—"recommended for ninth-graders and then decide whether to approve it" (n.p.). That statement, Leung noted, "caught the attention of some school board watchers and community members who fear that a Dunn-led board could successfully block a young adult novel approved by teachers and curriculum experts." An organized protest soon led "about 15 people, mostly members of Indivisible Conejo," a local liberal, anti-Trump group, to stand "outside the district offices in the midst of a heat wave holding up signs that read 'Banning books is immoral'" (n.p.).

> "Mr. Dunn is not an expert on what is and is not appropriate for students of different grade levels to read," said Jon Cummings, co-founder of Indivisible Conejo. "He was not elected on the basis that he's an expert in curriculum. He should be trusting the experts to know what's appropriate and not appropriate." (n.p.)

Dunn, a conservative, said that he had "read parts of [Alexie's book] and found 'profanity, vulgarity, excessive violence and pornography'" (n.p.) "But he said he's inclined to approve the book if parents have the choice to opt out for their children. 'Chances are, I'll vote for it,' Dunn said in an interview earlier this week" (Leung). Even at this point, then, Dunn indicated that he did not want to "censor" the book in the sense of preventing students from reading it. He only wanted to give parents the chance to "opt out" of having the book assigned if they disapproved of the novel. Dunn never claimed to be a proponent of book banning or censorship per se, merely of giving parents greater choice in determining what their children would or would not read, especially in the ninth grade.

Leung reported, however, that according to "Jennifer Boone, director of curriculum, the book is being recommended for board approval as a ninth-grade core literature title. *Like all core literature titles, students and parents can opt out,* she said" (my emphasis). If Boone and Dunn both agreed that students and parents could indeed opt out, then what was all the controversy about? As often happens in many disputes, there was fundamental disagreement about what a simple term such as *opt out* might mean. But even if students *could* opt out, some local citizens argued (as Leung reported) that Dunn was "effectively censoring the book" by intentionally or unintentionally delaying a decision: "'No teacher would use the book in preparation for the fall semester if it has not been approved by the board,' said Sally Hibbitts, president of American Association of University Women, Thousand Oaks. 'If it's never going to be [put on the board's agenda], then it's a form of censorship,' Hibbitts said. 'It's de facto banning.'" Dunn, however, saw no need to make what he considered a rushed decision: "'I think protecting children takes precedent,' Dunn said. 'If we have to wait a couple of weeks, I'm sure it's worth it'" (Leung). Others, however, were not so sure at all.

The school board soon began receiving letters of protest from groups both inside and outside the local community, including one from the National Coalition Against Censorship, which implied that the board, by putting off a decision, was deliberately engaging in a delaying tactic. An NCAC official, although noting that Alexie's novel was often challenged, also conceded that it was in fact rarely banned. The NCAC advised the board to listen to qualified "experts in the field of literature." Dunn, in contrast, thought that the board should be responsive to majority opinion in the local district: "'The first question I ask myself is, "Does the majority of this community want children in public school to read this book right now?" ...'I'm not so sure.'" Dunn said he considered himself not a censor but "a parent concerned about child abuse. I consider books that promote pornography, that school districts require children to read, a type of child abuse. No child should be forced to read pornography'" (n.p). Cummings, one of Dunn's most frequent and vocal critics, was paraphrased as believing that "board members do not have the right to deny a book based on moral guidelines. 'I feel like it's one person who is in a position of power imposing his values on my child, my family and my community,' Cummings said" (Leung).

Of course, Dunn and his supporters would (and did) reply that they were not denying anyone anything and that they were not imposing their values on anyone. Instead, they claimed that they merely sought to make parents better informed, that they merely wanted to give parents greater freedom and input, and that in fact those who designed curricula might actually be the ones guilty of trying to impose values on children. Even in this very early article, then, one could already see the complexities of the issue revealing themselves. Dunn would later make a severe mistake in trying to defend his views—a mistake that would lead him to be censured by the rest of the board—but initially, at least, he presented himself as a very reasonable person voicing reasonable concerns. His opponents, however, prompted by what they considered good reasons, distrusted his motives from the start.

The Controversy Expands
One week prior to the appearance of Leung's article, the local liberal group known as "Indivisible: Conejo" had begun urging its members, and others, to write to the school board to oppose "censorship." A document dated June 15, headed "Censorship by CVUSD School Board," suggested that IC's members should tell the board to "follow the guidance of educational experts" in deciding whether to allow Alexie's novel to be taught. "Their judgment of the thematic and literary merits of a book as a whole, and not a board member's concerns about language or events taken out of context," IC wrote, "must determine the suitability of that book for age-appropriate students in our schools." IC claimed that "numerous court decisions have recognized that the First Amendment does not allow banning materials from a school curriculum because of some community

members'—or board members'—objections on 'moral' grounds."
IC also advised that

> Censorship is a risk that is not likely to pay off for the board, either in
> the court of public opinion or in a court of law. Furthermore, banning
> *Part-Time Indian* or other novels would be an outrageous risk to our
> community's stature. Our schools in the Conejo Valley are recognized
> as some of the finest in California, and colleges nationwide recognize
> the quality of the education our high school students receive. That
> reputation must not be sacrificed in order to cater to the narrow values
> of a small, vocal segment of community members, or to satisfy a
> board member's personal feelings.

As will be seen, Dunn and his defenders had numerous replies
to all these claims and all this advice. Sometimes they challenged
the impartiality and objectivity of the so-called experts. Mostly they
insisted that they were not interested in "banning" or "censoring"
anything but were instead interested in giving parents greater
information and input. They noted, in fact, that enrollment in the
local schools had been falling recently: roughly 25 percent of local
students were now either being homeschooled or were attending
private schools—partly (Dunn and his allies claimed) because the
parents of those children were concerned about the quality and
objectivity of the education their children were receiving in CVUSD
schools. Defenders of the local schools pointed to the schools'
supposedly excellent reputation; skeptics suggested that the schools
were losing students precisely because parents *already* did not trust
the quality of education their students were receiving.

Perhaps the most interesting sentences in the letter written by IC
were these two: "If individual parents have problems with any book
in the curriculum, district policies already allow them to substitute
an alternative text for their own children. It would be an enormous
mistake for [the school board members] to impose [their] own values
on all the students of CVUSD." Dunn and his defenders responded
by simply claiming that they wanted to alert parents, explicitly, that
they did indeed have the right "to substitute an alternative text for
their own children." Dunn and his defenders also claimed that by

encouraging parents to become more involved in making decisions about what their children would read, the conservative members of the board were in fact trying to ensure that *no one person or group* would have the ability to "impose [their] own values on all the students of CVUSD."

Dunn and his defenders—or people sympathetic to them—might have noted that disputes of the sort taking place in the Conejo Valley public schools were almost inevitable in any *public, government-funded* school system. In fact, almost all the disputes, over many decades, about banned books or book censorship or challenged books have involved *public* schools, not private schools. People who are already skeptical about the value of the entire public school system—and, in particular, people who believe that the government should not be involved in imposing its values on schools at all but should simply give parents vouchers to use at whatever schools they choose for their children—might point to the repeated controversies about alleged censorship to support their views about the value of vouchers.

Back to Conejo Valley
To return, however, from this larger issue to the particular issues in Conejo Valley, it seems important to note that by mid-August of 2017, the board had voted 4 to 1 to *approve* giving teachers the option of teaching Alexie's novel. An article by Dawn Megli-Thuna published on August 17 in the *Thousand Oaks Acorn* noted that much of the conversation at a recent board meeting had "revolved around the district's *unwritten* opt-out policy, which allows parents who object to a certain book on moral, religious or other grounds to request an optional title for their child" ("School Board" n.p.; my emphasis). Megli-Thuna reported that "Trustees Sandee Everett and John Andersen both expressed concern that the policy was not explicit enough for parents," although "the pair ultimately voted to approve the book based on the assurance that upcoming discussions between educators and parents would help craft a clearer policy" (n.p.). According to Megli-Thuna, the "lone dissenter, board president Mike Dunn, said he couldn't support

the title. 'My position is the book is very controversial, and I will not vote *to force or require* a child to read this book,' he said" (my emphasis). Thus, even though Dunn did not want to "force or require" a student to read the book, he was still not advocating that it be banned or censored. He was still making the point he had made all along: that parents should have the right to opt out. Some local figures claimed that parents already *had* that right; others claimed that the right was "unwritten" or "not explicit enough." Once again, it would seem, there were grounds for considering this whole dispute a reasonable disagreement.

In fact, Jennifer Boone, the district's director of curriculum, conceded (in Megli-Thuna's paraphrase) that while "California law [did not] guarantee students the right to opt-out of core titles, CVUSD [had] a decades-long policy of honoring those requests. 'We do offer options,' she said. 'Our focus is to find a solution.'" Megli-Thuna paraphrased Betsy Connolly, a "liberal" member of the board, as asserting that "it was not her job to decide what teachers can teach. 'The job of this board cannot be to substitute our personal beliefs for the judgment of parents or the judgment, in this case, of classroom teachers,' she said. 'This is a diverse community, and I believe that it is a mistake to restrict what is taught in the classroom'" (n.p.). An outside observer, however, might note how frequently Dunn's opponents claimed that he was trying to "decide what teachers can teach," or was trying to "substitute ... personal beliefs for the judgment of parents ... or classroom teachers," or was trying to "restrict what is taught in the classroom." These claims were made over and over again, even though Dunn and his defenders claimed, repeatedly, that they merely and simply wanted to give parents more information about *what* their students *were required* to read and more explicit options for opting out of such requirements. Dunn, a controversial local figure, was apparently *so* distrusted by his opponents that they refused to take him and his supporters at their word. Dunn was disappointed that he was the lone vote against making an immediate decision about Alexie's novel. But everyone seemed to agree, at this point, that it was probably a good idea to develop a more formal, more explicit set of rules for why, when, and how a parent might exercise the opt-out option.

A Supporter of Dunn

Having already quoted at length from IC, the liberal group whose members opposed Dunn, it seems only fair to quote at length from the other side as well. One of the most effective spokespersons for that "other side" was Amy Chen, a local parent whose views were published in yet another local newspaper, this one called the *Citizens Journal*. The *Journal*'s take on the whole controversy was basically conservative, but the *Journal* also, routinely, published lengthy lists of many relevant sources, including links to articles from other local newspapers. Anyone who wants to read the voluminous amount of prose generated by the Conejo Valley dispute will find plenty of it—and links to even more—in the *Citizens Journal*.

Chen's essay was especially interesting, because Chen had actually taken the trouble to read some of the books at the center of the dispute. Part of the point of her essay was to provide parents with actual excerpts from those books—excerpts, frankly, that I cannot quote here. Before providing those excerpts, however, Chen asserted that

> accusations of censorship against the school board are distorted and preposterous. For example, some falsely accuse them of censoring the best quality works, betraying the trust of students and parents, threatening our students' futures, and threatening our students' acceptance success to colleges. These accusations are fallacious and melodramatic because the process of approving the best books inherently involves selecting certain books while rejecting others. Inevitably, some quality works will not make the approved list for various reasons. We have layers of checks and balances on a book's journey to approval, the last layer being with the school board for final approval. The school board is obligated to represent the parents and community, preserve parental rights, and protect students. It is certainly not an empty formality. It is dirty politics to personally attack any school board member for doing his or her job with careful discretion. (n.p.)

Chen said that while some people had advocated the teaching of *Snow Falling on Cedars*, she herself had "talked to teachers that say they cannot even teach such a book," especially to students aged 15 to 17 years old, "because of its pornographic content." She then quoted from a passage on page 91 of the book—a passage that a reasonable person might in fact consider pornographic and, in fact, a passage that I cannot reproduce here. The same is true of the passage she quoted from pages 298-99. It is easy to imagine why some parents might not want a 15-year-old to be reading those passages, however valuable and worthy the rest of the book might be. Chen argued that

> after reading this book, we should question the credibility of experts who approved this, and individuals/groups such as Indivisible Conejo and the AAUW [American Association of University Women] who advocate for this book. *No one is trying to censor this from the libraries or prevent any family from reading this to their minor children.* However, it should concern us all when a school can require minors to read explicit graphic sex *without any enhanced parental consent.* Context does not matter here. Just as we would not require minors to watch a movie at school with just a few pornographic scenes no matter how good the rest of the movie is, we cannot require minors to read just a few pages of porn because some people say the rest of the book is extraordinary. (n.p.; my emphasis)

Like almost all of Dunn's supporters, Chen stressed that she was not trying to ban a book from libraries or even prevent it from being read. She simply wanted to make sure that parents knew precisely what their children were being assigned to read. In fact, various supporters of Dunn noted that a parent's approval was required merely for a student to watch an R-rated movie at school. The passages from which Chen quoted certainly might be rated R (at the very least) and might even be rated X if the actions described were explicitly enacted on screen.

To say this is not to say that Chen had the only valid or even the most persuasive argument. It is only to say that her concerns will strike many people as reasonable, especially when the intended audience consisted of 15-year-olds. In the Conejo Valley dispute, as in many disputes about many topics, *both* sides had reasonable arguments to make—a point that is sometimes lost when the topic is censorship or book banning. Anyone who automatically dismisses the concerns of a person like Chen is, ironically, helping to further undermine the already weak trust that many Americans have in the public schools. It is easier and easier these days to homeschool one's children, and more and more parents, dismayed by numerous problems in many public schools ("pornography" being one of the least of these), are taking advantage of that option. To claim that a person like Chen is anything other than a concerned parent may only further erode trust in the whole public school enterprise.

Chen, dealing more precisely with the specific issue at hand, then quoted a passage from *Diary of a Part-Time Indian* that managed to use both the N-word and the F-word in the same sentence, and in a way that might also easily offend Native Americans. By this point, of course, the board had already decided, by a 4-to-1 margin, to approve the teaching of Alexie's book. Nevertheless, here is the sentence that bothered Chen—a joke leveled by one character at another: "Did you know that Indians are living proof that n******* f*** buffalo?" It is easy to imagine how sentences like this might be justified by situating them very clearly within the larger context of the book. Obviously the book is not inviting readers to sympathize with the joke itself or with the character who makes the joke. But, again, one can easily imagine why an African American parent might want not his or her child to read that sentence; why a Native American parent might agree; and why a parent opposed to use of the F-word (which, after all, is one of seven words that cannot be broadcast on the public airwaves) might be similarly skeptical. My point is not to agree with Chen; my point is only to suggest that Chen and people with similar concerns deserve to be listened to with respect rather than dismissed as fascists.

Interestingly, Chen made another intriguing claim:

> Once a book is approved, the book is available for the teacher to use as required reading for the class. Currently, despite the misinformation

put out there, a student cannot legally opt out of public school curriculum including books. It is up to the teacher's discretion to grant the request. The student must also face the possibility of discrimination and retaliation for speaking up and disagreeing.

Whether this claim was true would become a much-debated issue. Some people (mostly teachers and their supporters) claimed that the existing opt-out policy was satisfactory and sufficient. Others, such as Chen, disagreed and raised noteworthy concerns, especially about the possibility of "discrimination and retaliation" from teachers and peers. A comment added by William Hicks at the bottom of the digital version of Chen's piece raised another question that many people such as Chen might ask: "What's the point of electing school board members if they have to rubber stamp the 'experts' [sic] decision of book choices?"

Although Alexie's novel had been approved for teaching by the time Chen wrote her essay, it remained a subject of controversy. In fact, a letter from Timothy J. Bond (founder of a conservative alternative to IC called Unified Conejo) continued to doubt the merits of requiring students to read *Part-Time Indian*. His letter, published in the *Thousand Oaks Acorn* on September 7, appeared under the headline "Book Will Have Kids Spouting Racist Slurs." Bond began by asserting that the "Conejo Valley school board voted 4-1 to approve a book in your public schools that contains profanity, racism, vulgarity and more." But then he made a more interesting claim: "If these books are read aloud verbatim in classrooms, or simply discussed between students, our schools' own rules of conduct will be violated" (n.p.). In other words, the local schools would not tolerate a student, say, wearing a T-shirt using the N-word or the F-word or especially a T-shirt simply quoting the disputed sentence from Alexie's novel. (Imagine what would happen to a student wearing such a shirt to school or even to the local mall!) Why, Bond implied, should students be *forced* to read language the school would never approve in other contexts? The obvious answer, of course, is that context is everything: that the offending sentence *would* be offensive—and might even seem a deliberate provocation—if worn on a T-shirt but should not be considered offensive if read within the pages of a novel. But as everyone knows, making that claim and convincing *others* (especially students and parents) of that claim's correctness are two different things, particularly when racial and ethnic sensitivities are involved.

In any case, Bond made the same point that would be made over and over again by the people who were being accused of censorship: "Let's be clear, school board members never suggested any book be removed from school libraries, and none of them ever suggested any book be banned." All the alleged censors wanted, they claimed, was to give parents greater information and involvement. Bond concluded his letter with another intriguing claim—a claim designed to defeat the assertion that, in judging which language is appropriate in a book, one must judge the author's intentions. Bond asked, "If alleged good themes justify compulsory reading of obscene content, what's next? T-shirts with "[expletive] Cancer" on them in school?" Who could disagree with the well-intentioned advice that cancer should be F'd? Who could fail to understand the positive, admirable meaning of that assertion and the worthy motives behind it? And yet Bond was probably right that a student wearing such a T-shirt would be sent home from school and asked to return wearing something else.

Opting Out

Many parents and other community members who had qualms about some of Conejo Valley's required reading assignments were mollified by the thought that they and their children could, if they felt the need, opt out of such requirements and substitute other reading material. Dunn and his defenders seemed satisfied with this idea but wanted the opt-out policy clarified and made more widely known. A September 28 article by Dawn Megli-Thuna ("School Community") reported that the "Conejo Valley school board is forming an ad hoc committee to take a closer look at the district's opt-out practices" (n.p.). Megli-Thuna noted that although the board had approved the inclusion of Alexie's novel in the core, that decision had done "little to quell the debate over how ... officials should approach controversial core literature titles and the parents who don't want their children reading them." In fact, Megli-Thuna reported that "Trustees Sandee Everett and John Andersen [had] said at the Aug. 17 meeting that they voted to approve the book based on the assurance from staff that discussions between educators and parents would help craft a clearer policy. Until now," the article continued, "the district has relied on an unwritten policy whereby teachers provide students who wish to opt-out of a book with an alternate assignment. If an agreement cannot be reached with the teacher, the principal and ultimately the district becomes involved to resolve the situation." Various teachers and administrators claimed that this policy had long been working well, although one parent who had exercised the opt-out option asserted that the policy, as presently constituted, created problems for all involved.

Perhaps the most interesting revelation contained in this article, however, came from "Joanna Burns, chair of the English department at TOHS," who "said she's not sure state law allows for a broader opt-out policy, *or even the one the district is already practicing*" (my emphasis). Megli-Thuna paraphrased Burns as saying that the "state education code provides only three instances where parents have the legal right to withdraw their children from participation: comprehensive sex education, HIV/AIDS training and surveys related to health like the annual California Healthy Kids Survey. She said the district's existing practice goes beyond that." In other words, the present opt-out policy might have been violating state law. This possibility apparently came as a big surprise to all involved.

But one day after the publication of Megli-Thuna's article, the liberal "Indivisible: Conejo" group published an article suggesting that *any* kind of opt-out policy was itself a form of censorship. The headline of the piece conveyed both its substance and its tone: "School Board Extremists Still Pursuing Censorship Via Curriculum 'Opt-Out.'" The article asserted that the school board had "entered the fall prepared to take on the entire English-literature curriculum"—a claim that seems exaggerated, to say the least. The article further claimed that "each of the board's three conservatives betrayed ignorance of the teaching process, an extremist predilection for keeping challenging books out of students' hands, and a general detachment from reality." IC opposed efforts to let parents know that the state department of education had already flagged some books as intended for mature readers. The group criticized trustee Sandee Everett's suggestion that these "potentially offensive books"—which had already been identified as such by the state (which, in essence, had given them an R rating) "could be marked on the Core Lit list with a simple asterisk—with no context provided." According to CI, Everett had "also suggested that parents should be able to arrange an opt-out via a simple email notification—a far cry from the current process, which requires a discussion of the book with the teacher and perhaps the principal as well." As the rest of the article made clear, CI definitely distrusted both the behavior and the motives of the board's conservative members. CI was particularly suspicious of the possibility that a new, clearer opt-out policy might make "opting out too easy & attractive for parents." The group worried that a new policy might place undue burdens on teachers, might intimidate teachers, and might encourage parents to try to opt out of the teaching of other forms of potentially controversial material, such as in history classes.

Basic Arguments, Pro and Con
The debate raged for the next three or four months, and there is no denying that Dunn and his allies made some fundamental tactical mistakes. For instance, one of the conservative trustees put forward a proposed opt-out policy of her own, without (it was alleged) seeking sufficient input from faculty and administrators. Most damagingly and disturbingly, Dunn contacted the employer of one of his most vocal critics and was accused of thereby trying to intimidate both the employee and her boss. The employer publicly defied Dunn, saying that he supported his employee's right to free speech, and Dunn was eventually censured by his colleagues for this perceived effort at intimidation.

More interesting than these or any other specific details, however, are the broader, more general arguments that arose out of the entire Conejo Valley controversy. In the present section of this essay, I want to focus on these larger assertions and counterassertions. One argument, for instance, involved the degree to which school boards should be involved in making decisions about schools' curricula. Most opponents of Dunn and his colleagues argued that teachers, administrators, and other experts should be trusted to make appropriate decisions; Dunn and his defenders argued that parents should have the ability to opt out of reading assignments that they or their children found inappropriate.

Perhaps the largest issue of debate involved how much information parents should be given about possibly offensive books and *how* that information should be provided. Dunn told one reporter that "at a minimum, he want[ed] letters of notification sent to parents describing the books, including excerpts that might be deemed offensive" (qtd. in Miller, "Conejo Schools" n.p.). The same reporter, in the same article, noted that at one board meeting "quite a few members of the public weighed in, preponderantly in favor of parental opt-out or even elimination of offensive books from the core literature list. One score keeper told us that 18 spoke in favor of some form of opt-out/restriction and four against." Sometimes, however, at other meetings, opponents of Dunn far outnumbered supporters. One other larger issue raised by this controversy, in fact, involved the degree to which curricular decisions should be made based on turnout at meetings. Dunn claimed that the school board members themselves had been elected by the entire community, rather than by just one segment of it or only by those who happened to show up at any given meeting. He felt that board members, as elected representatives of the community as a whole, should for that very reason have an important say in determining policy (see Miller, "Conejo Schools" n.p.).

Another claim made by Dunn—with which some people, however, disagreed—was the assertion that the "government should not force a child to read an obscene book. Forcing a child to read an obscene book is psychological child abuse" (Miller, qtd in "Conejo Schools" n.p.). Even more interesting, however, was his argument that "children fear asking" for substitute books "because of retaliation from the teachers." Dunn reported that one parent had claimed that his child, who normally received As and Bs in her classes, "got an F in the class [in which] she requested a different book" (qtd. in Miller, "Conejo Schools" n.p.). Dunn also claimed that the local public school system's enrollment had been declining while enrollment at a local Christian school was increasing, despite the fact that the latter school charged yearly tuition of $25,000. Dunn blamed part of the school system's declining enrollment on a widespread perception that parents had little say, in the public schools, over how their children would be educated (Miller, "Conejo Schools" n.p.).

One argument made several times by supporters of Dunn was that parents should have at least as much input over what their children would read as they presently had over what those children would see in the form of movies shown at school or, in fact, at local theaters. Timothy Bond, a Dunn supporter and leader of a local conservative group, wrote that "we cherish the contributions of teachers and we want their support in providing the best Opt-In policy we can offer, perhaps even better than the policies required to gain approval from parents for their kids to watch PG-rated movies in the classroom, and at least as stringent as the readily accepted standards applied at movie theaters around the country" (qtd. in Miller, "Conejo Schools" n.p.). Even some conservatives, however, felt (in the words of Paul White, a local conservative leader) that Dunn had not used his "political capital wisely" in objecting to Alexie's book. In fact, White defended *Part-Time Indian* at length (qtd. in Miller, "Conejo Schools" n.p.). George Miller, although conservative himself, provided a very helpful overview of the entire controversy, quoting often from both supporters and opponents of Dunn as well as from Dunn himself. Miller also provided extensive links to many sources of information, not all of them conservative by any means. Miller concluded, sensibly, that both sides had genuine, reasonable concerns: "Those who want restrictions fear that their kids may suffer reprisals" for trying to opt out of the core curriculum. "Those who don't [support Dunn] fear that good books will be squeezed out by those trying to shield their kids from what they believe is offensive or even harmful literature" ("Conejo Schools" n.p.). Later, however, offended by the tactics of some of Dunn's opponents, Miller moved closer to supporting Dunn.[1] Miller and others noted that the state of California itself had flagged a couple of hundred books for their potentially disturbing "adult" content; he and others saw no problem with letting parents know (by appending a simple asterisk, comparable to an R movie rating) that those books had in fact been flagged by the state.

Further Local Debate

Jon Cummings of IC, however, in a letter dated November 6, 2017, called the proposed asterisk rating system "despicable" and warned that it would "turn CVUSD into a laughingstock" and would "force university admissions counselors to re-evaluate the quality of education our district provides" (n.p.). Cummings claimed that the policy the board was considering "would not merely allow, but encourage, opt-out—requiring teachers to include out-of-context 'content warnings' on the syllabi they distribute each August" ("Despicable" n.p.). Proponents of the policy claimed, of course, that it would merely alert parents to warnings that had already been issued by the state. Cummings asserted that local "English teachers are understandably up in arms over this proposal, which insults their professionalism while encouraging parents to defy their curriculum choices." (It seems safe to say that many parents would be offended by Cummings's use of the verb *defy*.)

Dawn Megli-Thuna, in an article on the dispute published the same day as Cummings's letter, reported that local English teachers felt that trustee Sandee Everett was attempting "to revise the district's instructional material policy against their will" and with insufficient teacher input ("Teachers, Trustee" n.p.). Megli-Thuna observed that "among the proposals in Everett's draft policy" was "a requirement that district teachers alert parents before their children are assigned to read books that have been identified by the California Department of Education as having mature content." Some teachers complained "in an interview that Everett's policy replaced rather than amended the policy created by teachers and administrators and focused on the selection of new core literature titles, which the board specifically said was not the purpose of the committees when they were formed." They also complained that Dunn had allegedly refused to let the teacher-supported proposal be considered alongside Everett's. One teacher explained that "'We all know that once these labels are placed on any book, that text is dead in the water, and many parents will opt out without even investigating further'" ("Teachers, Trustee" n.p.). For her part, Everett said that her

> "goal in updating this policy is to encourage parents to be more involved in their children's education, not to overhaul our district's literary system or place unnecessary burdens on teachers . . . . By informing parents, in advance, of the books their children will be reading, we will be better equipping them to take an active role in the education process and even read along." ... Regarding her recommendation to notify parents about books with adult themes, Everett said the state education office already annotates certain titles on its website with a warning that reads: "This book was published for an adult readership and thus contains mature content. Before handing the text to a child, educators and parents should read the book and know the child." Whenever a book with that annotation appears on the course reading list, Everett said, she'd simply like teachers to include the wording on class syllabi and notify parents via email and on parent-teacher night. (Megli-Thuna, "Trustee Takes" n.p.)

However, one teacher opposed to Everett's ideas "called on teachers to show up in force" at a scheduled meeting, writing, "If you want to fight back against this nightmare becoming your reality, it is critical that everyone show up." The same teacher urged people

> to show up in big numbers; get anyone who has concerns about the impending lack of diversity in our curriculum and who doesn't want their kids to just read safe books written by only dead white guys. This is our last line of defense against impending doom, and it's not too late: if we go down, "at least we die with a harness on our back." (qtd. in Megli-Thuna, "Trustee Takes" n.p.)

Everett, more calmly, said that "study after study has shown that one of the most important factors in a successful education is parental involvement and only by parents and teachers working together can we ensure the best possible education for our community's kids." Teachers complained, however, that in fact Everett had *failed* to work with them, especially by putting forth a policy proposal of her own (see Megli-Thuna, "Trustee Takes").

Larger Issues Again

As the debates dragged on, several more "larger" issues arose—issues relevant not just to the Conejo Valley dispute but to similar discussions elsewhere. These included the following:

- The claim, by one student, that "requiring a parent signature on syllabi would place an unfair burden on students who have difficult home lives" (qtd. in Megli-Thuna, "Trustee Takes").
- The claim, by one letter writer, that some of the reading material that would be flagged by asterisks "contain[ed] graphic descriptions of sex acts that if sent to a minor" would make the sender guilty of a criminal offense (Savalla, n.p.).
- The claim, by Paul D. White, that high schools routinely "censor" students by, for instance, frequently banning candy and soda from campus "to encourage students to develop better eating habits"; by prohibiting "risque and inciteful clothing"; by outlawing drinking and smoking on campus; by prohibiting and punishing "vulgar language and disrespectful behavior"; etc.
- The claim, also by White, that teachers these days tend to share the same basic sociopolitical values, that these values are often at variance with those of many parents, and that teachers who do not fall into line with their peers are often subjected to peer pressure to conform.
- The claim, again by White, that many teachers were being "forced to assume a growing parenting role regarding moral issues—due to irresponsible moms and dads who refuse to do their job."
- The argument, made by George Miller, that "the medical industry is required to obtain parental approval for medical procedures on children (except abortions). Many schools require parental permission for field trips and even certain in-school celebrations, such as pagan Halloween fetes. R-Rated movies shown in the

district have an opt-IN requirement. So why," Miller asked, "would books be so different?" ("Conejo Valley" n.p.)[2]

Conclusion

The Conejo Valley debate never really ended, but it did, over the next few months, die down. The unanimous censuring of Dunn by his colleagues badly hurt him. Having professed all along that he had had no intention of censoring anything, he was accused by his opponents of trying to censor one of his most vigorous critics by allegedly trying to intimidate her employer. By the early months of the new year, coverage of the larger controversy had diminished because the larger controversy itself had diminished. By May, 2018, it emerged that the California Department of Education had removed, from its massive list of books, the "warning language" about some books that would have been called to parents' attention by using asterisks. Why had this change been made? Had the department itself succumbed to, or engaged in, a kind of censorship (or self-censorship) of its own? A spokesman for the department denied any such possibility:

> "The California Department of Education process for annotations was not changed in response to the way they were being used at Conejo Valley Unified," said Scott Roark, a public information officer for the California Department of Education. "The process is periodically reviewed."
> Roark also told *The Star* that because California is a local-control state, specific decisions about classroom instruction are made at the local level by teachers and local administrators as opposed to in Sacramento. (D'Angelo n.p.)

Skeptics, however, might wonder about the timing and motives of the process that led to the apparently sudden deletion of the content warnings. But for the time being, at least, the ball was back in Conejo Valley's court.

Notes

1. In an editorial dated November 9, 2017 ("Next Tuesday"), Miller expressed less sympathy than he had earlier for Dunn's opponents. He thought that they had "tried to overwhelm [a recent] meeting with numbers, intensity, arguments and sheer offensiveness, bordering on, if not crossing over, into intimidation. We heard estimates of an overflow crowd of 150-175, mostly opponents and about 50 of them students" (n.p.). Miller opined that "opponents have been accusing the three board members" who wanted a clearer opt-out policy of "'censorship,' religious fundamentalism, white supremacy and more. But what the [proposed opt-out] policy does," Miller thought, "is clarify how literature will be selected and provide a straightforward and fairly objective method of identifying potentially objectionable material, informing parents and allowing them to opt out their children if they object. To say that this is 'censorship,'" he concluded, "is absurd. Parents deciding whether their children should view objectionable materials is far from *Fahrenheit 451. Since there are only a couple of hundred such books out of over 8000 on the state's literature ["adult warning"] list and very few of these make it to CVUSD's list*, the potential impact is not that large" ("Next Tuesday," n.p.; my emphasis). Opponents of Dunn had begun to lose the respect and sympathy of people like Miller.

2. As usual, Miller, in this piece, provided a balanced overview of the whole debate as well as an updated list of relevant links of representative commentary and reporting.

Works Cited

Bond, Timothy J. "Book Will Have Kids Spouting Racist Slurs." *Thousand Oaks Acorn*, 7 Sept. 2017. www.toacorn.com/articles/book-will-have-kids-spouting-racist-slurs.

"Censorship Attempt by CVUSD School Board." *Indivisible: Conejo Weekly Newsletter*, 15 June 2017. www.indivisibleconejo.org/daily-actions/2017/6/15/daily-action-stop-a-censorship-attempt-by-the-cvusd-school-board.

Chen, Amy. "Do You Know What YOUR Child Is Reading?" *CitizensJournal.us*, 5 Sept. 2017, www.citizensjournal.us/know-child-reading.

Cummings, Jon. "Despicable Conejo Proposal." *Ventura County Star*, 6 Nov. 2017. www.eu.vcstar.com/story/opinion/readers/2017/11/06/despicable-conejo-proposal/838615001.

D'Angelo, Alexa. "Conejo School Board Brings Back Contentious Literature Policy." *Ventura County Star*, 2 May 2018. www.vcstar.com/story/news/education/2018/05/02/conejo-school-board-brings-back-contentious-literature-policy/569725002.

Leung, Wendy. "Conejo School Board Hesitation Sparks Book Ban Fears." *Ventura County Star*, 22 June 2017. https://eu.vcstar.com/story/news/2017/06/23/conejo-school-board-hesitation-sparks-book-ban-fears/417207001.

Megli-Thuna, Dawn. "School Board OKs Controversial Novel." *Thousand Oaks Acorn*, 17 Aug. 2017. www.toacorn.com/articles/school-board-oks-controversial-novel.

_____. "School Community Talks 'Explicit' Books." *Thousand Oaks Acorn*, 28 Sept. 2017. www.toacorn.com/articles/school-community-talks-explicit-books.

_____. "Teachers, Trustee Clash Over Literature Policy." *Thousand Oaks Acorn*, 6 Nov. 2017. www.toacorn.com/articles/teachers-trustee-clash-over-literature-policy.

_____. "Trustee Takes on Book Policy." *Thousand Oaks Acorn*, 9 Nov. 2017. www.toacorn.com/articles/trustee-takes-on-book-policy.

Miller, George. "Conejo Schools 'BookGate' War Continues." *Citizens Journal*, 7 Oct. 2017, http://citizensjournal.us/conejo-schools-bookgate-war-continues.

_____. "Conejo Valley Schools Parental Choice Book Dispute Status: Spinning the Narrative, Attacking Board Members, etc." *Citizens Journal*, 4 Feb. 2018. www.citizensjournal.us/conejo-valley-schools-parental-choice-book-dispute-status-spinning-narrative-attacking-board-members-etc.

_____. "Next Tuesday in T.O.: Who 'Owns' the Children? Who Sets School Policy?" *Citizens Journal*, 9 Nov. 2017. www.citizensjournal.us/next-tuesday-t-o-owns-children-sets-school-policy.

Savalla, Deborah Baber. "Just the Facts." *Citizens Journal*, 12 Nov. 2017. www.citizensjournal.us/true-news-conejo-valley-school-board-proposed-curriculum-policy-bookgate.

"School Board Extremists Still Pursuing Censorship Via Curriculum 'Opt-Out.'" *Indivisible: Conejo Weekly Newsletter*, 29 Sept. 2017. www.indivisibleconejo.org/news/2017/8/18/indivisible-conejo-weekly-newsletter-54bke-czcxb-5n4ma-exw5c8-8y2hm-2fsd9-9f4jj-jjxht-lnxlr-jw3yc.

White, Paul D. "Conejo Valley Faux Book Banning Controversy: Just the Tip of a Dangerous Iceberg," *Citizens* Journal, 24 Nov. 2017, http://citizensjournal.us/conejo-valley-faux-book-banning-controversy-just-tip-dangerous-iceberg.

RESOURCES

Further Reading

Amnesty International. *Voices for Freedom*. AI Publications, 1986.

Ashbee, Henry S., and Peter Fryer. *Forbidden Books of the Victorians*. Odyssey, 1970.

Atkins, John. *Sex in Literature*. 4 vols. John Calder, 1982.

Barton, Frank. *The Press of Africa: Persecution and Perseverance*. Macmillan, 1979.

Berninghausen, David K. *The Flight from Reason: Essays on Intellectual Freedom in the Academy, the Press, and the Library*. ALA, 1978.

Bernstein, Matthew. *Controlling Hollywood: Censorship and Regulations in the Studio Era*. Rutgers UP, 1999.

Biesen, Sheri Chinen. *Film Censorship: Regulating America's Screen*. Columbia UP, 2018.

Bobbitt, Randy. *Free Speech on America's K-12 and College Campuses: Legal Cases from Barnette to Blaine*. Lexington, 2018.

Bosmajian, Haig, compiler. *Censorship, Libraries, and the Law*. Neal-Schuman, 1983.

Boyer, Paul S. *Purity in Print: The Vice Society Movement and Book Censorship in America*. Scribner's, 1968.

Bristow. Edward J. *Vice and Vigilance*. Gill and Macmillan, 1977.

Broun, Heywood, and Margaret Leech. *Anthony Comstock: Roundsman of the Lord*. Boni, 1927.

Bryson. Joseph E., and Elizabeth W. Detty. *Legal Aspects of Censorship of Public School Libraries and Instructional Materials*. Michie, 1982.

Buranelli, Vincent. *The Trial of Peter Zenger*. New York UP, 1957.

Burress. Lee. *Battle of the Books: Literary Censorship in the Public Schools, 1950-1985*. Scarecrow. 1989.

Calder-Marshall, Arthur. *Lewd, Blasphemous & Obscene*. Hutchinson, 1972.

Carmen, Ira H. *Movies, Censorship, and the Law*. U of Michigan P, 1966.

Chadwick-Joshua, Jocelyn. *The Jim Dilemma: Reading Bias in Huckleberry Finn*. U of Mississippi P, 1998.

Chiari, Sophie, editor. *Freedom and Censorship in Early Modern English Literature*. Routledge, 2018.

Chris, Cynthia. *Indecent Screen: Regulating Television in the Twenty-First Century*. Rutgers UP, 2019.

Clor, Harry M. *Obscenity and Public Morality: Censorship in a Liberal Society*. U of Chicago P, 1967.

Craig, Alec. *The Banned Books of England and Other Countries*. Allen & Unwin, 1962.

_____. *Suppressed Books: A History of the Conception of Literary Censorship*. World, 1963.

Daniels, Walter. *The Censorship of Books*. Wilson, 1954.

Davis, James E., editor. *Dealing with Censorship*. National Council of Teachers of English, 1979.

De Grazia, Edward. *Censorship Landmarks*. Bowker, 1969.

_____, and Robert K. Newman. *Banned Films: Movies, Censors and the First Amendment*. Bowker, 1982.

Dewhirst, Martin, and Robert Farrell. *The Soviet Censorship*. Scarecrow, 1973.

Ditchfield, P. H. *Books Fatal to Their Authors*. Stock, 1903.

Donnelly, Michael. *Freedom of Speech and the Function of Rhetoric in the United States*. Lexington, 2018.

Downs, Donald A. *The New Politics of Pornography*. U of Chicago P, 1989.

_____. *Value and Limits of Academic Speech: Philosophical, Political, and Legal Perspectives*. Routledge, 2018.

Duker, Sam. *The Public Schools and Religion: The Legal Context*. Harper & Row, 1966.

Ernst, Morris L. *Censorship*. Macmillan, 1964.

Farrer, J. A. *Books Condemned to Be Burnt*. Stock, 1892.

Fellion, Matthew, and Katherine Inglis. *Censored: A Literary History of Subversion and Control*. British Library, 2017.

Findlater, Richard. *Banned! A Review of Theatrical Censorship in Britain*. McGibbon & Kee, 1967.

Foerstel, Herbert N. *Banned in the U.S.A.: A Reference Guide to Book Censorship in Schools and Public Libraries*. Greenwood, 1994.

Forster, Chris. *Filthy Material: Modernism and the Media of Obscenity.* Oxford UP, 2018.

Fronc, Jennifer. *Monitoring the Movies: The Fight over Film Censorship in Early Twentieth-Century Urban America.* U of Texas P, 2017.

Gardiner, Harold C. *Catholic Viewpoint on Censorship.* Hanover House, 1958.

Geller, Evelyn. *Forbidden Books in American Public Libraries (1876-1939).* Greenwood, 1984.

Geltzer, Jeremy. *Film Censorship in America: A State-by-State History.* McFarland, 2017.

Gillespie, Tarleton. *Custodians of the Internet: Platforms, Content Moderation, and the Hidden Decisions That Shape Social Media.* Yale UP, 2018.

Gillett, Charles R. *Burned Books,* 2 vols. 1932. Greenwood, 1975.

Glass, Loren. *Rebel Publisher: How Grove Press Ended Censorship of the Printed Word in America.* Seven Stories, 2018.

Grendler, Paul F. *The Roman Inquisition and the Venetian Press, 1540-1605.* Princeton UP, 1977.

Haight, Anne L. *Banned Books,* 2nd ed. Bowker, 1955.

_____, and Chandler B. Grannis, *Banned Books, 387 B.C to 1978 A.D.,* 4th ed. Bowker, 1978.

Haney, Robert W. *Comstockery in America.* 1960. Da Capo, 1974.

Hentoff, Nat. *The First Freedom: The Tumultuous History of Free Speech in America.* Delacorte, 1980.

_____. *Free Speech for Me—But Not for Thee: How the American Left and Right Relentlessly Censor Each Other.* HarperCollins, 1992.

Hohenberg, John. *Free Press/Free People.* Collier-Macmillan, 1973.

Hoyt, Olga, and Edwin P. Hoyt. *Censorship in America.* Seabury, 1970.

Hurwitz, Leon. *Historical Dictionary of Censorship in the United States.* Greenwood, 1985.

Jenkinson, Edward B. *Censors in the Classroom: The Mind Benders.* Southern Illinois UP, 1979.

Karolides, Nicholas J., editor. *Censored Books II: Critical Viewpoints, 1985-2000.* Scarecrow, 2002.

_____, et al., editors. *Censored Books: Critical Viewpoints.* Scarecrow, 1993.

Kristof, Nicholas D. *Freedom of the High School Press.* UP of America, 1983.

Lamont, Corliss. *Freedom Is as Freedom Does: Civil Liberties in America.* Continuum, 1990.

Lederer. Laura. *Take Back the Night: Women in Pornography.* William Morrow, 1980.

Legman. G. *Love and Death: A Study in Censorship.*1949. Hacker. 1963.

Levy, Leonard W. *Legacy of Suppression: Freedom of Speech and Press in Early American History.* Belknap, 1960.

_____. *Freedom of the Press from Zenger to Jefferson: Early American Libertarian Theories.* Bobbs-Merrill. 1966.

Liston, Robert A. *The Right to Know: Censorship in America.* Watts, 1973.

Long, Robert E., editor. *Censorship.* Wilson, 1990.

MacInnes, Mairi. *Versions of Censorship.* Routledge, 2017.

Marx, William. *Hatred of Literature.* Translated by Nicholas Elliott, Belknap, 2018.

McClellan, Grant S. *Censorship in the United States.* Wilson, 1967.

Moon, Eric. *Book Selection and Censorship in the Sixties.* Bowker, 1969.

Moore, Nicole. *Censorship and the Limits of the Literary: A Global View.* Bloomsbury Academic, 2017.

Nelson, Jack. *Captive Voices: The Report of the Commission of Inquiry into High School Journalism.* Schocken, 1974.

Nelson, Jack, and Gene Roberts Jr. *The Censors and the Schools.* Little, Brown, 1963.

New York Public Library. *Censorship: 500 Years of Conflict.* Oxford UP, 1984.

O'Higgins, Paul. *Censorship in England.* Nelson,1972.

O'Neil, Robert M. *Classrooms in the Crossfire: The Rights and Interests of Students, Parents, Teachers, Administrators, Librarians, and the Community.* Indiana UP, 1986.

Palfrey, John. *Safe Spaces, Brave Spaces: Diversity and Free Expression in Education.* MIT, 2018.

Perrin, Noel. *Dr. Bowdler's Legacy: A History of Expurgated Books in England and America*. Macmillan, 1970.

Phelps, Guy. *Film Censorship*. Gollancz, 1975.

Piper, Daniel. *The Rushdie Affair: The Novel, the Ayatollah, and the West*. Carol, 1990.

Rauch, Jonathan. *Kindly Inquisitors: The New Attacks on Free Thought*. U of Chicago P, 1993.

Rembar, Charles. *The End of Obscenity: The Trials of* Lady Chatterley, Tropic of Cancer *and* Fanny Hill. Andre Deutsch, 1969.

Robertson, Geoffrey. *Obscenity: An Account of the Censorship Laws and Their Enforcement in England and Wales*. Weidenfeld & Nicolson, 1979.

Robertson, James C. *The British Board of Film Censors, 1896-1950*. Croom Helm, 1985.

_____. *Hidden Cinema: British Film Censorship in Action 1913-1972*. Routledge, 2017.

Ruud, Charles A. *Fighting Words: Imperial Censorship and the Russian Press, 1804-1906*. U of Toronto P, 1982.

Schumach, Murray. *The Face on the Cutting Room Floor: The Story of Movie and Television Censorship*. William Morrow, 1975.

Shanor, Donald R. *Behind the Lines: The Private War against Soviet Censorship*. St. Martin's, 1985.

Siebert, Frederick S. *Freedom of the Press in England, 1476-1776*. U of Illinois P, 1952.

Simmons, John S., editor. *Censorship: A Threat to Reading, Learning, Thinking*. International Reading Association, 1994.

Skinner, James M. *The Cross and the Cinema: The Legion of Decency and the National Catholic Office for Motion Pictures, 1933-1970*. Praeger. 1993.

Snyder, Gerald S. *The Right to Be Informed: Censorship in the United States*. Julian Messner, 1976.

St. John-Stevas, Norman. *Obscenity and the Law*. Seeker & Warburg, 1956.

Stephens, J. R. *The Censorship of English Drama, 1824-1901*. Cambridge UP, 1980.

Strassel, Kimberley. *Intimidation Game: How the Left Is Silencing Free Speech.* Twelve, 2017.

Strossen, Nadine. *HATE: Why We Should Resist It with Free Speech, Not Censorship.* Oxford UP, 2018.

Sutherland, John. *Offensive Literature: Decensorship in Britain, 1960-82.* Junction, 1985.

Swayze, Harold. *Political Control of Literature in the USSR, 1946-1959.* Harvard UP, 1962.

Thomas, A. H. *Censorship in Public Libraries.* Bowker, 1975.

Thomas, Donald. *A Long Time Burning: A History of Library Censorship in Britain.* Routledge, 1969.

Trevelyan, John. *What the Censor Saw.* Michael Joseph, 1973.

Tribe, David. *Questions of Censorship.* St. Martin's, 1973.

Vitz, Paul C. *Censorship: Evidence of Bias in Our Children's Textbooks.* Servant, 1986.

Wagner, Peter. *Eros Revived.* Seeker & Warburg, 1988.

Webb, Peter. *The Erotic Arts.* Rev. ed., Seeker & Warburg, 1983.

Werbel, Amy. *Lust on Trial: Censorship and the Rise of American Obscenity in the Age of Anthony Comstock.* Columbia UP, 2018.

West, Mark I. *Children, Culture, and Controversy.* Archon, 1988.

Whittington, Keith F. *Speak Freely: Why Universities Must Defend Free Speech.* Princeton UP, 2018.

Widmer, Kingsley, and Eleanor Widmer. *Literary Censorship: Principles, Cases, Problems.* Wadsworth, 1961.

Woods, L. B. *A Decade of Censorship in America, 1966-1975.* Scarecrow, 1979.

Zerman, Melvyn Bernard. *Taking on the Press: Constitutional Rights in Conflict.* Crowell. 1986.

Bibliography

Abel, Richard L. *Speaking Respect, Respecting Speech*. U of Chicago P, 1998.

Atkins, Robert, and Svetlana Mintcheva, editors. *Censoring Culture: Contemporary Threats to Free Expression*. New Press, 2006.

Bald. Margaret. *Literature Suppressed on Religious Grounds*. Facts on File, 2006.

Boyer, Paul S. *Purity in Print: Book Censorship in America from the Gilded Age to the Computer Age*. U of Wisconsin P, 2002.

Byrd, Cathy, and Susan Richmond, editors. *Potentially Harmful: The Art of American Censorship*. Georgia State University, 2006.

Cate, Fred H. *The Internet and the First Amendment: Schools and Sexually Explicit Expression*. Phi Delta Kappa Educational Foundation, 1998.

Coetzee, J. M. *Giving Offense: Essays on Censorship*. U of Chicago P, 1996.

Collins, Ronald K. L., and David M. Skover. *The Death of Discourse*. Westview, 1996.

Couvares, Francis G., editor. *Movie Censorship and American Culture*. Smithsonian, 1996.

Curry, Ann. *The Limits of Tolerance: Censorship and Intellectual Freedom in Public Libraries*. Scarecrow, 1997.

DelFattore, Joan. *What Johnny Shouldn't Read: Textbook Censorship in America*. Yale UP, 1992.

Delgado, Richard, and Jean Stefancic. *Must We Defend Nazis? Hate Speech, Pornography, and the New First Amendment*. NYUP, 1997.

Dell, Pamela. *You Can't Read This! Why Books Get Banned*. Compass Point, 2010.

Dines, Gail, et al. *Pornography: The Production and Consumption of Inequality*. Routledge, 1998.

Dooling, Richard. *Blue Streak: Swearing, Free Speech, and Sexual Harassment*. Random House, 1996.

Doyle, Robert P. *Banned Books: Challenging Our Freedom to Read*. ALA, 2010.

Dworkin, Andrea. *Life and Death: Unapologetic Writings on the Continuing War Against Women.* Free, 1997.

Edwards, June. *Opposing Censorship in the Public Schools: Religion, Morality, and Literature.* Erlbaum, 1998.

Felshin, Nina, and Richard Meyer. *Potentially Harmful: The Art of American Censorship.* Georgia State University, 2006.

Finan, Christopher M. *From the Palmer Raids to the Patriot Act: A History of the Fight for Free Speech in America.* Beacon, 2007.

Fish, Stanley Eugene. *There's No Such Thing as Free Speech, and It's a Good Thing, Too.* Oxford UP, 1997.

Fiss, Owen M. *The Irony of Free Speech.* Harvard UP, 1996.

_____. *Liberalism Divided: Freedom of Speech and the Many Uses of State Power.* Westview, 1996.

Gates, Henry Louis, et al. *Speaking of Race, Speaking of Sex: Hate Speech, Civil Rights, and Civil Liberties.* New York UP, 1995.

Godwin, Mike. *Cyber Rights: Defending Free Speech in the Digital Age.* Times Books, 1998.

Goldstein, Robert Justin. *Burning the Flag: The Great 1989-1990 American Flag Desecration Controversy.* Kent State UP, 1996.

Greenawalt, Kent. *Fighting Words: Individuals, Communities, and Liberties of Speech.* Princeton UP, 1995.

Gurstein, Rochelle. *The Repeal of Reticence: America's Cultural and Legal Struggles Over Free Speech, Obscenity, Sexual Liberation, and Modern Art.* Hill & Wang, 1996.

Haworth, Alan. *Free Speech.* Routledge, 1998.

Heins, Marjorie. *Not in Front of the Children: "Indecency," Censorship, and the Innocence of Youth.* Rutgers UP, 2008.

Hentoff, Nat. *Living the Bill of Rights: How to Be an Authentic American.* HarperCollins, 1998.

Heumann, Milton, et al., editors. *Hate Speech on Campus: Cases, Case Studies, and Commentary.* Northeastern UP, 1997.

Heyman, Steven J, editor. *Hate Speech and the Constitution.* Garland, 1996.

Houle, Michelle M. *Mark Twain: Banned, Challenged, and Censored.* Enslow, 2008.

Karolides, Nicholas J. *Literature Suppressed on Political Grounds*. Facts on File, 2006.

_____, et al. *120 Banned Books: Censorship Histories of World Literature*. Checkmark, 2005.

Klingler, Richard. *The New Information Industry: Regulatory Challenges and the First Amendment*. Brookings Institution, 1996.

Knuth, Rebecca. *Burning Books and Leveling Libraries: Extremist Violence and Cultural Destruction*. Praeger, 2006.

Kors, Alan Charles, and Harvey A. Silverglate. *The Shadow University: The Betrayal of Liberty on America's Campuses*. Free, 1998.

LaMarche, Gara, editor. *Speech and Equality: Do We Really Have to Choose?* New York UP, 1996.

Lederer, Laura J., and Richard Delgado, editors. *The Price We Pay: The Case Against Racist Speech, Hate Propaganda, and Pornography*. Hill & Wang, 1995.

Lewis, Anthony. *Freedom for the Thought That We Hate: A Biography of the First Amendment*. Basic, 2007.

Lowenthal, David. *No Liberty for License: The Forgotten Logic of the First Amendment*. Spence, 1997.

Lyons, Charles. *The New Censors: Movies and the Culture Wars*. Temple UP, 1997.

MacDonald, Joan Vos. *J. K. Rowling: Banned, Challenged, and Censored*. Enslow, 2008.

Marcus, Laurence R. *Fighting Words: The Politics of Hateful Speech*. Praeger, 1996.

Maschke, Karen J., editor. *Pornography, Sex Work, and Hate Speech*. Garland, 1997.

McElroy, Wendy. *XXX: A Woman's Right to Pornography*. St. Martin's, 1995.

McNair, Brian. *Mediated Sex: Pornography and Postmodern Culture*. Arnold, 1996.

McNicol, Sarah, editor. *Forbidden Fruit: The Censorship of Literature and Information for Young People*. Brown Walker, 2008.

Morrison, Toni, editor. *Burn This Book: PEN Writers Speak Out on the Power of the Word*. HarperStudio, 2009.

Nygaard, William. *The Price of Free Speech*. Translated by Rosemary Fearn, Scandinavian UP, 1996.

Petersen, Klaus, and Allan C. Hutchinson, editors. *Interpreting Censorship in Canada*. U of Toronto P, 1997.

Post, Robert C., editor. *Censorship and Silencing: Practices of Cultural Regulation*. Getty Trust Publications, 1998.

Ravitch, Diane. *The Language Police: How Pressure Groups Restrict What Students Learn*. Knopf, 2003.

Robbins, Louise S. *Censorship and the American Library: The American Library Association's Response to Threats to Intellectual Freedom, 1939-1969*. Greenwood, 1996.

Sanford, Bruce W. *Don't Shoot the Messenger: How Our Growing Hatred of the Media Threatens Free Speech for All of Us*. Free, 1999.

Scales, Pat R. *Teaching Banned Books: 12 Guides for Young Readers*. ALA, 2001.

Schwarz, Ted. *Free Speech and False Profits: Ethics in the Media*. Pilgrim, 1996.

Shiell, Timothy C. *Campus Hate Speech on Trial*. Lawrence: UP of Kansas, 1998.

Soley, Lawrence. *Censorship, Inc.: The Corporate Threat to Free Speech in the United States*. Monthly Review, 2002.

Sova, Dawn B. *Literature Suppressed on Sexual Grounds*. Facts on File, 2006.

_____. *Literature Suppressed on Social Grounds*. Facts on File, 2006.

Strossen, Nadine. *Defending Pornography: Free Speech, Sex, and the Fight for Women's Rights*. Scribner's, 1995.

Thomas, R. Murray. *What Schools Ban and Why*. Praeger, 2008.

Walker, Samuel. *Hate Speech: The History of an American Controversy*. U of Nebraska P, 1994.

Weinstein, James. *Hate Speech, Pornography, and the Radical Attack on Free Speech Doctrine*. Westview, 1999.

West, Mark. *Trust Your Children: Voices Against Censorship in Children's Literature*. New York: Neal-Schuman, 1997.

Whillock, Rita Kirk, and David Slayden, editors. *Hate Speech*. Sage, 1995.

Wolfson, Nicholas. *Hate Speech, Sex Speech, Free Speech*. Praeger, 1997.

Wright, R. George. *Selling Words: Free Speech in a Commercial Culture.* New York UP, 1997.

About the Editor_____

Robert C. Evans is I. B. Young Professor of English at Auburn University at Montgomery, where he has taught since 1982. In 1984 he received his PhD from Princeton University, where he held Weaver and Whiting fellowships as well as a university fellowship. In later years his research was supported by fellowships from the Newberry Library (twice), the American Council of Learned Societies, the Folger Shakespeare Library (twice), the Mellon Foundation, the Huntington Library, the National Endowment for the Humanities, the American Philosophical Society, and the UCLA Center for Medieval and Renaissance Studies.

In 1982 he was awarded the G. E. Bentley Prize and in 1989 was selected Professor of the Year for Alabama by the Council for the Advancement and Support of Education. At AUM he has received the Faculty Excellence Award and has been named Distinguished Research Professor, Distinguished Teaching Professor, and University Alumni Professor. Most recently he was named Professor of the Year by the South Atlantic Association of Departments of English.

He is a contributing editor to the John Donne *Variorum Edition* and is the author or editor of more than fifty books (on such topics as Ben Jonson, Martha Moulsworth, Kate Chopin, John Donne, Frank O'Connor, Brian Friel, Ambrose Bierce, Amy Tan, early modern women writers, pluralist literary theory, literary criticism, twentieth-century American writers, American novelists, Shakespeare, and seventeenth-century English literature). He is also the author of roughly four hundred published or forthcoming essays or notes (in print and online) on a variety of topics, especially dealing with Renaissance literature, critical theory, women writers, short fiction, and literature of the nineteenth and twentieth centuries.

Contributors_____

Jane Addams (1860-1935), the first woman winner of the Nobel Peace Prize, was famous as an author, sociologist, public intellectual, defender of civil rights, champion of women's rights, and advocate for world peace.

C. E. Bentley (1859-1929) was an African American dentist from Chicago, where he became a leader of the local branch of the NAACP. He eventually became national treasurer of that organization. He was recognized as a leader in dental medicine during his era, especially as an advocate of oral hygiene.

Robert Donahoo is professor of English at Sam Houston State University in Texas. A former president of the Flannery O'Connor Society, he is the coeditor of *Flannery O'Connor in the Age of Terrorism: Essays on Violence and Grace* (2010) and the forthcoming *Approaches to Teaching the Fiction of Flannery O'Connor* from MLA. In 2014, he codirected a National Endowment for the Humanities Summer Institute, "Reconsidering Flannery O'Connor," and he has published essays and journal articles on O'Connor, as well as on the drama of Horton Foote, Larry Brown's *Dirty Work*, the novels of Clyde Edgerton, postmodern American science fiction, and Tolstoy's *Resurrection*.

Liyang Dong, an independent scholar who holds two masters degrees in English from Chinese and American universities, has extensive collegiate teaching experience both in the United States and in China, her country of birth. Her extensive research into a variety of literary topics has been funded repeatedly by a number of different agencies in China. Her published work includes the following essays: "On the Limitation of Task-Based Teaching Methods in College English Teaching," "The Features and Function of Register and Its Application in English Teaching," "A New Photographic Interpretation on the Formation Mechanism of Context Metaphor," "On the Application of Eclectic Interactive Teaching Approaches in English Teaching," and "A Well-Wrought Metaphor—Doctorow's Pessimism in *The March.*"

Alan Gribben, editor and publisher of the *Mark Twain Journal: The Author and His Era*, is the biographer of the University of Texas library founder Harry Ransom, editor of multiple editions of Mark Twain's *The Adventures of Tom Sawyer* and *Adventures of Huckleberry* Finn, coeditor of *Mark Twain on the Move: A Travel Reader*, and author of dozens of articles on Twain's intellectual background. For fifteen years he reviewed books and articles about Mark Twain for *American Literary Scholarship, An Annual*. His three-volume *Mark Twain's Literary Resources: A Reconstruction of His Library and Reading* (2019) reflected five decades of research. www.alangribben.com.

Darren Harris-Fain is an honors professor of English at Auburn University at Montgomery, where he teaches British and American literature and American film history. He is the author of *Understanding Contemporary American Science Fiction: The Age of Maturity, 1970-2000* and the editor of three volumes on British fantasy and science fiction writers for the *Dictionary of Literary Biography*. He has published essays on literary fiction, science fiction, fantasy, and comics in more than thirty books, including *Teaching the Graphic Novel, The Cambridge Companion to the Graphic Novel, The Cambridge History of the Graphic Novel*, and *The Cambridge Companion to American Science Fiction*. His previous contributions to the Critical Insights series include essays in the volumes on Harlan Ellison, Rebellion, Ken Kesey's *One Flew over the Cuckoo's Nest*, and Survival.

Phill Johnson earned a doctorate in law and a masters in library science and has spent thirteen years in law school administration, mainly with the University of Illinois and the University of Missouri—Kansas City (UMKC) law schools. In addition to being involved with the libraries at each institution, he managed the IT Department at UMKC and regularly taught on a variety of topics. He assumed his current role of dean of the library at Auburn University at Montgomery, Alabama, in 2015. His publication history mostly involves topics related to libraries, though he also continues to publish in the legal field. A recent article on attempts to censor Ralph Ellison's *Invisible Man* was widely praised by experts on Ellison.

Mary Childs Nerney (1865-?) was the executive secretary of the NAACP from 1912 to 1916. She led the campaign against the film *The Birth of a Nation* after W. E. B. Du Bois, the organization's leader, refused to do so.

Richard Obenauf graduated Phi Beta Kappa from the University of New Mexico before earning his MA and PhD in medieval and Renaissance English literature at Loyola University Chicago. His research centers on tolerance and intolerance, censorship, political and religious heresy, and the history of ideas, with secondary interests in satire, textual criticism, and genre theory. Since 2010 he has taught interdisciplinary courses on literature, history, and politics in the Honors College at the University of New Mexico.

Kelly Snyder is an independent scholar with a special interest in pluralistic and thematic approaches to literature.

Basil Tozer (1868-1949) was a prolific British author of essays and books, including such works as: *The Horse in History*; *The Riddle of the Forest*; *Vengeance*; *Confidence Crooks and Blackmailers: Their Ways and Methods*; *The Story of a Terrible Life: The Amazing Career of a Notorious Procuress*; *Practical Hints on Shooting*; *The Elusive Lord Bagtor*; and various others.

Nicolas Tredell is a writer and lecturer who has published 20 books and more than 350 essays and articles on authors ranging from Shakespeare to Zadie Smith and on key issues in literary, film, and cultural theory. His recent books include *C. P. Snow: The Dynamics of Hope*, *Shakespeare: The Tragedies*, *Novels to Some Purpose: The Fiction of Colin Wilson*, *Conversations with Critics* (an updated edition of his interviews with leading literary figures), and *Anatomy of Amis* (the most comprehensive account so far of the fiction and nonfiction of Martin Amis). He formerly taught literature, drama, film, and cultural studies at Sussex University and is currently consultant editor of Palgrave Macmillan's Essential Criticism series, which now numbers 86 volumes, with many more to come. He is a frequent speaker at a wide variety of venues, most recently at the 2018 Literary London Conference at the University of London and the Second

International Colin Wilson Conference at the University of Nottingham, UK.

Abe, Frank 217
Absolutely True Diary of a Part-Time Indian, The xi, 245
absurdist narrative 156
academic freedom 26, 27, 235, 241, 242
activism 67
Adams, Joseph Quincy 53
Adventures of Huckleberry Finn vii, xiii, xvii, 26, 74, 77, 172, 173, 179, 181
Adventures of Tom Sawyer, The vii, xiii, xv, xvii
aesthetics 145, 152, 164, 167
African American vii, xxii, xxiii, xxiv, xxv, xxvi, 63, 65, 66, 69, 70, 175, 176, 195, 196, 197, 199, 205, 211, 213, 254
alcoholism 72, 171
Alexie, Sherman xi, 245
allegory 38, 54, 66
Almereyda, Michael 152
altered text 3, 219
alternate version xv
American Association of University Women 247, 253
Americanized 216
American Library Association 28, 29, 170, 233, 235
anarchism 90
Anaya, Rudolfo 245
Angelou, Maya 26, 245
Anglophone fiction 151
Anglo-Saxon 12, 13
"Annus Mirabilis" 133
anti-racism 60
anti-Semitism 141

apotheosis 149, 152
"Are Your Kids Reading Rot?" 28, 34
Arnold, Matthew 96, 146, 148
arson 62
"Artificial Nigger, The" 57, 58, 59, 61, 62, 66, 70, 72, 73, 75, 76
Arundel, Thomas 37
Asian American 209, 210, 211, 212, 213, 214, 215, 216, 219, 222, 223, 224, 225, 226, 228
Atwood, Margaret 245
Austen, Jane 96, 97, 134
autobiography 118, 212, 215, 216, 217, 218, 231

Baker, William 38
Bald, Margaret 22, 34
Baldwin, James 59, 67
Banned Books Week 29, 30, 32, 33
banned literature iv
Barnes, Jake 139
Barry, William 82, 99
Batman: The Dark Knight Returns 238
Battiste, Jerry 191
Beat generation 151, 163, 165
Bechdel, Alison 229, 231, 233, 235, 237, 239, 241, 242, 243, 244
Bechdel test 229
Becket, Thomas 11
Beckett, Samuel 152
Beckett, Stephanie 28

Bell for Adano, A 61
Beloved 30
Bennett, Joan 135
Bible, the 233
Big Read initiative xiii
bildungsroman 169
Birth of a Nation, The ix, 100,
    103, 107, 109, 113, 114,
    115, 116
black community 197, 198
Blackerby, Sharon 196, 203
Blackfriars' Council of 1382 9
Blake, William 143
Blankets 231, 233, 239
blasphemy 37, 45, 46, 53
Bless Me, Ultima 245
Bless the Beasts and the Children
    245
Bluest Eye, The 245
Bollman, Richard 38
book burning 11, 62, 81, 203
Boyle, T. C. 245
Brandl, Alois 53
Brantley, Jessica 38
Bronte, Charlotte 96, 97
bullying 31
burdened Southern conscience 57
Burke, Edmund 148
Burroughs, William S. x, 151,
    153, 155, 157, 159, 161,
    163, 165, 167

Caine, Hall 96
canonical 5, 52, 151
Canterbury Tales 7, 8, 91
Carlin, George xxiv
Catcher in the Rye, The 26, 171,
    245

Catholic Church Index of
    Prohibited Books 60
Catholicism 74
Cavafy, Constantine 117, 119,
    121, 123, 125, 127, 129, 131
Caxton, William 4
censorship vii, viii, ix, x, xi, xii,
    xiii, xiv, xix, xx, xxi, xxii,
    xxv, xxvi, 3, 4, 5, 6, 7, 8, 9,
    10, 11, 12, 13, 14, 15, 16,
    18, 22, 23, 25, 26, 27, 29,
    35, 37, 38, 39, 40, 43, 50,
    51, 52, 53, 54, 81, 89, 91,
    92, 94, 97, 115, 118, 119,
    123, 125, 126, 130, 131,
    151, 158, 166, 174, 177,
    188, 190, 192, 193, 194,
    199, 200, 209, 210, 213,
    223, 224, 225, 227, 241,
    245, 247, 248, 250, 252,
    254, 256, 257, 264, 265
Censorship of the Church of Rome,
    The 4, 6, 20
challenged books 24, 26, 31, 233,
    250
Chan, Charlie 211
Charles, Ron 32
Chatterley, Connie 143
Chatterley, Lady Constance 137
Chatterley, Sir Clifford 138
Chaucer, Geoffrey 7, 8, 9, 19, 20,
    77, 91
Chicago Review 151
Chicano 24
Chickencoop Chinaman, The 211
China Men 212
Chinese America 215
Chinese civilization 214, 216, 217

Chinese culture 214, 215, 216, 219, 223
Chinese history 216, 217, 218
Chinese myth 219
Chin, Frank xi, 209, 210, 220, 221, 224
Chopin, Kate 234, 283
Christian 7, 24, 35, 42, 54, 56, 96, 98, 215, 216, 217, 218, 219, 227, 237, 260
Church of Rome 4, 5, 6, 20
civil rights xiv, xv, xviii, 58, 67, 100, 177, 189
Civil Rights era 202
civil rights movement xviii, 189
Civil War 103, 104
Clansman, The 100
classroom vii, xiv, xvi, xviii, xxi, xxii, xxiii, xxv, xxvi, 25, 173, 174, 175, 178, 179, 181, 195, 202, 231, 241, 251, 260, 264
Clegg, Cyndia Susan 5
Clemens, Raymond 6
Color Purple, The 213
comic book 229
Comic Book Legal Defense Fund 235, 244
"Coming Censorship of Fiction, The" 81, 83, 85, 87, 88, 89, 90, 91, 93, 95, 97, 98, 99
condemnation viii, 3, 6, 97, 103
Condren, Chelsea 30
Conejo Valley xi, 245, 246, 247, 249, 250, 251, 252, 253, 254, 255, 256, 257, 258, 259, 261, 263, 264, 265, 266, 267

Conejo Valley controversy 246, 258
conformity 3, 4, 6, 7, 12, 17, 19, 40, 43, 49, 55
Connery, Sean 117
Conrad, Joseph 134, 149, 153
conservative 59, 241, 246, 250, 252, 255, 258, 260
Constitution 26, 171, 183, 184, 209, 236
consumer culture 152
content warning 261, 264
controversy viii, xi, xx, xxiii, 27, 82, 188, 190, 191, 194, 196, 198, 200, 203, 204, 239, 245, 246, 247, 252, 255, 258, 259, 260, 264, 267
core curriculum 260
Corelli, Marie 96
corruption 35, 38, 39, 50
counterculture 151, 152, 163
Crisis, The 100, 107, 111, 113, 116
Cromwell, Sharon 25
Cultural Revolution 211
Curious Incident of the Dog in the Night-Time, The 233
curriculum xiv, xxi, xxii, 24, 26, 169, 170, 171, 173, 176, 181, 182, 233, 242, 246, 247, 248, 249, 251, 255, 257, 260, 261, 262, 266

Day-Lewis, C. 135
Dead Fingers Talk 151
Death 50
Declaration of Independence 236
de Hamel, Christopher 7
democracy 25

de Sola Pinto, Vivian 135, 149
dilemma viii, 129, 239
disability 133, 138, 139, 140
Dixon, Thomas 100
Doctor Benway 157, 158, 160
Doctor Faustus 51, 52
Drugstore Cowboy 152
dual personality 216
Du Bois, W. E. B. 111
Dunn, Mike 246, 250
Dykes to Watch Out For 229

East of Eden 61
ecology 146
educators xxiii, 26, 213, 250, 257,
    262
Eisner, Will 238
Eliot, George 96, 97, 134, 143,
    149, 157
Eliot, T. S. 127, 153
Ellison, Ralph 59
empathy 32
environmentalism 145, 146, 200,
    237, 242
Eroticism 122, 123
erotic novel 92
ethnicity viii, xi, 136, 201
ethnic sensitivity 256
Everyman 50, 51, 52

Faerie Queen 91
"fake" writer 214
fantasy 161, 163
Far Left xxvi
Far Right xxvi
fascism 213
Faulkner, William 59
Federalist Papers 236
Fei, Yue 214, 219

feminism 135, 138, 217
Fifty Shades of Gray 233
Finch, Atticus 205
First Amendment 26, 209, 235,
    248
Fitzgerald, F. Scott 155
Fleshly Fiction 81
"Fleshly School of Fiction, The"
    82, 99
Forest-Hill, Lynn 37
Forster, E. M. 135
Frantzen, Allen 12
free speech x, xxv, 23, 62, 258
free will 43
Fulton, Thomas 38, 55
fundamentalist Christian 24
Fun Home: A Family Tragicomic
    229
F-word xxiv, 254, 255

Gaiman, Neil 234
Gaines, Ernest J. 59
gay/lesbian xi
gay literature xi, 243
Gebbie, Melinda 240
Geck, John A. 39
gender 70, 128, 136, 174, 209,
    219, 229
gender equality 219
genre 45, 50, 51, 52, 215
Gershwin, George 153
Gibbons, Dave 238
Ginsberg, Allen 151
Girodias, Maurice 151
Goodbye to Berlin 165, 167
Good Man Is Hard to Find, A 58,
    59
Goosebumps series 26
Gor Yun, Leong 216

Graham, Timothy 6, 19
Granlund, Dave xx
graphic memoir 230, 231, 233,
    234, 237, 243
graphic novel xi, 229, 231, 237,
    238, 239, 240, 241, 242
Green, John 233
Griffith, Ben 58
Griffith, D. W. ix, 100
Grundy, Mrs. 81, 87, 89
Guterson, David 245
Gysin, Brion 153

Haddon, Mark 233
Hagelin, Rebecca 28
Hamlet 26
Handmaid's Tale, The 245
Hansberry, Lorraine 172
Haraway, Donna 139
Hardy, Thomas 86, 88, 89, 97
Harry Potter series 30
Hawthorne, Nathaniel 26
Hayden, Robert 230
Head, Mr. 66, 69, 70, 71, 73, 75
Heart of Darkness 153
Heinlein, Robert 215
Heitman, Danny 59
Hemingway, Ernest xix
heresy 5, 13, 14, 35, 37, 40
heroic tradition 218, 219
Hersey, John 61
heteronormative 136
Heyward, DuBose 153
hierarchy 3, 41
Higgins, Gwen 173
Hoggart, Richard 135
Holmes, Suzette 196
Holocaust, the 229
homoerotic verse 118

homosexual 24, 28, 62, 123, 155,
    230
homosexuality 171, 229, 232
Hosseini, Khaled 245
Hough, Graham 135
Howe, Frederic C. 107, 111
Hudson, Genevieve 231
Hwang, David Henry 214, 218

identity crisis 216
ideology 25, 134, 136
I Know Why the Caged Bird Sings
    26, 245
imagery 52, 127, 143, 232
imprisonment 6, 8, 47
Indianapolis Star 173, 185
Indivisible: Conejo (IC) 248, 257,
    265, 267
industrialization 146
Industrial Revolution 143
informal censorship 209, 211, 213,
    215, 217, 219, 221, 223,
    225, 227
interzone 152, 153, 161
intolerance 3, 4, 5, 9, 12, 13, 14,
    15, 16, 17, 18, 35, 37, 38,
    39, 40, 42, 43, 44, 47, 49,
    50, 54, 55
Isherwood, Christopher 165
Islamic Revolution 229
Iwata, Edward 210

James, E. L. 233
James, Henry 134, 140, 149, 165
James, William 140, 149
Joachite, Franciscan 10
Jones, Bill T. 69, 75, 76
Joyce, James 234

Kafka, Franz 157
Kahane, Claire 58
Karim, Persis M. 23
Karolides, Nicholas J. 22
Kempe, Margery 18
Kerby-Fulton, Kathryn 9, 20
Kermode, Frank 133
Kerouac, Jack 153, 222
King, Buddy 205, 206
Kingston, Maxine Hong xi, 209,
    210, 214, 216, 223, 225,
    227, 228
Kite Runner, The 245
Kron, Lisa 231
Krug, Judith 170
Ku Klux Klan ix, xv, 100, 103,
    105

Lady Chatterley's Lover x, 133,
    135, 136, 138, 142, 149,
    151, 154
Langland, William 9
Larkin, Philip 133
La Rosa, Suzanne xv, xvi, xviii,
    xxv
LaRue, James 32
Laursen, John Christian 42, 56
Lawrence, D. H. x, 133, 134, 137,
    149, 151
Leavis, F. R. 133, 134
Lee, Harper x, 24, 30, 169, 182,
    185, 187, 205
Lee, Maryat 58
lesbianism 229, 230, 237, 240
Levithan, David 32
Lewis, John 67
Lewis, W. H. 115
LGBTQ 229, 236
LGBTQ newspapers 229

liberal 101, 229, 241, 246, 248,
    251, 252, 257
library xiv, xvii, xxvii, 25, 28, 29,
    30, 32, 33, 82, 86, 88, 166,
    170, 172, 179, 180, 182,
    191, 231, 232, 233, 238, 240
Library of Congress (LoC) 116,
    117, 237
life writing 229
literary feud 209
literary merit 31, 82, 93, 133
Lolita 151, 154
Lollards 37
London, Jack 215
Looking for Alaska 233
Los Angeles Times 210, 225, 228
Lost Girls 240

Macro Plays, The 52, 53, 55, 56
male heroism 219
Manchu, Fu 211
Mankind ix, 35, 36, 37, 38, 39, 40,
    41, 42, 43, 44, 45, 46, 47,
    48, 49, 50, 51, 52, 53, 54,
    55, 56
Manly, John M. 53
Marlowe, Christopher 51
Marx, Eleanor 53
Marx, Karl 53
Maus 229, 238
McCawley, Harry 192, 195, 197
McCunn, Ruthanne Lum 245
McMahon, Regan 31
medieval literature 3, 43, 45
Megli-Thuna, Dawn 250, 256, 261
memoir 230, 231, 233, 234, 235,
    237, 239, 242, 243
Mendelsohn, Daniel 119, 120,
    130, 132

Mercy 35, 36, 37, 40, 41, 42, 43,
    44, 45, 46, 47, 48, 49, 52,
    54, 69, 76
metamorphosis 156, 160
Metamorphosis 157
Middle Ages 3, 4, 7, 11, 13, 14,
    15, 16, 17, 20, 35, 49, 50,
    52, 54
Mikulecky, Larry 27
Millett, Kate 135
Mills, Louise 231
Mischief 36, 41, 47
misogyny 216, 217, 219, 225
modern fiction 61, 149
monasticism 12
Moore, Alan 238, 240
Moore, Carl 205
morality ix, 32, 36, 37, 39, 40, 48,
    50, 51, 96, 195
morality play ix, 36, 37, 39, 40,
    50, 51
moral satire 38, 45
More, Thomas 18, 19
Morrison, Toni 30, 59, 65, 77, 245
Ms Magazine 63
Muir, Kenneth 135
Mulan, Fa 214, 218
murder 62, 191
mutilation 13
My Life in China and America 215
Myrtius 120
mythology 218, 219

Nabokov, Vladimir 151
Naked Lunch x, 151, 152, 153,
    154, 155, 156, 157, 158,
    159, 160, 161, 162, 163,
    164, 165, 166, 167

National American Woman
    Suffrage Association, The
    111
National Association for the
    Advancement of Colored
    People (NAACP) ix, 100,
    113, 173, 187
National Board of Censorship
    107, 108, 109, 111
National Coalition against
    Censorship (NCAC) 181,
    247
National Endowment for the Arts
    xiii
National School Boards
    Association (NSBA) 26
Native American 254
negro 103, 104, 105
Nelson 66, 69, 70, 71, 180, 185
"New Assault on Libraries, The"
    23
New Historicism 16
New Testament 7
New World 219
New York Times xvi, 70, 76, 209,
    231, 243, 244
Nichols, Ashton 147
No More Pornography 234
N-word xiii, xv, xvi, xvii, xx, xxii,
    xxiii, xxiv, xxv, xxvi, 73,
    183, 189, 203, 205, 254, 255

obedience 12, 55, 126
Obermeier, Anita 8
O'Brien, Tim 245
obscenity xx, 24, 54, 55, 239
O'Connor, Flannery ix, 57, 58, 59,
    61, 63, 65, 67, 68, 69, 70,
    71, 73, 74, 75, 76, 77

O'Donnell, Edward 58
Of Mice and Men 172, 173
Oldcastle, John 37
"One of Their Gods" 121
On the Road 156
oppression xiv, 4
opt-in 260
opt-out 250, 251, 252, 255, 256,
    257, 258, 259, 261, 265
Origin of Others, The 66, 76

parental involvement 29, 262
parents vii, viii, xi, xxii, 24, 25,
    26, 27, 28, 29, 30, 59, 61,
    91, 95, 155, 171, 172, 173,
    174, 175, 178, 179, 181,
    182, 189, 204, 205, 230,
    235, 238, 241, 246, 247,
    248, 249, 250, 251, 252,
    253, 254, 256, 257, 258,
    259, 260, 261, 262, 263,
    264, 265
Parker, Matthew 12
Parks, Rosa xviii
Patrick, William 38
Patterson, Annabel 4
Peabody, George Foster 113, 114
pedophilia 240
permissive society 133
persecution 16, 37, 42, 43
Persepolis 229, 234
Phillpotts, Eden 86, 88, 89
picaresque narrative 156
Piers Plowman 9
Playing in the Dark 65, 66, 76
political correctness xxvi, 59
political intolerance 5, 38
pornography 232, 234, 246, 247,
    248, 254

postmodern 285
post-publication censorship 5
post-structuralist 165
poverty xviii
Powers, Ron xviii, xxi
prejudice 31, 87, 103, 105, 124,
    178, 192, 193, 195, 218, 235
premodern censorship 3
profanity 61, 62, 171, 172, 246,
    255
protest 26, 29, 67, 85, 108, 112,
    114, 115, 234, 244, 246, 247
Prufrock, J. Alfred 127
public school x, xiii, xviii, xxii,
    169, 183, 247, 250, 254,
    255, 260
Putnam, G. H. 4

race viii, ix, xi, 57, 58, 64, 66, 69,
    70, 71, 74, 76, 103, 105,
    113, 170, 181, 188, 193,
    200, 201, 215, 217
race calumny 100, 101, 103, 105,
    107, 109, 111, 113, 115, 116
race prejudice 103
racial slur xx, 72, 173, 177, 179
racial tensions 193
racism vii, 30, 32, 60, 66, 72, 73,
    74, 170, 175, 176, 181, 182,
    183, 190, 191, 192, 196,
    200, 202, 203, 204, 223,
    224, 226, 255
racist language x, 62, 73, 74, 169
racist mind 216
Raisin in the Sun, A 172, 173
Ranck, Andrew 196, 197
Ransom, John Crowe 57, 58, 76
*Reading, Mercy and the Artificial
    Nigger* 69, 76

reconciliation 71
Reconstruction xvii, 63, 103
Reed, Ishmael 211, 213
Reformation, the 5, 13, 16, 35
Regina v. Penguin Books Limited 133, 150
religious zealotry 7
Renaissance, the 16, 18, 35, 55
Republic, The 188, 189, 192
required reading 59, 169, 170, 171, 172, 173, 180, 192, 233, 245, 254, 256
Richard III 138
right-wing groups 24
Robertson, Randy 5
Robinson, Tom 188, 190
Romanticism 134, 143
Ruskin, John 145

Salinger, J. D. 26, 171, 245
Samsa, Gregor 157
Sandman 234
Sant, Gus Van 152
satire 7, 8, 38, 45, 54, 154, 163, 164
Satrapi, Marjane 229
Scarlet Letter 26
scholarship 4, 5, 54, 65
school board xi, 27, 61, 170, 171, 175, 176, 179, 180, 189, 191, 246, 247, 248, 249, 252, 255, 256, 257, 259
school district xi, 172, 179, 180
science fiction xi, xxiii, 156, 160, 161
Scott, Walter 86, 88, 97
scribal transmission 7
second-wave feminism 135
Selby, John 57

self-censorship x, 9, 16, 37, 38, 39, 43, 118, 119, 123, 126, 131, 264
Sergel, Christopher 187
Seven Deadly Sins 52
sexism xi, 30
sexual assault 31
sexual content 50, 233
sexual identity 31
sexuality 24, 32, 133, 135, 136, 137, 138, 140, 143, 183, 230, 234, 237, 239, 241, 242
sexually explicit 209, 238
Sexual Politics 135
Shakespeare, William 26, 51, 55, 91, 138, 168, 171
Shorter, Donald 70, 71
Shostakovich, Dmitri 119
"Show Must Go On, The" 174, 196, 207
Shrovetide 39, 45, 46, 52, 54
Shuger, Debora 5
Siebert, Frederick Seaton 4
silent censorship vii, xix, xxvi
Sing, Wittman Ah 219, 220
slander 7, 8
slavery 202
Snow Falling on Cedars 245, 253
social Darwinism 215, 216
Southern Gothic 169
Sova, Dawn B. 22, 34
Spencer, H. Leith 14
Spenser, Edmund 91
Spiegelman, Art 229
Steinbeck, John 61, 172
stereotype 138, 214, 215, 216, 217, 218
Stine, R. L. 26
suicide 32, 100, 230

Sun Also Rises, The 139
Sung, Betty Lee 217
Swarthout, Glendon 245
Swinburne, A. C. 118
S-word xxiv
syllabi xi, 134, 235, 261, 262, 263
Szatmary, Peter 173

Tan, Amy 214, 216, 218, 222
Tesori, Jeanine 231
textual purity xv
Things They Carried, The 245
Thompson, Craig 231
"Those Winter Sundays" 230
Thousand Pieces of Gold 245
thriller 154, 156
Thurlay, William 38
tithe 38
To Kill a Mockingbird x, 30, 169,
        170, 171, 173, 175, 177,
        179, 180, 181, 183, 185,
        187, 189, 190, 193, 199,
        201, 202, 204, 206
toleration 4, 18, 40, 41, 42, 44, 46,
        48, 49, 50, 55, 66, 89
Tortilla Curtain, The 245
transgender 233
"Trial of Lady Chatterley, The"
        134, 150
Tripmaster Monkey 219, 220, 228
triumphalist 58
trolling 134, 142
Twain, Mark vii, xiii, xiv, xv, xvi,
        xvii, xviii, xx, xxi, xxvi,
        xxvii, 26, 59, 74, 172
Twister 152
Two Boys Kissing 32

urban pastoral 153

Uses of Literacy 135

Van Dyk, Sally 193, 204
Vaughn, Brian 234
Venus and Adonis 91
victim 210, 217, 225
violence 23, 32, 103, 172, 219,
        234, 242, 246
Violent Bear It Away, The 62, 72
vouchers 250

Walker, Alice 63, 77, 213
Walzer, Michael 40
Warren, Nagueyalti 63
Wars of the Roses 36, 38
Washington, Booker T. 114
Washington Post xvi, 32, 33, 209
Waste Land, The 153, 164, 167
Watchmen 238, 242
Watson, Nicholas 18
Wells, H. G. 140
Werner, Nick 187, 189, 196
Westernized 229
West, Rebecca 135
white culture 226
white male 155
white supremacist 214, 217
white universality 217
Wiggins, Gwen 187, 189
Wiggins, Nioka 193
Williams, Melvin 58
Williams, Randall xv, xviii, xxv
Williams, Raymond 135
Wilsey, Sean 231
Wilson, Will 190
Wilson, Woodrow 100
Wing, Yung 215, 216
Wise Blood 57, 61, 62

Woman Warrior, The 210, 211, 212, 213, 214, 216, 221, 227

Women in Love 135

Wong, Jade Snow 215, 216, 217

Wood, Ralph 58

word hoard 164

World War II 134

Wycliff, John 9, 37

X, Malcom 211

Year of the Dragon 211

Young Adult 28

YouTube 117

Y: The Last Man 234